1968

his book may

The World of W. B. Yeats

The World of W. B. Yeats

REVISED EDITION

Edited by Robin Skelton and Ann Saddlemyer

UNIVERSITY OF WASHINGTON PRESS

Seattle

The original edition of this book was published as part of the
W. B. Yeats Centenary Festival of the University of Victoria
in February-March, 1965.

Photographs by Barnes Studio, Victoria, B.C.
Printed in the United States of America

Contents

Part Three CONTEMPORARIES

Illustrations

Introduction

THE title of this book is to some extent self-explanatory. W. B. Yeats was born on June 13, 1865, and died on January 28, 1939; his work has often been discussed but has less frequently been related to its background and to the work of the poet's friends and contemporaries. To celebrate the centenary of Yeats's birth we have compiled a symposium intended to present the poet in the context of his own time and place and to reflect his many enthusiasms; we hope this may serve to fill one or two gaps left by previous commentaries and works of criticism in this field.

In making our selection of topics and assembling them into a pattern, we have been governed by several considerations. We determined to include only one analytical study of a single work by Yeats, feeling that such criticism was already a heavily capitalized industry. We also decided that our symposium could usefully explore material that has been ignored, or regarded as unimportant, by previous writers, even though by so doing we might be obliged to omit restatements of the obvious or comments upon work long realized to be of central significance. Thus our contribution upon Synge concentrates on his theories rather than his plays, and we have paid more attention than is usual to the work of such widely different figures as Jack Yeats, Susan Mitchell, Edward Martyn, George Moore, Gordon Craig, T. Sturge Moore, and Charles Ricketts. We have been fortunate in being able to make use of much unpublished material and in having the generous cooperation of many people whose libraries and resources are superior to our own. We would like particularly to mention our gratitude to Mrs. W. B. Yeats, without whose assistance so many

Yeats scholars would have been lost in impenetrable confusion, to Mrs. L. M. Stephens, to Mr. Gordon Craig, to Mrs. Sybil le Brocquy, to Mr. Owen Linnane, and to Mr. Alf MacLochlainn of the National Library of Ireland.

Limitations of space have prevented our making full use of all the help we have been given, or our commenting upon more than a small number of those aspects of Yeats's life and environment which still demand further attention if a complete perspective upon his lifework is to be gained. Several of these essays are more in the nature of prolegomena than complete studies, but we hope that they may lead to further explorations and discoveries.

The original edition of this book included a catalogue of the University of Victoria W. B. Yeats Exhibition; this material has been omitted from the present version.

The creation of this book has meant a great deal of work for a large number of people. We would like to express our gratitude to all those who have helped us, and in particular to Mr. Gerald Auchinachie and Miss Moyra Nisbet for their assistance with many matters of detail, to Miss Joan Coldwell for her labors upon the proof, to Mrs. Joan Whitfield for her help in preparing the book for the printer, and to Mr. Charles Morriss of the Morriss Printing Company for his patient understanding of our difficulties and his solving of many typographical problems in the creation of the original edition.

R.S., A.S.

University of Victoria

Part One

BEGINNINGS

The Cult of the Celt:
Pan-Celticism in the Nineties

ANN SADDLEMYER

We propose to have performed in Dublin, in the spring of every year certain Celtic and Irish plays, which whatever be their degree of excellence will be written with a high ambition, and so to build up a Celtic and Irish school of dramatic literature.

S O READ in part the 1897 manifesto of the Irish Literary Theatre, signed by Augusta Gregory, Edward Martyn, and William Butler Yeats. Years later Lady Gregory in her biography of the early days of the movement eased much of the bombast by explaining candidly that the "Celtic" was thrown in for Fiona Macleod. It is significant, however, that these Irish nationalists should have been compelled to flourish their prospectus under an allegiance broader than their own island, and indicates to what extent the mystical spell of Pan-Celticism had cast its own twilight.

This "celtic revival" of the last decade of the century was no new phenomenon in literature. It was essentially a re-naming and re-ordering of a familiar trait, the "folk spirit", marked by the heightened passions and superstitions common to all literature rising from the people, and given new life by the recent scientific studies of folklore and myth culminating in Sir James Frazer's *The Golden Bough* in 1890. In addition, it possessed a strong tendency towards melancholy which attracted the mystics of Maeterlinck's school. But the new element in the "celtic revival" was a sense of *place*, as opposed to a vague atmosphere. Life and mood became more pointed by the close relationship between nature and emotion. In a general sense this element of the Celtic spirit could be considered a natural outgrowth of the Pantheism or nature-worship of the Romantics influenced by the mystics' renewed interest in Druidism;

3

more specifically it arose from a self-conscious intellectual attempt to inject fresh life into well-known themes and develop a new approach to old form. Here again was a precedent: although fiercely nationalist himself, Richard Wagner in his great music-dramas of the Ring cycle had shown how effective the folk myth could be in the creation of new art, as a steady stream of pilgrims to Bayreuth testified. Gradually, however, the literary movement became a nationalist and language movement limited to one country, Ireland, with its own periodicals and political platform, thus losing much of its earlier depth and cosmopolitan significance.

As early as 1856 Ernest Renan explored Brittany and as he testifies in *The Poetry of the Celtic Races* discovered the Celt; ten years later in *The Cornhill Magazine* Matthew Arnold elaborated Renan's description of the Celtic movement in literature and advocated a Chair of Celtic Literatures at Oxford; in 1882 the Society for Promoting Christian Knowledge flirted with heresy by publishing *Celtic Britain* by John Rhys who later also published his lectures on *The Origin and Growth of Religion as Illustrated by Celtic Heathendom*. Meanwhile in France Henri d'Arbois de Jubainville supplemented his lectures at the Sorbonne with the publication of *Le Cycle mythologique irlandais et la mythologie celtique*, to be followed by Anatole Le Braz and *Le Théâtre Celtique*. By 1891 there had been such an increase in activity that Grant Allen could feel justified in making the Celt responsible for all the modern movements in England through the conservative pages of *The Fortnightly Review*, and by the end of the century innumerable scholars, organizations and periodicals were devoted to the recovery of the Celt. In his introduction to *Lyra Celtica*, one of the largest and most sweeping collections of Celtic literature, William Sharp devoted three and a half pages to a survey of the writings of Celtic specialists.

The greatest impetus came from Ireland, where for the first time Old Irish manuscripts had been exhumed and translated by such redoubtable German scholars as Kuno Meyer and made available to historians and literary scholars. Writers such as Yeats rejoiced in the "new fountain of legends" which was thus suddenly available, and both poetry and prose flowed with ancient Irish tales and exciting new symbols. However, this excitement was not limited to Ireland. Claimants and supporters arose in Scotland (although Fiona Macleod was in reality not a Scot nor indeed a lady), Brittany (the Celtic Theatre "The Troupe of Sainte-Anne" produced its first play in 1902, but Synge's Paris friends were encouraging him to attend Celtic festivals in Brittany in the late nineties), Wales, Cornwall, and even on the Isle of Man. The Pan-Celtic Society was founded in 1899; *Celtia: a Pan-Celtic Magazine* published its first number in 1901; the Society still exists. In their enthusiasm for the Celtic virtues, many writers of dubious national heritage claimed a share of the spoils: Arthur Symons qualified doubly as a member, being of Welsh birth and Cornish parentage; Lionel Johnson discovered a strain of Celtic ancestry and was duly admitted. Although perhaps not to be taken too seriously as argument, it is interesting to observe that Henrik Ibsen wrote to that Scottish translator William Archer in 1895, "one of the conclusions to which I have come is that there are very strong traces in me of my Scotch descent."

Although the case for Celtic ancestry was at times pushed beyond genealogical sanction, the Celtic movement as it gradually took form in the 1890's illustrated definite tendencies and prevalent character-istics, especially in the work of the major writers, Yeats, Fiona Macleod, and Ernest Rhys. To the "natural magic" and "sense of the mystery of life" recognized by Arnold and Renan was added, Yeats claimed in an article for *The Bookman*, "a franker trust in passion and in beauty than was possible to the poets who put their trust in the external world and its laws." The sense of melancholy and the vague longings associated with "the Celtic twilight" gradu-ally gave way to specific references to ancient legend and mythology, which in turn sharpened imagery and diction and rooted experience in time and space. That the time was the distant past and the space some far-off corner of the world strengthened the appeal and well demonstrated William Blake's belief, Yeats felt, that "art is a labour to bring back again the golden age." A critic of this cult of the Celt might see in the renewed emphasis on the virtues of the peasant and the glamour of the remote past a natural development of the roman-ticism of Rousseau and Ruskin. But to devotees such as Yeats, here was one more source of

> Traditional sanctity and loveliness;
> Whatever's written in what poets name
> The book of the people . . .

"The Noble and the Beggar-Man": Yeats and Literary Nationalism

ANN SADDLEMYER

"His occult mission, it seemed, was to celebrate the wedding of Madame Blavatsky and Finn MacCumhail." FRANK HUGH O'DONNELL

"There are things a man must not do to save a nation." JOHN O'LEARY

Writing in 1901 of his distaste for contemporary English life, Yeats referred to the two passions men might still find in Ireland, "love of the Unseen Life and love of country"; [1] it might truthfully be stated that much of Yeats's own nationalism was a result of the search for the one love in the arms of the other. Moreover, any discussion of Yeats's nationalism must take into consideration the many interests, diverse though they may seem, which compounded and conspired to produce the Irish man of letters. Poet, playwright, mystic, magus and finally, inevitably, politician, the more he tried to move away from his country, the more involved he became in it. But propagandist he would never be. "I have always felt that my mission in Ireland is to serve taste rather than any definite propaganda," he wrote to Lady Gregory in 1901, and a few years later he reiterated his theme:

I am a Nationalist.... But if some external necessity had forced me to write nothing but drama with an obviously patriotic intention, instead of letting my work shape itself under the casual impulses of dreams and early thoughts, I would have lost, in a short time, the power to write movingly upon any theme. [2]

[1] "Ireland and the Arts," *Essays and Introductions* (London: Macmillan, 1961), 204.
[2] "An Irish National Theatre," *Collected Works*, 1908, IV, 121-22.

6

The secret to Yeats's nationalism, then, belongs among those "dreams and early thoughts," at the point where two loves meet.

I

"When I began to write," Yeats recalled in 1913 in his essay "Art and Ideas," "I sought some symbolic language reaching far into the past and associated with familiar names and conspicuous hills that I might not be alone amid the obscure impressions of the senses." Reaching back to "that early phase of every civilization . . . where everything is prescribed, as buried under dream and myth," he found his source in "the oldest of the aristocracies of thought," folk art,[3] the golden dream of king and peasant. He was fortunate, for the work of those ahead of him — the Celtic Folklore Commission, the translations of Kuno Meyer and Douglas Hyde, the poems of Sir Samuel Ferguson — already yielded a rich harvest of legend:

Alone among nations, Ireland has in her written Gaelic literature, in her old love tales and battle tales, the forms in which the imagination of Europe uttered itself before Greece shaped a tumult of legend into her music of the arts; and she can discover, from the beliefs and emotions of her common people, the habit of mind that created the religion of the muses.[4]

His search for that habit of mind led him first to his own study of the folk myth, later to his researches with Lady Gregory, and finally to his renunciation of the "great Celtic phantasmagoria whose meaning no man has discovered nor any angel revealed"[5] in favour of his own mythology, A Vision. But by then his nationalism had taken its mature form and even its most vociferous offspring, the Abbey Theatre, had moved away from him.

Stories of the countryside, of Them and Their ways, had been told in his mother's kitchen at Sligo. In 1888 he published Fairy and Folk Tales of the Irish Peasantry, then followed it in 1893 with The Celtic Twilight, in which he wrote,

3 "By the Roadside" (1901), Mythologies (London: Macmillan, 1959), 139; also his introduction to The Cat and the Moon, in Wheels and Butterflies (London: Macmillan, 1934), 136.

4 "The Literary Movement in Ireland," Ideals in Ireland, ed. Lady Gregory (London: Unicorn Press, 1901), 98.

5 "A Visionary" [AE], The Celtic Twilight (Dublin: Maunsel, 1905), 22. This passage is omitted from Mythologies.

I have desired, like every artist, to create a little world out of the beautiful, pleasant, and significant things of this marred and clumsy world, and to show in a vision something of the face of Ireland to any of my own people who would look where I bid them.

Lady Gregory's *Cuchulain of Muirthemne* (1902), *Poets and Dreamers* (1903), and *Gods and Fighting Men* (1904), followed much later by the two volumes of *Visions and Beliefs of the West of Ireland* (1920), were further documents of the search for the peasant's imagination: "she and I felt that we had got down, as it were, into some fibrous darkness, into some matrix out of which everything has come." [6] As early as 1899 he could write to a friend, "I have worked at Irish mythology and filled a great many pages of notes with a certain arrangement of it for my own purposes; and now I find I have a rich background for whatever I want to do and endless symbols to my hands."

But long before he had systematized that mythology, Yeats's mind had turned towards Ireland for subject-matter. "England is old . . . but Ireland has still full tables," he commented in a review of Todhunter's play *The Banshee* in 1892. "Here in Ireland the marble block is waiting for us almost untouched, and the statues will come as soon as we have learned to use the chisel." His memory and imagination took him always back to the Irish countryside, and especially to the wild beauty of the west country, haunted by its legends of the past and events of the near-present: "I had a conviction, which indeed I have still," he writes in 1902, "that one's verses should hold, as in a mirror, the colours of one's own climate and scenery in their right proportion." [7] "We should make poems on the familiar landscapes we love, not the strange and rare and glittering scenes we wonder at," he wrote to his fellow-poet Katharine Tynan in 1888. Not only would this bring sincerity and originality to one's work, but greater interest as well. "One should love best what is nearest and most interwoven with one's life," he wrote to another poet the following year.

But one writer alone could not create a literature. A body of artists united in aim and an audience educated to appreciate them were also necessary. "One wants to write for one's own people, who come to the playhouse with a knowledge of one's subjects and with hearts ready to be moved," he wrote to his American patron John

[6] Introduction to *An Indian Monk, Essays and Introductions*, 429.
[7] "What is 'Popular Poetry'?" (1902), *Essays and Introductions*, 5.

Quinn. Having achieved this, literature will then once more become folk art, "the possession of a people," and her artists once more be honoured as the spiritual leaders of the age, speaking "out of a people to a people." Because of this belief, Yeats chose to be numbered "one/With Davis, Mangan, Ferguson."

II

The Ireland the young poet turned to for subject-matter was in many ways still a cultural outpost of the England he loudly denounced. For despite indications of a new impulse in Irish literature, the intellectual climate of Dublin was not markedly different from that of the earlier decades of the century. Writers of Irish literature in the English language could roughly be separated into two main parties: the "West Britons" or literary Unionists whose residence in Ireland from a literary point of view seemed a mere accident, and the true Anglo-Irish writers, who if not always writing for Ireland, wrote of it.

Professor Edward Dowden of Trinity College might be considered the grand old man of literary Unionism. Poet, scholar, critic, and boyhood friend of John Butler Yeats, "for perhaps a couple of years he was an image of romance" to the artist's son. His "quiet influence" was praised by Nationalist and English alike, but he did not have the imagination (or in the Yeatses' opinion the courage) to believe in an Irish Renaissance, and remained distrustful of any movement that broke away from the great traditions of the English Renaissance. Perhaps his closest contact with the new movement occurred when an unknown young college student, John Synge, recorded and preserved his lectures on the ethical qualities of Elizabethan literature. Still others contributed to the picture of Trinity College as the bulwark of anti-nationalism. Professor Atkinson incurred lasting opprobrium by publicly declaring that the "Gaelic Irish literature" was "intolerably low in tone" with "very little idealism in it, and very little imagination"; in 1914 Provost Mahaffy prohibited "the man Pearse" from lecturing within the College walls. Even when favourably disposed towards the new movement, such college men as George Savage-Armstrong and John Todhunter remained English both in output and outlook, preferring the spirit of Shelley, Keats and Wordsworth to the ancient idealism of the Celt.

The term describing the second general category of Irish writers, "Anglo-Irish," has always been a difficult one to define. It was used most accurately perhaps by Thomas MacDonagh, now celebrated as one of the patriots of 1916, known then not only as "helper and friend" to the schoolmaster Pearse, but as an astute literary critic and one of the more hopeful poets. In a collection of essays published in the fateful year 1916 MacDonagh wrote,

The term Anglo-Irish literature . . . is worth having as a term only to apply to the literature produced by the English-speaking Irish, and by those in general only when writing in Ireland and for the Irish people . . . so much in love with Ireland, . . . in consonance with the Irish rhythm of life and literature, in converse with Irish people and out of converse with others.

By applying this measure, MacDonagh felt justified in rejecting certain writers of Gaelic stock as "more Greek than Gael," and accepting such alien friends as Lionel Johnson and Nora Chesson.[8]

Like all successful autocrats inclined to create, alter, or discard on the sincerity of the moment, Yeats was willing to extend his interpretation of Anglo-Irish letters not only to embrace his good friends Lionel Johnson and Arthur Symons, but to sense an undefined Celtic sympathy even in such opposite forces as William Blake and Maurice Maeterlinck. But if he allowed himself extremes in one direction, he channelled his enthusiasms in others. Like two other major Irish critics, the brilliant but testy historian Standish O'Grady and "our one philosophical critic" John Eglinton, Yeats never succumbed to the Irish language as thoroughly as George Moore or Edward Martyn, believing instead that "we must put Irish emotion into the English language if we were to reach our generation." Like MacDonagh, he accepted those authors who wrote for Ireland and the Irish, while maintaining their belief in literature "as an expression of such insight into life and nature as man can gain by any means in his power."[9]

The Anglo-Irish tradition of letters which Yeats turned to for support had been a long and noble if not always consistent one, achieving its greatest breadth and following in the nineteenth cen-

---

8 *Literature in Ireland: Studies Irish and Anglo-Irish* (Dublin: Talbot Press, 1916), 28-29 *et passim*.

9 John Eglinton, "A Word for Anglo-Irish Literature," *United Irishman*, March 22, 1902.

tury. It in turn could be sub-divided as to motive and character, between those who, although self-consciously Irish, wrote with one eye on the English market, and those who were content, sometimes naïvely so, to sing their native woodnotes wild. While recognizing the advantages of claiming such forbears as William Allingham, Samuel Lover, Charles Lever, Gerald Griffin, and Maria Edgeworth, Yeats sought the company of the latter group, those novelists and poets who wrote not only of Ireland but only for Ireland as well. He admired the "square-built power" of their realism and, foreshadowing Synge, applauded their determination to see "the whole of everything they looked at . . . the brutal with the tender, the coarse with the refined." In 1889 Yeats edited a selection of stories by William Carleton, "the Walter Scott of Ireland," and two years later gave him pride of place in his *Representative Irish Tales*. As late as 1901 he mentions proudly that his publisher found him equal with Carleton in unpopularity among Dublin booksellers.

A less virile strain had entered Irish literature with the poetry of Thomas Moore, whose "dazzling lightness and insincere sentiment" were frowned upon by later sterner critics. But the tenderness and pathos of Moore's *Irish Melodies* and *National Airs* coloured poets' visions of Ireland for almost a century. The popular sentiment of his poetry in turn paved the way for the sentimental nationalism and propaganda of *The Nation*, whose founders "united literature to their politics and civil morality to literature." [10] Charles Gavan Duffy, editor of the newspaper, and Thomas Davis, leading spirit of *The Nation*'s political school of poetry, together inspired and created the picture of Ireland still broadcast by sentimental Irish emigrants, raising Irish patriotism to "a sort of religious or idealistic status" later realists have never been allowed to alter. By encouraging and publishing the poems of Irish men and women of all classes and creeds, *The Nation* truly became the voice of Ireland, but the sacrifice of quality to quantity built up an idealistic concept of Ireland which became so mingled with patriotism that criticism automatically implied a denial of national values as well. "If we said that *The Spirit of the Nation* was but salutary rhetoric," complained Yeats, "England might overhear us and take up the cry." Although recognizing the importance of such "images for the affections . . . the Soldier, the Orator, the Patriot, the Poet, the Chieftain, and

[10] See *A Treasury of Irish Poetry in the English Tongue*, edited by Stopford A. Brooke and T. W. Rolleston (London: Smith, Elder and Co., 1900).

above all the Peasant," Yeats and his colleagues deplored the rhetoric, convention and sentimentality begotten by this levelling process. Believing that "the sentimental mind is the bourgeois mind"
(and the Irish are descendants of kings), they in their turn dreamed
of the unspoilt peasant untouched by "the mind of the town," at
times just as artificial an ideal as the one against which they so
violently reacted. A great deal of Yeats's own unpopularity in Ireland can be traced to his frequent and vehement denunciations of
what AE called "boyscoutish" propaganda. Many years later Yeats
still had difficulty shaking off memories of "the Tower and wolf-
dog, harp and shamrock, verdigris-green sectaries who wrecked my
movement for the time." [11]

But deplorable as its aesthetic qualities might be, "the rhymed
lesson book of Davis" provided not only an outlet for hitherto mute
inglorious patriots, but a source and goal to which they could direct
previously scattered or unexpressed hopes and ideals. Even in the
"rhetoricians" and "newspaper hacks" Lady Gregory could note
"a certain dignity, an intensity born of continuity of purpose." For
the first time since the rebellion of 1798, Ireland had a rallying
point. Without this step away from localized or provincial loyalties
towards nationalism, no matter how artificial the conjuration, the
later hopes of the literary nationalists could never have been realized,
new "images for the affections" forged. "They taught fervour, and
labour, and religious toleration," Yeats recognized, "and left that
memory for an inspiration to the young men of Ireland." Nor was
that inspiration reserved for the "Young Ireland" of the middle
class and peasantry. Thomas Davis's impressive funeral cortège
gave rise to the poetry of "Speranza," the future Lady Wilde. And
as a young girl Lady Gregory chose for her birthday gift that same
collection of *The Nation*'s poetry which inspired Speranza. (Nor·
was her youthful enthusiasm dampened when a doubtful sister
qualified the gift by the inscription, "Patriotism is the last refuge
of the scoundrel.")

Two other poets excited interest for their originality and genius
during the early part of the nineteenth century, James Clarence
Mangan and Sir Samuel Ferguson. Notable for their technical virtuosity and breadth of treatment, both poets, and to a lesser extent
Aubrey de Vere, in a sense helped initiate the true Celtic revival

[11] Letter to Olivia Shakespear, August 1, 1921. Mrs. Shakespear was the
"Diana Vernon" of his early years.

which gained such prominence in the nineties. William Allingham had re-worked and distributed old street ballads; the poets of *The Nation* had invoked the name of the ancient Gael; Ferguson and Mangan moved even closer to the national heritage. Not only did they translate the ancient literature of the Gael, but reintroduced his very spirit, the "peculiar strain of mingled homeliness and grandeur, of simplicity and elaboration, of sensuousness and mysticism." Both differed strongly from the propagandist verse of the time, though both were in their own ways strongly nationalist; both tempered their patriotism to their art, and by doing so provided the models the writers of the nineties were seeking. In a review of Katharine Tynan's *Ballads and Lyrics* in 1891 Yeats acknowledges this debt to the past:

If literatures are to go on they must add art to impulse and temper their fire with knowledge. Literary Ireland is going through such a training. The days of Davis were followed by those of Allingham's Ballyshannon songs and de Vere's "Innisfail" and his "Legends of St. Patrick" and Ferguson's later and greater work, his "Deirdre" and "Conary". Those men were all experimenters, trying to find out a literary style that would be polished and yet Irish of the Irish. Those who follow them have their work made more easy through their experiments.

Ferguson's *Lays of the Western Gael* (1864) in particular, the first work of any length to deal with the epic cycles of Ireland, can perhaps be considered the Chronicle on which later writers based and developed and expanded their work. But neither Ferguson nor Mangan achieved the recognition they deserved, and Yeats may have been thinking of these two writers when he explained his own intentions in writing *The Secret Rose*:

It is at any rate an honest attempt towards that aristocratic esoteric Irish literature, which has been my chief ambition. We have a literature for the people but nothing yet for the few.

III

But Yeats and his colleagues were also the logical and legitimate successors to a movement that had been quietly but steadily acquiring momentum and followers throughout the preceding decade, not only in literature but in other areas also.

Although generally referred to as the "Celtic Renaissance," the increasing interest in the early literature of the Gael might with more accuracy be termed a revival of Irish scholarship. For its original impetus was critical and corrective rather than creative; indeed, one of the permanent characteristics of this movement throughout its various phases has been its emphasis on teaching, whether of individuals, particular groups, or the general public. Its beginning was rooted in traditional scholarship, however, thereby limited to the isolated few who, in the nineteenth century, were not only familiar with the Irish language but qualified to work with the twelve or fourteen hundred octavo volumes of manuscripts then available. It is perhaps significant, also, that this astonishing mass of relatively untouched material should be popularized outside Ireland before receiving general recognition within the country itself. Long before Arnold had delivered his memorable plea for the study of Celtic literature or Trinity College had made room in its curriculum for the study of Irish history, German scholarship was attacking the field with customary industry: first Zuess in 1853 with his *Grammatica Celtique*, followed by Windisch and Zwemmer, and, most popular and industrious of all, Dr. Kuno Meyer, who came to study and remained to teach. Irish scholars and their colleagues in England and America took up the work, and interpretation, often exceedingly free, followed translation, so that by the latter part of the century an increased awareness of the literature of their own country prompted a renewed interest in Irish history, archæology, theology, legend, and, finally, the language itself.

There had, of course, been individual forays into these related fields before, especially in the field of Irish folk music and song, which had long held a fascination for the collector and musicologist. Collections of traditional music had been made by Bunting (1796), Hudson (1841), Petrie (1855), Pigot (1842), and P. W. Joyce (1873); Thomas Moore had composed verses for many anonymous tunes. But whereas the earlier historians had been prompted simply to collect, the renewed interest in the songs of the Fileas, Brehons and Seanachies of the Druidic age, the harpers of the thirteenth century, the wandering songsters of a later period, reflected a more personal, immediate approach. Yeats, Douglas Hyde, Lady Gregory concerned themselves more with the character of the bard himself than with his representative or collectors' value; Douglas Hyde's translation of *The Love Songs of Connacht*, while retaining the charm and naïveté of the original, was a work of art in itself; Yeats's search for legends and traditions of fairy and folklore was, as we

have seen, to a great extent part of his lifelong search for himself
in a world scheme; Lady Gregory haunted the cottages of her tenants
and sought out the blind poet Raftery's lonely, unmarked grave. In
fact Yeats felt that he and Lady Gregory moved closer to the true
spirit of the Celt while moving away from organized research:

We had little scientific curiosity, but sought wisdom, peace, and a
communion with the people. . . . Dr. Hyde and his [Gaelic] League . . .
sought the peasants . . . but we sought the peasant's imagination.

The reaction in other branches of the "Renaissance" similarly
reflected this personal interest. Petrie and Stokes with their archæo-
logical and architectural studies of early Ireland paved the way for
a fresh interest not only in history but in theology; Edward Martyn
strove to preserve traditional music and improve church decoration,
interests perhaps resulting largely from his own aesthetic asceticism;
Katharine Tynan and Eleanor Hull wrote of the lives of the saints.
And just as the folklore and peasant scholarship of Douglas Hyde,
Yeats, Lady Gregory and Synge idealized the Celt as peasant, the
popular folk history and mythology of Standish O'Grady, Lady
Gregory, Alfred Nutt, T. W. Rolleston, William Larminie and
Eleanor Hull (as well as countless other minor popular historians)
exalted the Celt as hero. The epic cycles of romance, taken from the
Book of the Dun Cow, the Book of Leinster, the Speckled Book,
and the Yellow Book of Lecan, confirmed this mixture of ancient
mythology with great heroic battles. The new generation desired, in
fact, not a realistic knowledge of past history, but an indication for
the future, a "deliberate creation of a kind of Holy City in the
imagination" erected over the cairns of ancient gods and heroes.
AE confided in Yeats of his hope for an Irish millenium; Yeats
planned a "Légende des Siècles of Ireland," and Lionel Johnson
and Lady Gregory furthered the dream; Synge alone objected to
their pattern of fairy belief and epic legend, retaining his *Aran
Islands* within a realistic framework.

Occasionally there were objections to this method of regaining a
national literature: Standish O'Grady rebuked Lady Gregory for
her "refinement" of the Saga story, then somewhat paradoxically
objected on moral grounds to the dramatization of the Deirdre
legend. John Eglinton questioned whether "anything but belles
lettres, as distinguished from a national literature, is likely to spring
from a determined pre-occupation" with these ancient legends of

Ireland. Even AE worried over his ability to cope: "I am afraid it would be a futile task to try consciously for the Celtic traditional feeling," he wrote to Yeats. "A certain spirit of it I have but I am not Celt inside, not for many lives." And when Yeats and Moore dared to interpret the legend of Diarmuid and Grania in their own way, the general public joined the protest.

Meanwhile, however, this renewed interest in things Irish prompted a slight industrial renaissance also. *The All-Ireland Review*, edited by Standish O'Grady, campaigned for the use of Irish matches and patronage of the Irish Industrial Fair; gradually a new nationalism arose which attempted to displace the old hatred of England with a concern for Ireland. In 1889 Horace Plunkett formed the first agricultural organization society in an effort to beat the Danish market for England in bacon, eggs, and butter. In ten years there were over two hundred societies and a system of agricultural banks, organized under Plunkett's banner by AE. Ireland was beginning to stir.

Alongside Plunkett's Society of Agricultural Co-operation grew a revival of interest in the Irish language, mainly through the efforts of Douglas Hyde and Dr. George Sigerson. The Gaelic League was founded in 1893, a society which aimed "not at getting rid of English, but at 'keeping Irish spoken where it is spoken still'." The agricultural organizations prospered in comparative peace, but the language question remained controversial. Douglas Hyde spoke frequently and vehemently on "the necessity for de-Anglicizing Ireland"; of his own book of Gaelic poems he wrote, "I would like better to make even one good verse in the language in which I am now writing, than to make a whole book of verses in English. For if there should be any good found in my English verse, it would not go to the credit of my mother, Ireland, but of my stepmother, England." At the height of his Irish enthusiasm George Moore threatened to disown his brother's children if they did not immediately learn to speak Irish, and Edward Martyn was for many years a member of the *Coisde Gnotha*, governing body of the Gaelic League. Lady Gregory, on the other hand, advocated bilingualism, and Yeats, although in his usual politic manner remaining on friendly terms with the Gaelic Leaguers (at one time he even advocated the establishment of a Gaelic touring company for the Abbey), never seriously studied the language. But Synge, who had studied Irish at Trinity College and practised it on the Aran Islands, vehemently denounced the Gaelic League as "founded on a doctrine that is made up of ignorance, fraud, and hypocrisy"; and John Eglinton advised a "thought movement" rather than a "language movement" as the path towards true nationality.

However, despite the varying attitudes towards the Gaelic League, and the vehemence with which the opposing parties built their platforms, the renewed interest in the Irish language served the double function of increasing the general knowledge of the mythology and folklore utilized by the new writers, and helping Ireland regain her self-respect as a nation.

IV

Politically speaking, Ireland had been suffering for some time from the extremes of both hero-worship and its inevitable disillusionment. In 1875 a newly-elected member of Parliament, Charles Stewart Parnell, had fired the imagination of the Irish people; five years later he became President of the Land League and largely through his efforts the Gladstone government finally passed the Land Act in 1881, recognizing "the three F's" of Tenant-rights: Fixity of Tenure, Free Sale and Fair Rents. Hopes of Home Rule once more rose, to be swamped in 1889 by Captain O'Shea's petition for divorce, citing Parnell as co-respondent. The machine Parnell had so carefully constructed, in which for the first time he had successfully "reconciled the Nationalist Party with the Fenians, and brought both in contact with the economic needs and desires of the peasantry," irreparably broke down. Economically, matters were not much better. The great Clearances of the 1850's and the evictions of the 1870's still rankled in the minds of the older peasants; the vast emigrations (unaided by the government) which had begun after the famine of 1846 continued. All political action seemed to have come to nothing. And so, after the fall of Parnell, the active element adopted a complete reversal of tactics. Parliamentary action gave way to direct action; hope of British aid was replaced by "independent voluntary effort within the domain of economics and social action."[12] Social development became more important than political growth, and the energy which had previously been governed by Parnell, or allowed to drain off into unorganized individual

[12] Ernest Barker, *Ireland in the Last Fifty Years*, 2nd ed. (Oxford: Clarendon, 1919), 16-25.

interests, was channelled into the agricultural co-operative efforts, the Gaelic League, and, for those like the printer-patriot John Mitchel, who still felt the only remedy lay in "the edge of the sword," the Irish Republican Brotherhood. The first two movements as we have seen continued their efforts to "rehabilitate Ireland from within"; the third aimed at complete separation of Ireland from England.

Nationalism, religious consciousness, and the land are laced into the heartstrings of every Irishman; they are in turn the basis of Irish literature. But they are also the cause of sensitivity to Irish literature, and further resentment of the "stage Irishman," now inextricably linked with the fall of Parnell, continued to cause suspicion of any portrayal of the national character on stage or printed page. Extremists of the Sinn Fein movement banned any import of English culture as well as English goods, and the Anglo-Irish writers, who chose the English language as their literary medium, were frequently under fire. The new ideal of Irish literature in a foreign language, English, was accused of heresy. And the Gaelic League, although ostensibly non-political, was encouraged by these extremists as the only truly "national" literary movement.

Fortunately about this time a new "Young Ireland" movement arose, mainly Fenian in its source, but finding as its leader a man who while declaring, "We protest against the right of patriots to perpetrate bad verses," had sufficiently proved his patriotism by going to jail for it. It was through the personal influence of John O'Leary that the younger group of patriots, Yeats, AE, Maud Gonne, the red-haired orator John F. Taylor and others, found a new call to patriotism, "beautiful, lofty things." And O'Leary, in turn, fired their enthusiasm for Irish folklore and history. Once again the hopeful young nationalists had a goal, and the "acts and happenings which are long since forgotten" softened the bitter downfall of "the Great Comedian," Parnell.

v

Each of these young nationalists reacted according to his own nature. Yeats, involved in the literary societies of London, found encouragement for his own pursuits. His mission in Ireland was "to serve taste rather than any definite propaganda," to create a National Theatre of Beauty. O'Leary gave him Irish history to read, and bid him create for the sake of Ireland. He in turn used Ireland as the focal point required for his art. "Remember," he warned Katharine Tynan in 1887, "by being Irish as you can, you will be more original and true to yourself and in the long run more interesting, even to English readers." And a few years later, "Much may depend in the future on Ireland now developing writers who know how to formulate in clear expressions the vague feelings now abroad — to formulate them for Ireland's not for England's sake." "I would have Ireland re-create the ancient arts, the arts as they were understood in Judaea, in India, in Scandinavia, in Greece and Rome, in every ancient land; as they were understood when they moved a whole people and not a few people." [13]

But Yeats was also aware of the dangers of too narrow a nationalism. Many years later he commented, "A nation should be like an audience in some great theatre — 'In the theatre' said Victor Hugo 'the mob becomes a people' — watching the sacred drama of its own history; every spectator finding self and neighbour there, finding all the world there as we find the sun in the bright spot under the burning glass." [14] And, like the audience, the nation should participate and at the same time criticize. "Young Ireland," he felt, had taught "a study of our history with the glory of Ireland for event." Their leader, Davis, had been concerned with "conscious patriotism." "His Ireland was artificial, an idea built up in a couple of generations by a few commonplace men." Because of this emphasis on a propaganda that appealed to the commonplace rather than to the individual, "hardly any Irish writer can liberate his mind sufficiently from questions of practical reform for this contemplation. Art for art's sake . . . seems to him a neglect of public duty." The "poetry of the middle class" must be exchanged for "a speech for our private griefs and sorrows." One of the faults of Irish writers (including Shaw, Wilde, and George Moore) was their inability to restrain this habit of writing "not for our own delight but for the improvement of our neighbours."

Politically speaking, Yeats refused to commit himself wholeheartedly to any particular party. In part this attitude was due to his cosmopolitan interest in art, which he felt transcended any narrow nationalism, but also he wisely refrained from involving himself

[13] "Ireland and the Arts" (1901), *Essays and Introductions*, 206.
[14] Commentary on "Three Songs to the Same Tune," *King of the Great Clock Tower*, 1934, 36-38.

with any partisan group which might prevent him from receiving the co-operation of any other group for his own literary aims. "I had withdrawn from politics because I could not bear perplexing, by what I said about books, the simple patriotic men whose confidence I had gained by what I said about nationality," he commented in his autobiography. The "infinite triviality of politics" was not, he felt, his business. And, even though O'Leary had great influence on his thought, perhaps the model he took for his own political platform was William Morris. In one sense certainly his nationalism was a reaction against the Victorian materialism and ugliness he saw in England and found reflected in Dublin. Speaking at a Wolfe Tone banquet in London in 1898 he tries to transmute this into a nationalism he himself could believe in:

We hated at first the ideals and ambitions of England, the materialisms of England, because they were hers, but we have come to hate them with a nobler hatred. We hate them now because they are evil. We have suffered too long from them, not to understand, that hurry to become rich, that delight in mere bigness, that insolence to the weak are evil and vulgar things.

Where Morris and the Pre-Raphaelite Brotherhood turned to the past for their models, Yeats turned to the Ireland he wished to create.

His Utopian Ireland, too, owes much of its spirit to Morris. He foresaw a nicely ordered world in which people lived aesthetically but everything got done; enough workers felt inclined to reap when the grain had ripened:

First of all, we Irish do not desire, like the English, to build up a nation where there shall be a very rich class and a very poor class. . . . I think that the best ideal for our people . . . is that Ireland is going to become a country where, if there are few rich, there shall be nobody very poor. Wherever men have tried to imagine a perfect life, they have imagined a place where men plough and sow and reap, not a place where there are great wheels turning and great chimneys vomiting smoke. Ireland will always be a country where men plough and sow and reap.

His ideal was by no means a classless society, but like Morris's might be termed an aristocratic socialism: *A Dream of John Ball* for the arts and intellect. One must "accept the baptism of the gutter," if necessary, but he was convinced that "public order cannot long persist without the rule of educated and able men." Like Morris,

Butler, and Shaw, his aim if he had one at all was to create that aristocratic society of the intellect. "The end of all government, the end of all politics, the end of all movements is the making of character," and that political movement was best that made "the most men of high and stable character" in a country.

Towards this aim he was willing to contribute time and energy, and for ten years he struggled towards its fulfilment. About the same time that he met John O'Leary, he joined a discussion group called the "Contemporary Club," organized by Charles Hubert Oldham, leader of a group of nationalists at Trinity College and largely responsible for founding the *Dublin University Review* which published Yeats's first work. In 1889, the year before Parnell's fall, he met the nationalist beauty Maud Gonne, whose hatred of England was rivalled only by her passionate desire to "free Ireland." The following year he paid his first visit to the Southwark Irish Literary Club of London, whose objects were "the cultivation of Irish history, art, and literature, and the providing of a medium of social and intellectual intercourse for Irish people of both sexes." And in 1891 he and T. W. Rolleston founded the London Irish Literary Society. He then moved across to Ireland and proceeded to establish the Irish Literary Society of Dublin. In a letter to the morning papers, June 2, 1892, he outlined the aims the founder-members had in mind:

... to circulate a new "Library of Ireland" through the existing Literary Societies and by establishing new bodies for the purpose ... to aid the educational influence of the library by well-organized lectures and discussions. ... These books and lectures will be national but not political in any narrow sense of the word. They will endeavour to make the patriotism of the people who read them both deeper and more enlightened, and will set before them the national and legendary heroes as they present themselves to the minds of scholars and thinkers.

Yeats's plans for a New Irish Library were taken over by Charles Gavan Duffy and eventually the control of the National Literary Society passed from his hands, but by then he had turned his nationalist endeavours elsewhere. In 1898, when the Irish Literary Theatre sought sponsorship, the National Literary Society was on hand to grant its benison.

He had, in fact, turned not to London but to Paris. Encouraged by Maud Gonne, in 1896 he joined the Irish Republican Brotherhood, and for the next two years travelled between London and

Paris in preparations for the great Wolfe Tone Centennial celebrations. Yet still he did not commit himself; his aim became a "union of the Gael," which would once more restore the ancient sovereignty to the race, through culture, not through politics. For in order to achieve the Utopia of the arts he dreamed of for Ireland, union of the various political parties must first be arranged, this time through the common celebration of the great union of 1798. Again he succeeded, and again turned once more to a new scheme, the experiment of an Irish Literary Theatre. But this time the experiment outlasted the limits set for it, and he became involved in a project which was to occupy much of his time and many of his plans for the rest of his life. The last deliberate political move we see him making was a formal letter of protest over Queen Victoria's visit to Ireland in 1900, and his contribution to Maud Gonne's successful counter-display through the streets of Dublin.

VI

Yeats's nationalism, then, while in itself a strong emotional need, was in part a result of a much larger dream of art. Art must belong to all and come from all. His aim, therefore, was "to restore what is called a more picturesque way of life . . . in which the common man has some share in imaginative art." Once securely rooted in the nation, art then had an audience. By bringing "the imagination and speech of the country, all that poetical tradition descended from the Middle Age, to the people of the town," the artist was once more free to develop in his own way, secure in his own subject and in the understanding of those for whom he wrote:

I thought we might bring the halves together if we had a national literature that made Ireland beautiful in the memory, and yet had been freed from provincialism by an exacting criticism, a European pose.

In so doing, literature could once more be united to the "great passion of patriotism," thereby ennobling both. For these reasons, then, he and his colleagues dreamed of "a school whose declared purpose is to create in Ireland a true, cultivated, patriotic class, and which for the first time unites Montagu and Capulet in the one movement." This would require scholarship as much as patriotism, artistic freedom as well as collective energy. "Creative work has always a fatherland," as he wrote in his Introduction to *A Book of Irish Verse*, for

...in greater poets everything has relation to the national life or to profound feeling; nothing is an isolated artistic moment; there is a unity everywhere, everything fulfils a purpose that is not his own; the hailstone is a journeyman of God, and the grass blade carries the universe upon its point.

However, he warns, "though a poet may govern his life by his enthusiasms, he must, when he sits down at his desk, but use them as the potter the clay." He must write in the language of his thoughts, for only then can he be true to himself. And if he finds examples elsewhere, he must be free to choose his models from another nation. Nationalism must be tempered by cosmopolitanism; "it is the presence of a personal element alone that can give it nationality in a fine sense"; "a writer is not less National because he shows the influence of other countries and of the great writers of the world." National literature could therefore be defined as

the work of writers, who are moulded by influences that are moulding their country, and who write out of so deep a life that they are accepted there in the end.

What Yeats required for his art was stability in the culture of his nation, and at the same time a free passport to the wisdom of the ages, as befitting that roving aristocrat of the intellect, the artist. If necessary he would by means of his art mould the first to his ideal, in spite of his art challenge his right to the second.

"The Art of Happy Desire": Yeats and the Little Magazine

JOAN COLDWELL

I N DECEMBER 1902, Yeats told Lady Gregory of a projected magazine to be called, after his play, the *Hour-Glass*. He was to write a preface defining the editorial policy he had persuaded Pamela Colman Smith to accept:

> The magazine is to be consecrated to what I called, to their delight, the Art of Happy Desire. It is to be quite unlike gloomy magazines like the *Yellow Book* and the *Savoy*. People are to draw pictures of places they would have liked to have lived in and to write stories and poems about a life they would have liked to have lived. Nothing is to be let in unless it tells of something that seems beautiful or charming or in some other way desirable.

Unfortunately the *Hour-Glass* did not get beyond preliminary suggestions that Ricketts and Shannon should provide illustrations and Lady Gregory some Irish stories. Had it materialized, its history would no doubt have been similar to that of the dozens of "little magazines" that emerged during the eighteen-nineties as the peculiar offspring of that self-conscious age of transition and experiment. Its life-span would have been brief, perhaps fewer than half a dozen numbers; it would have contained the work of a small group of artists, appealed to a limited group of intellectual readers, and besides being a showplace for the contributors would have been an *objet d'art* in itself, beautifully printed and bound.

Yeats's career had been closely connected with magazines of this kind, for much of his earlier work made its first appearance in them before being collected, often in revised versions, for book publication. But his interest in the magazines extended beyond the practical, for they represented a unique venture in periodical publication. Never before had there been such an attempt to create an object of lasting beauty out of this ephemeral form. The influence of William Morris's Aits and Crafts movement is apparent in the belief of periodical editors that a magazine need not necessarily have the air of a glorified newspaper but could be designed to merit a permanent place on the library shelf.

The prospectus for *The Yellow Book*, issued in March 1894, announced:

It will be a *book* — a book to be read, and placed upon one's shelves, and read again; a book in form, a book in substance; a book beautiful to see and convenient to handle...

Book form quickly became popular. The early numbers of *The Savoy* were bound in uncovered boards; the Scots produced four solid issues of *The Evergreen*, while even magazines that came out originally in paper covers were quickly bound into de luxe volumes and sold in limited editions. "Handsomely bound" sets of *The Dome* were offered as status symbols: "No more satisfactory purchase can be made for the bookshelves of the man of taste or for the tables of a country house."

Most of the magazines followed the policy of *The Yellow Book* in printing no advertisements other than publishers' lists. This step towards the purification of art from any taint of commercialism resulted in financial unsteadiness and was largely responsible for the short lives of the periodicals.

The Yellow Book gave art and literature equal status in the magazine, pictures being included in their own right and not simply as illustrations of the text. This stemmed partly from a feeling that artists needed more of a public outlet than was available in the galleries, where exhibitions were often controlled by conservative academicians opposed to *avant-garde* methods. It was also an opportunity for the many painter-writers who wished to show both sides of their work. Beardsley, for example, though primarily an artist, contributed part of a novel and several poems to *The Savoy*, while of the five men contributing drawings to *The Dial*, only Lucien Pissarro did not also publish written pieces there.

This dual interest in art and literature reflects that age's growing sense of the need for cultural education and also the belief, fostered by continental theorists, of the inter-relation of all the arts. *The*

Dome in particular reflects the eclecticism of *fin de siècle* culture. Its First Series was described as "A Quarterly containing Examples of All the Arts," the arts, however, being represented only under the four headings of Architecture; Literature; Drawing, Painting and Engraving; and Music. The first number includes a mock review of itself, laughing at its own ambitiousness (and also at the prevalent arts and crafts craze): "while promising Examples of All the Arts, there is not so much as a reference to Sculpture, Poker-work or Self-defence; and to make the sub-title good, something should surely have been said about Amateur Bent-iron work (Revived Young Ladies Victorian)."

Though the early numbers made a valiant attempt to distribute space equally among the four arts, the literary contributions gradually became more numerous and the music and architecture sections sometimes less apparent. When the New Series was started in October 1898, *The Dome* became a monthly magazine, with a tendency to fall back upon critical articles. Where in the early numbers scores by Edward Elgar for pianoforte solos had graced the music section, in the New Series an informative article on early plainsong would suffice as the only musical contribution.

The music section of the January 1900 issue contains a setting by Thomas F. Dunhill of Yeats's song "Aodh to Dectora," the third of a group of poems which had previously appeared in *The Dome* of May 1898. It was this relatively long-lived magazine which published more of Yeats's work than any other London periodical in the eighteen-nineties; the two articles explaining the principles of the Irish Literary Theatre were first published here.

A puzzled reader of Yeats's poem "The Desire of Man and Woman" in the June issue of 1897 wrote in *The Daily Mail* a scornful comment on this twelve-lined "sonnet" which had sent him "careering back to commonplaces with a sigh of relief." The deliberate appeal of the little magazines to an intellectual coterie is emphasized by the editor of *The Dome* in a subsequent patronizing note: "All humane men and women will feel glad that *The Daily Mail* person returned to his own place so safe and sound after his venturesome little excursion in foreign parts."

Other regular contributors to *The Dome* were Arthur Symons, Laurence Binyon, Laurence Housman, Fiona Macleod and Oswald Sickert, and the most memorable art work came from Edward Gordon Craig. His woodcuts in the New Series include a likeness of his actress mother, Ellen Terry, while the March issue of 1899 contains his striking poster design for *The Dome* and a detachable postcard with a *Dome* picture. Later, Craig was to be involved with his own periodical publication *The Mask*, edited by John Semar in Florence from 1908 to 1929. Like *The Dome* this, though it contained no music, was an eclectic magazine but its bias was theatrical. A European venture, it did not confine itself to English-speaking interests but contained reviews of the arts throughout Europe, including interviews with actors and actresses. Craig's own ideal of the actor as "über-marionette" pervades *The Mask*, whose title points to his interest in a highly stylized form of drama. The April 1911 issue shows Craig's design for the mask of the Fool in Yeats's *The Hour-Glass* and a new version of that play appeared in the April 1913 number. Yeats's essay on "The Tragic Theatre" also had its first printing in *The Mask*.

Yeats's appearance in the most notorious of the little magazines, *The Yellow Book*, was brief: he was promised as a contributor in the prospectus but it was not until the thirteenth and last number that his poem "The Blessed" fulfilled his obligations. But he was closely associated with the artistic group supplying the contributions and with the art editor, Aubrey Beardsley. It was Beardsley who designed the poster for Yeats's first publicly performed play, the Avenue Theatre production of *The Land of Heart's Desire*; this poster design was reproduced for the cover of the first English and American editions of the play.

The Yellow Book made its dramatic entrance on April 15, 1894. The idea for the magazine seems to have arisen in casual conversation between Beardsley and the literary editor, Henry Harland, and Beardsley suggested the title. Yellow had been a favourite colour with the Pre-Raphaelites; Whistler had given "yellow breakfasts" and Oscar Wilde adopted the sunflower as a symbol of aestheticism, so that already in the public mind yellow was the colour of the *avant-garde*, and "art for art's sake." Beardsley's cover design alone, made more audacious by the substitution of yellow for white, was enough to shock the critics, and *The Westminster Gazette* called for an "Act of Parliament to make this kind of thing illegal." Others described it as "semi-obscene" and "sham erotic"; within a week, three editions of the first number had been exhausted and *The Yellow Book* was the talk of the town!

A bibliographic curiosity was produced at the time of Beardsley's removal from the post of art editor. Unfounded rumours that he was one of Wilde's circle were responsible for his dismissal, and in the general panic surrounding Wilde's trials, Harland and the publisher John Lane played safe by dispensing with the one person who made *The Yellow Book* a daring and original publication. Beardsley had already prepared designs for the April 1895 number; these were all removed before publication — except by an oversight the back cover. But one volume with the original Beardsley plates survived and it was given by Harland to Edmund Gosse with the inscription, "This is, so far as I know, the only copy of this suppressed Yellow Book in existence." This book was last heard of at a New York sale some years ago and it is probably still in the United States.[1]

The last *Yellow Book* appeared in May 1897. It had survived a long time for a little magazine, but since Beardsley's withdrawal its financial state had slowly worsened. But its fame and influence did not die; its name is inextricably bound with the eighteen-nineties and any study of that period must take it into account. Almost all the major figures on the artistic scene had at least one work in *The Yellow Book*; the notable exception is, ironically, Oscar Wilde.

In the summer of 1895, Beardsley, already very ill, was invited by Arthur Symons to be art editor of a new magazine, *The Savoy* (again a title suggested by Beardsley). This was intended as a rival to *The Yellow Book*; a rejected cover design for the first *Savoy* depicts by the crudest of insulting gestures Beardsley's contempt for the magazine that had spurned him. Dramatic colouring for the covers was again attempted, but less successfully in a blancmange pink, later changed to pale blue. *The Savoy*, however, was quarto size, principally to give Beardsley's drawings more effective reproduction on a larger scale, and it attempted to undersell its competitor by charging only half the price, two and sixpence. There were eight numbers published, all of them in 1896, for the initial success of the venture led Symons to change *The Savoy* at the third number into a monthly magazine, reducing the price by only sixpence and making the general format less substantial.

Yeats's criticism of *The Yellow Book* and *The Savoy* as "gloomy magazines" was echoed by many people who felt that not even Max Beerbohm's contributions avoided ponderous self-consciousness

[1] For a full description of the history of *The Yellow Book*, see Katherine Lyon Mix, *A Study in Yellow* (London, 1960).

or lightened the atmosphere of grotesque decadence. But Beardsley's work, though deliberately decadent, does much to relieve the gloom by its obvious humour which, though sometimes indelicate, is often gently affectionate or wittily self-directed. On the title-page of the third *Savoy* appeared a delightful drawing of a Puck on the winged horse Pegasus, with the motto *Ne Iuppiter quidem omnibus placet.* This figure was repeated in all subsequent numbers of *The Savoy* and it could appropriately have become Beardsley's personal emblem. It reflects his youthful conceit and his flair for a pose, as well as the justifiable sense of his own genius. It shows too that Beardsley thought of himself as a mischievous humorist, "a shrewd and knavish sprite."

Beardsley's preoccupation with Pierrot figures indicates a similar pose. During the *Yellow Book* days he had designed an invitation card for John Lane, showing an *avant-garde* Pierrot sitting beside a copy of *The Yellow Book* and smoking a small cigar. His last designs frequently incorporate Pierrot figures, inspired by the illustrations he made for Dowson's play *The Pierrot of the Minute.* In the sixth number of *The Savoy* appears the very moving picture "The Death of Pierrot," in which the comedian's friends come to pay their last respects. Beardsley was beginning to dramatize his own approaching death, and the Pierrot, traditionally a white-faced clown, appealed to his sense of humour as a fitting pose, for almost every description of Beardsley's appearance comments on the pallor of his face.

In the last three numbers of *The Savoy*, Beardsley's self-dramatization in the face of death has a painful poignancy. "The Death of Pierrot" in number six is followed in seven by his literal but graceful translation of Catullus' "Carmen CI," the poem of funeral rites for the beloved brother. The accompanying illustration shows a sorrowing quasi-Roman youth, one arm outstretched in salutation, with the words "Ave atque Vale" printed near the top of the design. In the final number, where the contributions are entirely by the two editors, is Beardsley's version of the "Et in Arcadia Ego" theme; in a formal flowery park, a slightly aging dandy inspects through his monocle a pillar, bearing an ornamental urn, on which the inscription is engraved. Fourteen months after the publication of this picture Beardsley was buried in the hillside graveyard above Mentone.

Beardsley dominates *The Savoy*, but the magazine had many

distinguished contributors. The opening article of the first number was George Bernard Shaw's "On Going to Church," an essay advocating beautiful church buildings but incidentally summarizing much of Shaw's religious attitudes at the time. Havelock Ellis contributed informative critical articles on Zola, Hardy and Nietzsche, presenting the latter to the English public for the first time. Conrad published a new story *The Idiots* in the sixth number, and Yeats sent poems, stories or essays to all but two of the issues. When Beardsley wrote to thank the publisher Smithers for his copy of the third number, he commented, "Yeats again provides the most interesting item." This item was probably not Yeats's poem "O'Sullivan Rua to Mary Lavell" but the first of his three articles on William Blake's illustrations to Dante's *Divine Comedy*. Strangely enough, it was this article which brought *The Savoy* to disrepute. W. H. Smith and Son refused to place on their respectable stands a magazine which reproduced Blake's naked "Antaeus, setting Virgil and Dante upon the Verge of Cocytus," and travellers by train were that month deprived of *The Savoy*.

The early death that terminated Beardsley's brief, four-year career as a professional artist helped to make him almost a symbol of the many young men of the nineties whose lives glowed with an intense but soon extinguished flame, who "lived in joy and laughed into the face of Death." These words by Yeats come from a group of seven poems "Upon a Dying Lady," inspired by the frequent visits Yeats made to Beardsley's sister Mabel, the beautiful red-haired actress, who died in 1916. Yeats was much impressed by her courage and gaiety, the renewal of "her dead brother's valour," and in letters to Lady Gregory describes the cheerful Sunday afternoons when Aubrey's friends and Mabel's came to see her. He tells how the dolls described in the second and third of the poems had been made by Charles Ricketts, the dresses designed and the faces carefully modelled to look like people in Beardsley's drawings. Ricketts was a devoted friend of the Beardsley family, bearing no malice though he felt that in at least one direction his work had been overshadowed: "My book-illustration work has been swamped for ever by the success of Beardsley . . ." [2]

Ricketts is revealed in his *Self-Portrait* as one of the most likeable characters of the period. Completely dedicated to art for its own sake, he is nevertheless the most unassuming and unaffected man

[2] *Self-Portrait*, comp. T. Sturge Moore, ed. Cecil Lewis (London, 1939), 227.

of that self-conscious age. He can on occasion turn as witty an epigram as his friend Oscar Wilde, but there is not the slightest suggestion of a pose. T. Sturge Moore writes that "he was supremely natural," full of infectious humour and capable of bursting the bubble of any affectation so that "laughter restored sanity."

Described by another contemporary as "the only legitimate children of the Pre-Raphaelites," he and the painter Charles Hazlewood Shannon spent all of their lives in quest of beauty, which was for Ricketts "the nearest approach possible to permanence." Wide knowledge of art, exquisite taste and a willingness to sacrifice their own physical comfort enabled them to build up one of the most fabulous private art collections in the country, left at their death to the nation. The body of the collection was housed in the Fitzwilliam Museum at Cambridge, while the Japanese prints and drawings went to the British Museum.

Ricketts was a constant experimenter in many fields. A designer, painter, wood-engraver and sculptor, he was also a writer for many periodicals and author of a number of books, some under the pseudonym of Jean-Paul Raymond. He was a connoisseur of music and the theatre, and designed sets and costumes for over thirty plays, including first performances of work by Shaw, Yeats, Bennett and even Gilbert and Sullivan. As founder with Shannon of the Vale Press, he created beautiful books, for which he not only designed woodcut illustrations, decorative borders and covers, but also three entirely new founts of type. Eighty-eight volumes, of which forty were editions of Shakespeare's plays, were issued between 1896 and 1906, Ricketts personally supervising every stage of the production.

It is not surprising then that the two periodicals produced by Ricketts and Shannon should be the most tasteful and elegant of late-Victorian magazines. For many years Ricketts' reputation rested on *The Dial*, an occasional publication founded by him in 1889 when he was a young man in his early twenties. The limited editions of the five numbers were quickly exhausted, and though the venture was abandoned in 1897, it had spread Ricketts' fame among artistic circles in England and on the continent.

The Dial was technically a private enterprise and more than any other magazine of the period it was a showplace for the work of a very small group. Besides Shannon and Ricketts, only Reginald Savage, T. Sturge Moore and Lucien Pissarro contributed art work; the same men, with the exception of Pissarro, furnished the literary matter, supported by six others who included Emile Verhaeren and Laurence Housman. The editors were frank about their project: "The sole aim of this magazine is to gain sympathy with its views . . . we are out of date in our belief that the artist's consciousness cannot be controlled by the paying public."

William Morris wrote to thank the editors for a copy of *The Dial* and expressed an opinion that may be aptly applied to most of the magazines of the nineties: ". . . the talent and the aberration of the talent seemed to me to be in about equal proportion." He declined to comment on the literary section, which indeed has little inspiration. It is the art work that keeps the magazine alive, and the tastefulness of the production that makes it valuable.

The fourth number, published in 1896, presents a specimen of the new Vale type, with illustrated initial. Ricketts was motivated in his printing experiments by much the same enthusiasm as William Morris, who had been largely responsible for the revival of the art of printing. Between 1891 and 1897 the Kelmscott Press produced books more beautiful than any printed since the Renaissance, and Morris and his followers expressed their aims in speeches and essays: "Therefore, granted well-designed type, due spacing of the lines and words, and proper position of the page on the paper, all books might be at least comely and well looking; and if to these good qualities were added really beautiful ornament and pictures, printed books might once again illustrate to the full position of our Society that a work of utility might be also a work of art, if we cared to make it so." [3]

Like Morris, Ricketts expressed his aims for a revival of printing, in a treatise entitled "De la typographie et de l'harmonie de la page imprimée." Here, and elsewhere in his writings, it is obvious that for Ricketts printing was an intensely creative act to which he dedicated himself wholeheartedly. He frequently stressed that these were not just ordinary books to him but part of a special artistic mission, and in 1904 he noted in his diary, "Took up Vale Press Bibliography again. Was touched and charmed while rehandling the old books, the old file copies full of associations and gold dust of life — to me at least."

The two volumes of *The Pageant*, edited by Charles Shannon and T. Gleeson White in 1896 and 1897, illustrate Ricketts' success in the art of creating beautiful books. He designed the bindings for

3 William Morris and Emery Walker, *Arts and Crafts Essays*, 1893.

these sumptuous quartos in a muted orange cloth, the designs embossed in gold. The first volume contains an article on the work of Ricketts in which Gleeson White writes, "Cloth-binding, but latterly a thing of horror, has suddenly become illuminated with intelligence; and for this no second name need be coupled with that of Mr. Ricketts." The interest of the editors in the beauty of the format is reflected in the frontispiece note to volume one, in which they acknowledge the designers of the end-papers, the binding, the title-page and even of the outer wrapper.

There was more variety in this magazine than in *The Dial* and the tone was less obviously earnest. In the first volume the twenty-three-year-old Beerbohm announced his retirement to the hermitage of a London suburban home: "Already I feel myself to be a trifle outmoded. I belong to the Beardsley period. Younger men . . . have pressed forward since then. *Cedo junioribus.*"

Yeats's story "Costello the Proud, Oona MacDermott and the Bitter Tongue" was first printed in *The Pageant* but there were closer associations than this between him and Ricketts. "My education in so many things" was Yeats's description of the man for whose conversation he set aside Friday evenings when he was in London and who as personal friend and as designer for some of his plays greatly influenced Yeats's development as a playwright. Ricketts' practical criticism must have helped to moderate the often too esoteric plays Yeats wrote. Of *Where There is Nothing* he writes, "It is much too long and showed halts in construction, but it could be cut down to a telling thing."[4] The day after the performance Yeats visited Ricketts, who then noted in his diary, "Yeats in the evening. We spoke about the failure of his play. He showed himself critical and shrewd. When he does not pontify he is all right."

Ricketts' interest in the Irish Literary Theatre brings us to those magazines edited by Yeats himself. The idea of this theatre as it had been outlined in the April 1899 number of *The Dome* was realized in the performance in May 1899, at the Antient Concert Rooms in Dublin, of *The Countess Cathleen* and Edward Martyn's *The Heather Field*. To the recording of the subsequent history of the Irish dramatic movement, the Abbey Theatre bulletins, all edited by Yeats, made no small contribution.

At that first performance in May 1899, copies were sold of *Beltaine*, "The Organ of the Irish Literary Theatre." The title

4 *Self-Portrait*, 198.

appropriately revives the name of an old Irish festival held at the beginning of Spring. For threepence, the reader had programmes for the two plays and analyses of them by Lionel Johnson and George Moore, a copy of the prologue to be spoken at the first performance and of the lyrics from *Countess Cathleen*, a reprint from the *Daily Express* of an article on the Scandinavian dramatists and another of Yeats's *Dome* articles, together with editorial outline of "Plans and Methods." Seldom was so much offered for so little.

In the second number a year later the price had judiciously doubled and there were no programmes in the magazine. Yet the offering was still generous. Lady Gregory presented reviews of the previous productions, the current plays were described and analysed, and Yeats's article "The Irish Literary Theatre" was reprinted from *The Dome*. But the most interesting passages in this number are from George Moore and Edward Martyn who, in the full tide of extravagant nationalism, both contributed comparisons of the English and Irish theatres. Having shown that all London had to offer was musical comedy, Moore concludes, "there is probably nothing in life so low as a musical comedy." Martyn describes England as a "rank garden . . . choked up with the rubbish of worn-out systems" and proclaims, "Literature is always the first to go at the downfall of an empire. There is no doubt that in England it has gone." Yeats, embarrassed perhaps by his own affiliations with England, tries in his editorial to smooth over this, preferring to throw the blame on commercialism and materialism and not on the race which had after all produced Arnold, Ruskin and Morris.

The third number of *Beltaine*, a mere halfpennyworth, had abandoned its thick paper cover and was nothing more than three sheets of Yeats's reviews of the previous year's plays. This was the last of *Beltaine*. In response to requests, the three numbers in their original wrappers were "encased in boards for preservation on the bookshelf."

In 1901, the company moved its performances to the autumn, and *Beltaine*'s services were now discharged more fully by *Samhain* (the old Irish name for the beginning of winter). There were seven issues, 1901-1908, and each contained texts of one or two of the plays written for the Irish theatre. Two of these plays, by Douglas Hyde, were printed in Irish, with Lady Gregory's translations. In the fifth number the process was reversed; Lady Gregory's *Spreading the News* was put into Irish by " Torna."

Samhain is useful for the researcher, for in addition to the annual report of progress it prints, in the sixth number, a complete list of the plays so far produced by the Society and, in the fourth, copies of Miss Horniman's letter offering financial help in the shape of a theatre building and of the Society's letter of acceptance. The few illustrations are also interesting: J. B. Yeats's drawing of Synge, Robert Gregory's drawing of Sara Allgood, and portraits of the Fay brothers, one of them by Jack Yeats.

Yeats notes in the last *Samhain* that it had not appeared for a couple of years "principally because an occasional publication, called *The Arrow*, took its place for a time." This was the period of the *Playboy* riots and the purpose of the pamphlet was to explain the Society's objectives to a hostile audience. A special number was prepared for the company's tour of England and Yeats wrote in it a defence of Synge's play:

> The failure of our audience to understand this powerful and strange work has been the one serious failure of our movement, and it could not have happened but that the greater number of those who came to shout down the play were no regular part of our audience at all but members of parties and societies whose main interests are political.

Two bibliographic curiosities resulted from *The Arrow*. At the time of the riots a group of Irish writers and artists composed a satirical pamphlet entitled *The Abbey Row*; it was designed to look like *The Arrow* but the cover, instead of depicting the figure of Eire, showed Mrs. Grundy with an umbrella in place of a quiver, and a wolf dog with the face of J. M. Synge. In 1939, after Yeats's death, a commemoration number of *The Arrow* was issued, edited by Lennox Robinson and with contributions from a number of Yeats's colleagues.

Like Ricketts, Yeats was concerned about the art of fine printing and it is to him and to his sister Elizabeth that the revival of that art in Ireland is to be attributed. In 1903 Elizabeth Yeats, who had been a pupil at Morris's Kelmscott House, founded the Dun Emer, later the Cuala, Press. Yeats styled himself the editor of the press and no book was published without his consent. The Cuala Press periodical, *A Broadside*, issued monthly from 1908 to 1915, was little more than a large card, always carrying three of Jack Yeats's charming woodcuts. Jack Yeats had contributed much to the magazine Pamela Colman Smith did finally publish instead of the projected *Hour-Glass*. In 1903 and 1904 thirteen numbers of her *Green Sheaf* appeared, with hand-coloured illustrations by herself and Jack Yeats and a reproduction of a pastel drawing by W. B. Yeats of *The Lake at Coole*. Yeats, Synge and Lady Gregory all contributed, and several writers, including Yeats, recounted dreams.

The artistic activity in Ireland was part of a larger movement, the so-called Celtic Renaissance, which produced a number of oddities in the way of magazines. Not the least of these was the "Pan-Celtic Monthly Magazine," *Celtia*, which covered all five Celtic nations including Brittany.

In Scotland, a "semi-collegiate group" of writers and artists endeavoured to follow in the footsteps of Allan Ramsay, who in 1724 had published his *Evergreen* in the hope of stimulating interest in local and national traditions. The Celtic obsession with the seasons, touched on in *Beltaine* and *Samhain*, is carried to strange lengths in the new *Evergreen*. Published quarterly, the magazine made itself wholly relevant to the season; in the first issue, for example, there are poems, stories, articles and pictures all trying to ring the changes on the theme of Spring. After four numbers, the subjects were exhausted and *The Evergreen* lived for only one year, 1896.

Like the London magazines this was a hard-bound book with full-page illustrations, and it carried eclecticism even further, for as well as imaginative matter it had articles on biology, natural history and sociology. It was, however, very conscious of its mission to oppose the principles of the decadent English and saw its aim as part of a grand evolutionary scheme, seeking "only to link the Autumn of our own age with an approaching Spring, and pass, through Decadence, towards Renascence." The proem to the first issue does not mince words about the artists producing the little magazines in the south: "so many clever writers emulously working in a rotten vineyard, so many healthy young men eager for the distinction of decay."

It was a similar, though less eccentric, type of Celtic miscellany that Yeats was concerned with in *The Shanachie*. Six numbers of this quarterly were published by Maunsel in 1906 and 1907, with works entirely by Irish contributors including Synge, Yeats, Bernard Shaw, Padraic Colum, J. B. Yeats and Jack Yeats. Lady Gregory refused to co-operate, claiming that "amateurish things of that kind were injurious to the whole movement." In the letter to Stephen Gwynn in which this statement is reported (June 13, 1906), Yeats defines his attitude to the principles of magazine publication. He criticizes the publishers of *The Shanachie* for vagueness of policy and general lack of co-ordination:

I do not find in the editing of this magazine any one selective mind or any one principle of selection . . . I don't believe it is possible to make a good magazine without making up your mind who it is for whom you are making it and keeping to that idea throughout . . . . what Dublin wants is some man who knows his own mind and has an intolerable tongue and a delight in enemies . . .

Yeats attempts to follow this creed in his last periodical venture, *On the Boiler* (modelled perhaps on Ruskin's *Fors Clavigera*). Cuala Press published the one issue in 1938 and the work is entirely from Yeats's pen. In the preface he repeats his policy, "In this new publication I shall write whatever interests me at the moment, trying, however, to keep some kind of unity."

Most of the experimental magazines of the eighteen-nineties did in fact operate according to these principles. The careers of *The Yellow Book* and *The Savoy* proved that for outstanding success a strong personality was needed, a man such as Beardsley, who knew his own mind, while the unabashed statements of appeal to minority groups showed the awareness of audience that Yeats recommended. But above all, the principles of selection were clear: nothing was to be let in unless it seemed in some way beautiful and worthy of a place in what was to be as nearly as possible a perfectly designed book. By striving to follow these principles, the artists of the eighteen-nineties succeeded in making of so ephemeral a form as the little magazine a thing of beauty that is, in Ricketts' words, "the nearest approach possible to permanence."

"Metaphors for Poetry": W. B. Yeats and the Occult

DAVID R. CLARK

ONE MIGHT WELL CONSIDER the subject of Yeats and the occult as "Yeats's Willing Suspension of Belief," for Yeats's problem was the opposite of Coleridge's. Coleridge, in directing his endeavours "to persons and characters supernatural," was striving to overcome his own disbelief in order to write the poem, and the reader's disbelief in order for him to read it. Yeats's problem, on the other hand, was, as indicated in the 1937 edition of *A Vision*, to accept the "unknown writer's" dictum that he had come, not to bring him "scattered sentences" of supernatural truth which he might "spend what remained of life explaining and piecing together," but to bring him "metaphors for poetry." It is clear from *A Vision* that, still late in life, he was repeating a dialogue with himself in which he struggled to recognize the creation of poetry, in and of itself, as his primary responsibility, and in which he resisted the temptation to codify articles of belief or to create poetic "manuals of devotion." But in his letter to Sturge Moore he still makes remarks like "I write not drama, but the ritual of a lost faith," and still he considers the nature of "the creation or enjoyment of a work of art" to be to "escape from the constraint of our nature and from that of external things, entering upon a state where all fuel has become flame where there is nothing but the state itself, nothing to constrain or end it." It is a one-sided approach to Yeats, then, to show impatience with his interest in the supernatural and to feel that it intrudes in his poetry. But it is a mistake of another kind to read the works as expressions of traditional neoplatonic or Eastern or occult philosophy without reference to their literary effect. Yeats was looking for authority for what he wanted to believe and for elaboration and clarification of his own ideas. Therefore he saw what was common among his sources, not what was different, and often he saw links where there were none.

The best source for Yeats's thoughts on these subjects up to 1903 is *Ideas of Good and Evil*, which collects essays from 1895 to 1903. The cardinal principles of his credo at this time from the 1901 essay "Magic" have been often quoted:

I believe in the practice and philosophy of what we have agreed to call magic, in what I must call the evocation of spirits, though I do not know what they are, in the power of creating magical illusions, in the visions of truth in the depths of the mind when the eyes are closed; and I believe in three doctrines, which have, as I think, been handed down from early times, and been the foundations of nearly all magical practices. These doctrines are:

1) That the borders of our mind are ever shifting, and that many minds can flow into one another, as it were, and create or reveal a single mind, a single energy.

2) That the borders of our memories are as shifting, and that our memories are a part of one great memory, the memory of Nature herself.

3) That this great mind and great memory can be evoked by symbols.

I often think I would put this belief in magic from me if I could, for I have come to see or to imagine, in men and women, in houses, in handicrafts, in nearly all sights and sounds, a certain evil, a certain ugliness, that comes from the slow perishing through the centuries of a quality of mind that made this belief and its evidences common over the world.

These cardinal principles were supported by a way, or set of ways, of regarding the universe, each aspect of which was derived from one of his sources or common to all or most of them. Yeats believed that kingdoms rise and fall as the grass grows and dies and grows again, that each cyclic movement of history is an "hour" within the "day" of a larger movement, and that all these cycles are caught within one all-inclusive "Great Year" which has a cosmic purpose. He believed too that the cycle of individual life repeated itself in many forms both in this world and beyond it until the possibilities have been exhausted and the soul either released or forced to "relive it all again." He believed that life is always a dramatic tension between warring opposites. He agreed with Blake (in the *Marriage of Heaven and Hell*) that "Without Contraries is no progression. Attraction and Repulsion, Reason and Energy, Love and Hate, are necessary to Human existence." It is the tension between opposite principles which creates the movement of the cycles. And for every cyclic movement, there is its opposite, a counter-cycle. Sun and moon, male and female, became basic symbols of the antinomies found in all of life. Two of these antinomies are the World of Being and the World of Becoming, the supernatural and nature. Between these may be found an elaborate series of Correspondences. The combination of the principle of correspondences and the principle of the antinomies may be illustrated by a passage from Yeats's play *The Hour-Glass*: "There are two living countries, one visible and one invisible, and when it is summer there, it is winter here, and when it is November with us, it is lambing-time there."

The individual soul, too, is at war with itself, or with its opposite within itself. And it must be transformed into its opposite. Here the Christian idea of the death of the old Adam and the birth of the new becomes fused with the idea of the ritual murder and rebirth of that nature god. The initiation rites of the Order of the Golden Dawn involved a series of spiritual deaths and rebirths through which one could climb the Tree of Life, whose roots are in earth and whose branches are in Heaven, from grade to grade until one achieved union with one's higher Self or God.

The fundamental opposition in which Yeats was interested is that between the "practical" objective man and the imaginative subjective man which he dramatized in his plays in such characters as Conchubar and Cuchulain and in his stories in Owen Aherne and Michael Robartes, more patently the two halves of himself. His own duty, clearly, was to transform his practical objective Aherne self into the imaginative subjective Robartes.

The body of ideas which Yeats got from his study and practice of the occult he identified with an ancient and universal belief which his writings were to make available to modern man. These ideas were incorporated into *A Vision* (1925), though transformed in the process. A convenient summary of some of the principal conceptions which went into *A Vision* may be found in the notes on "The Second Coming" in *Michael Robartes and the Dancer* (1920):

To the Judwalis, as interpreted by Michael Robartes, all living mind has . . . a fundamental mathematical movement, however adapted in plant, or animal, or man to particular circumstance; and when you have found this movement and calculated its relations, you can fore- tell the entire future of that mind. A supreme religious act of their faith is to fix the attention on the mathematical form of this move- ment until the whole past and future of humanity, or of an individual man, shall be present to the intellect as if it were accomplished in a single moment. The intensity of the Beatific Vision when it comes depends upon the intensity of this realization. It is possible in this way, seeing that death is itself marked upon the mathematical figure, which passes beyond it, to follow the soul into the highest heaven and the deepest hell. This doctrine is, they contend, not fatalistic because the mathematical figure is an expression of the mind's desire, and the more rapid the development of the figure the greater the freedom of the soul. . . . The human soul is always moving outward into the objective world or inward into itself; and this movement is double because the human soul would not be conscious were it not suspended between contraries, the greater the contrast the more intense the consciousness. The man, in whom the movement inward is stronger than the move- ment outward, the man who sees all reflected within himself, the subjective man, reaches the narrow end of a gyre at death, for death is always, they contend, even when it seems the result of accident, pre- ceded by an intensification of the subjective life; and has a moment of revelation immediately after death, a revelation which they describe as his being carried into the presence of all his dead kindred, a moment whose objectivity is exactly equal to the subjectivity of death. The objective man on the other hand, whose gyre moves outward, receives at this moment the revelation, not of himself seen from within, for that is impossible to objective man, but of himself as if he were somebody else. This figure is true also of history, for the end of an age, which always receives the revelation of the character of the next age, is represented by the coming of one gyre to its place of greatest expansion and of the other to that of its greatest contraction.

The philosophical system presented in *A Vision* was developed as a result of much varied reading, and as a consequence of many personal experiences. At an early age Yeats heard a voice, something like Socrates' daemon, which reproved him at moments of crisis, saw strange sights, "a supernatural bird in the corner of the room," and had psychic dreams in one of which he screamed out in his sleep and described an actual shipwreck in which his grandfather was involved. In an environment in which the servants and cottagers of Sligo believed in ghosts and fairies and told stories about them, these and other incidents were interpreted as evidences of the super- natural.

It is ironic that Yeats's father, sceptical J. B. Yeats, read to him *The Lay of the Last Minstrel* and gave him "a wish to turn magician that competed for years with the dream of being killed upon the sea-shore" [*Autobiographies*]. This dream of "heroic self-possession" which Yeats at this time also found in Irving's *Hamlet* later became associated in Yeats's mind with Irish myth and legend. He was to embody it in his own work in the figure of Cuchulain. The means towards attaining this self-possession, since his father's scepticism and the intellectual climate of the time would make orthodox religion impossible for him, was to become the study of magic. It is interesting to find end and means so clearly associated in this passage which must point to Yeats at about the age of twelve.

In May 1884 Yeats entered the Metropolitan Art School in Dublin where he met George Russell, and Russell immediately had an effect on Yeats through painting his visions rather than the model and through his interest in Asian religion and literature. Another friend interested in occult study was Charles Johnston. He read A. P. Sinnett's *The Occult World* (1881) in 1884. Presumably Madame Blavatsky's *Isis Unveiled* (1877) had also been consulted by these friends. Yeats read Sinnett's second book *Esoteric Buddhism* in the spring of 1885 and, communicating his excitement to these friends, joined them and some others in starting the "Dublin Hermetic Society" on June 16, 1885. In May 1887 Yeats visited Madame Blavatsky in London and joined the Blavatsky Lodge of the London Theosophical Society, becoming a member of the Esoteric section in 1888, the year in which Madame Blavatsky's *The Secret Doctrine* was published. G. R. S. Mead, author of *Thrice-Greatest Hermes: Studies in Hellenistic Theosophy and Gnosis* (1906) and other works, became a friend of Yeats at this time. In August 1890 Yeats was asked to resign from the Society because of his excessive interest in occult experiments.

Yeats had read *The Kabbalah Unveiled* by MacGregor Mathers (1887) before he met Mathers in 1890 and was persuaded by this Celtic Christian Cabbalist to join "The Order of the Hermetic Students of the Golden Dawn," which he did in March of 1890. The Order itself had been going since 1888. Yeats was active in this Cabbalistic and Rosicrucian organization from 1890 to about 1903 and again from 1906 to 1909. There was much in common between theosophy and the Golden Dawn, as is shown by the fact that the first public announcement of the Order appeared in Madame

Blavatsky's review *Lucifer* in June 1889. But whereas the theoso-phists' interests were theoretical, those of the Order of the Golden Dawn were practical — they were ritual and magic. Mathers gave Yeats a cardboard symbol to hold to his forehead, and when Yeats closed his eyes "there rose before me . . . a desert and black Titan raising himself up by his two hands from the middle of a heap of ancient ruins" [*Autobiographies*]. A symbol of fire had called up this shape "somewhere in sands of the desert" which reminds one of Yeats's "The Second Coming." Metaphors for his poetry and rituals of death and rebirth for his plays were found in the Golden Dawn.

Celtic heathendom had been full of ritual murders and of rebirth cycles. In 1888 appeared John Rhys's *Lectures on the Origin and Growth of Religion as Illustrated by Celtic Heathendom*. Yeats used the book in writing his *The Wanderings of Oisin* (1889). Sir James Frazer's *The Golden Bough*, Part I: *The Magic Art and the Evolution of Kings*, appeared in 1890. Yeats mentions this work in his notes to *The Wind Among the Reeds* (1899). But Yeats says that it was through John O'Leary, whom he met late in 1885, that he first discovered his theme (meaning, I take it, Irish unity of culture). O'Leary persuaded Yeats to read Thomas Davis and the other *Nation* poets who had written of and for the people. Earlier Yeats had read the heroic tales of Ireland in many forms including the *History of Ireland* by Standish James O'Grady (1882) and the verse versions of Sir Samuel Ferguson. Henri d'Arbois de Jubainville, author of *Le Cycle mythologique irlandais et la mythologie celtique* (1884) and the most distinguished celticist of his time, Yeats men-tions in a review February 22, 1890. Douglas Hyde's *The Story of Early Gaelic Literature* (1897), expanded into *A Literary History of Ireland* (1899), of course had an effect as did Lady Gregory's *Cuchulain of Muirthemne* (1902), and *Gods and Fighting Men* (1904). From 1896 to 1902 Yeats was interested in founding a specifically Irish cult in which rituals would be developed based on his reading of such books as these and on meditation. Maud Gonne, AE, William Sharp, MacGregor Mathers were involved in this pro-jected "Castle of Heroes" which was to have an island on Lough Key as its centre. His work prior to this time may be regarded as moving towards such an attempt, and very late in life he still saw Druidism as a major element in his credo.

Scholars point to Yeats's insistence on an Irish ancestry for William Blake as amusing evidence of Yeats's determination to accord all his other interests with his Irish ones. Yeats had known the works of Blake and Shelley from boyhood, thinking of *Prometheus Bound* as his "sacred book" when Edward Dowden (some time after May 1884) read to him and J. B. Yeats parts of his unpublished life of Shelley. But Blake's *Prophetic Books* could not have been a major influence until Yeats had worked out their interpretation in *The Works of William Blake, Poetic, Symbolic, and Critical* (1893) which he edited with Edwin John Ellis. (Yeats first mentions working on this in February of 1889.) The lyrics and the other more available literary works and the paintings and engravings were undoubtedly an influence much earlier. The explication of Blake's "Symbolic System" in volume 1 of the *Works* shows by allusion that Yeats had read and meditated on Jacob Boehme and Emmanuel Swedenborg before the book appeared in February 1893.

Richard Ellmann points out in *Yeats, the Man and the Masks* (1949) that although there was a considerable element of neoplatonism in theosophy and in the Golden Dawn ritual, Yeats apparently never got around to reading much of Plato himself until Lionel Johnson gave him a copy of the dialogues and made him read it. Yeats presumably knew Plotinus and his school through the translations of Thomas Taylor, whose *Porphyrus* he quotes at length in his essay "The Philosophy of Shelley's Poetry" (1900). Yet many years later in the spring of 1926 he avidly reads and re-reads the new translation by Stephen MacKenna of the *Enneads* (1917-1930) as if he had never read Plotinus before. He re-read Plato, too, in this period of the aftermath of having written *A Vision* (1925). As for the Cambridge Platonists, he quotes Joseph Glanvil in his essay on "Magic" in 1901, but read Henry More intensively in the summer of 1914 and used him in *Per Amica Silentia Lunae* (1918).

Yeats's knowledge of what was going on in continental literature and in particular the French symbolist movement and its connection with the occult undoubtedly came in large part through Arthur Symons. He may have read an article in the *National Observer*, a newspaper to which he himself contributed, in which Stephen Mallarmé, by way of commenting on a celebrated quarrel in occult and symbolist circles in Paris, described the relation of magic to art in much the way Yeats does in his "Magic" essay. Yeats left on a visit to Paris in February 1894 with introductions to Verlaine and Mallarmé. He escorted Maude Gonne to a performance of Villiers de l'Isle Adam's symbolist and Rosicrucian drama *Axel* and wrote a review for the *Bookman*. *Axel* became one of his sacred books and dominated his thought for years, influencing the ending of *The Shadowy Waters* (1900) and the matter of "Rosa Alchemica" (1896). In 1925 appeared a translation by H. P. R. Finberg with a preface by Yeats, with many designs by T. Sturge Moore.

Yeats moved into lodgings in the Temple adjoining those of Symons in late September or early October of 1895, staying there through January 1896, and had first-hand knowledge of Symons' translations from the symbolists. He worked with Symons to some extent on the latter's *The Symbolist Movement in Literature* (1899).

Yeats's interest in Indian philosophy is in the early years identified with his interest first in theosophy and then in the Order of the Golden Dawn. Three visiting Indians made an especial impression on Yeats. The Brahmin Mohini J. Chatterjee, an associate of Madame Blavatsky, to whom Yeats wrote in 1928 the poem which bears his name, came to Dublin in 1885 or 1886, lectured to the Dublin Society, and probably inspired such early poems as "Kanva on Himself" (1889), "Quatrains and Aphorisms" (1886), "Anashuya and Vijaya" (1887), "The Indian upon God" (1886), and "The Indian to His Love" (1886). Yeats gives an account of this visit in "The Pathway" in Volume Eight of the 1908 *Collected Works*. In June of 1912 Yeats met the Bengali poet Rabindranath Tagore and later helped to produce editions of Tagore's work in English — *Gitanjali* (1912), *The Post Office* (1914), and *Gitanjali and Fruit-gathering* (1919). But the Indian sage from whom Yeats learned most in the period between the two editions of *A Vision*, 1925 and 1937, was Shri Purohit Swami with whom he was closely associated from 1931 through 1936. Yeats was excited to learn, as Richard Ellmann notes, "that in the wisdom literature of the East the accepted belief was that 'the individual self, eater of the fruit of action, is the universal Self, maker of past and future.' At the highest moments of consciousness the individual self, detached from action, was aware of this identity. In the efforts which the Indian holy man makes to get rid of all that prevents this knowledge Yeats found his own image of the artist who purges away the inessential to get down to the bedrock of passion." [1] Yeats wrote important introductions to the Swami's autobiography, *An Indian Monk* (1932), to *The Holy Mountain* (1934), by the Swami's master Bhagwan Shri Hamsa, and to "A Short Upanishad," which was published in *Criterion* of July

[1] *Yeats, the Man and the Masks*, 279.

1935. Yeats and the Swami went to Majorca in 1936 to produce an English version of *The Ten Principal Upanishads* (1937), for which Yeats wrote an introduction as he did for the Swami's translations of Patanjali's *Aphorisms of Yoga* (1938).

In 1925 was published the first edition of Yeats's *A Vision*. A new version was, except for minor changes, completed in 1929 but not published until 1937. But his formal last word on subject matter and style appears in "A General Introduction for my Work," dated 1937 but not published until 1961. The essay is divided into the following sections: "I. The First Principle," "II. Subject-Matter," "III. Style and Attitude," and "IV. Whither?" The unifying concept in this essay is "the Self" of the Upanishads. The section called "The First Principle" makes four points. (1) The "poet writes always of his personal life, in his finest work out of its tragedy." (2) However, "he never speaks directly. . . . There is always a phantasmagoria. . . . Even when the poet seems most himself . . . he has been reborn as an idea, something intended, complete, . . . more type than man, more passion than type. He is Lear, Romeo, Oedipus, Tiersias; he has stepped out of a play. . . ." He has, in short, made the personal universal. (3) By so doing he enables his readers or audience to lose their daily minds "in the light of the Self. . . ." We adore the poet "because nature has grown intelligible, and by so doing a part of our creative power." By being "part of his own phantasmagoria" he enables us, who identify with him, to dominate a meaningfully ordered world. We lose our personal concerns in a larger perspective. " 'A wise man seeks in Self,' says the Chandogya Upanishad, 'those that are alive and those that are dead and gets what the world cannot give'." (4) The fourth point returns to the first. The poet, ascending into that higher "Self" which both writes and reads his poems, regains there what he had lost in his personal life. The remarkable sentence which ends this section — "The world knows nothing because it has made nothing, we know everything because we have made everything" — may merely be an expression of the exaltation one feels in the presence of great art. The poet provides a way of seeing the heterogeneous daylight world which creates it for the first time as a cosmos, an integral whole, and thus "nature grows intelligible" and "we know everything." On the other hand, the sentence may be a serious affirmation, going beyond what he has affirmed earlier — the poet's technique of using a phantasmagoria has been "transubstantiated" into the ultimate creative power. Either way, the poet's phantasmagoria has called up both in himself and in his hearers that "Self" which is the Creator, or at least a creator akin to the great Creator.

In Section II on "Subject Matter" Yeats tells how he found his theme through the poetry of Thomas Davis which "spoke or tried to speak out of a people to a people," through Standish O'Grady's versions of ancient Irish literature, and through stories of apparitions "heard in Irish cottages." "Behind all Irish history hangs a great tapestry" in which Druidism is interwoven with a Christianity still united to the ancient world. A modern man who studies Frazer's *Golden Bough* and Myers' *Human Personality*, works which emphasize the analogies among many beliefs and practices, can accept this ancient Christianity; Yeats, for example, can repeat the creed of St. Patrick thinking of "the Self" in the Upanishads instead of Christ. Even fragments of Neo-Platonism and Cabbalism have been woven into this tapestry which "filled the scene at the birth of modern Irish literature." Christian martyrdom joined with the heroism of Cuchulain in the men who, perishing before the firing squads of 1916, stepped back into the tapestry.

The faith in the interpenetration of natural and supernatural which was universal in the ancient world, the calendar of the Christian church for example having a direct relation to nature (and to the nature religions) when "Easter was still the first full moon after the Equinox," — this faith was preserved longest in Ireland. Yeats quotes Arnold Toynbee to the effect that the failure and decay of Far Western Christian Culture are signalized by the incorporation of Irish Christendom into Roman and that the formation of an independent Irish state marks the cessation of " 'a relic of an independent society'." Yeats hopes that Irish literature will keep the "Irishry" in this ancient sense living and that the Irishry will grow in interest in the supernatural as shown in Irish folk stories, contemporary spiritualism, Swedenborg, and Indian belief.

Yeats then states his credo:

I am convinced that in two or three generations it will become generally known that the mechanical theory has no reality, that the natural and supernatural are knit together, that to escape a dangerous fanaticism we must study a new science; at that moment Europeans may find something attractive in a Christ posed against a background not of Judaism but of Druidism, not shut off in dead history, but flowing, concrete, phenomenal. . . . I was born into this faith, have lived in it, and shall die in it; my Christ, a legitimate deduction from the Creed of St. Patrick as I think, is that Unity of Being Dante compared to a perfectly proportioned human body, Blake's 'Imagination,' what the Upanishads have named 'Self': nor is this unity distant and therefore intellectually understandable, but imminent, differing from man to man and age to age, taking upon itself pain and ugliness, 'eye of newt, and toe of frog.'

Yeats goes on to say, "Subconscious preoccupation with this theme brought me *A Vision*, its harsh geometry an incomplete interpretation." This remark warns us not to take *A Vision* as the last word in Yeats's thought. It also warns us that the credo above is the subject matter his work moves toward, not consciously recognized in full until late in his career.

Section III, "Style and Attitude," is consistent with "The First Principle" and the remarks on "Subject Matter." Yeats discovered around 1917 that " I must seek, not as Wordsworth thought, words in common use, but a powerful and passionate syntax, and a complete coincidence between period and stanza. Because I need a passionate syntax for passionate subject-matter I compel myself to accept those traditional metres that have developed with the language." The syntax is of the present; the traditional metre of the past. "The contrapuntal structure of the verse . . . combines the past and present." In a successful line of verse one may hear the living and the dead, the living in the passionate syntax, the dead in the "ghostly voice" of the metre; one is kept in that state between waking and sleeping which is most conducive to seeing visions. The regularity of the metre lulls one toward sleep, death's image, narrowing the range of one's attention, but the powerful syntax wakens the mind to a lively intensity in apprehending this narrow range of subject. The self that reads or writes these lines unites with the larger Self which seems superior to ordinary circumstance. "I am awake and asleep, at my moment of revelation, self-possessed in self-surrender. . . ." If either "vivid speech" or regular beat overset the balance and become obtrusive, then "I must wake or sleep," return completely to the individual self or its immediate situation or fall completely under the spell of an undifferentiated rhythm and sink into the dead past. The successful line renews the past in the present and joins "that ancient Self" to the living mind.

In talking about poetic speech, Yeats goes a little further than before in asserting that the characters who speak it also seem to expand beyond self to "that ancient Self." "The heroes of Shakespeare convey to us . . . the sudden enlargement of their vision, their ecstasy at the approach of death. . . . They have become God or Mother Goddess, the pelican, 'My baby at my breast,' but all must be cold. . . . The supernatural is present, cold winds blow across our hands, upon our faces, the thermometer falls. . . ."

In Section IV called "Whither?" Yeats rejects the modern school of poets who "express not what the Upanishads call 'that ancient Self' but individual intellect." They would "push the Renaissance higher yet, out-think Leonardo; their verse kills the folk ghost and yet would remain verse. I am joined to the 'Irishry'," Yeats says, "and I expect a counter-Renaissance."

It is true, as many have said, that in his youth Yeats had a large number of heterogeneous interests and ideas which he was furiously attempting to unify. His early work shows this lack of unity and at times seems a choir of everlasting voices which will neither be still nor chant in the same time and key. His later work has a certain remarkable thing to say and says it in one inescapable voice. In the early years it is as if Yeats, at least Yeats the poet, were in the position of the many seeking the one, objective heterogeneity seeking subjective unity and form. In later years the voice that speaks is the One, the Self, looking back toward the other side of the diagram toward the many and drawing all things into itself. The early Yeats talks insistently of Tir-nan-oge and the ideal world. The concrete reality is blurred, out of focus. The later Yeats, as the mortal man which speaks in his poems, still finds the theme of the ideal world to be of undiminished importance. Yet as the voice of the creative principle, as the Self speaking in the poems as their maker, he gives more attention to this "pragmatical preposterous pig of a world/Its farrow that so solid seem," because he can now absorb external reality powerfully, totally, into his subjective meditation.

> Such thought — such thought have I that hold it tight
> Till meditation master all its parts,
> Nothing can stay my glance
> Until that glance run in the world's despite
> To where the damned have howled away their hearts,
> And where the blessed dance;
> Such thought, that in it bound
> I need no other thing,
> Wound in mind's wandering
> As mummies in the mummy-cloth are wound.
>   *All Souls Night*

From the study of the occult Yeats evolved both the materials and the method for his achievement as a poet. Louis L. Martz, in his *The Poetry of Meditation* (1954) [p. 328], suggests that the orthodox meditative practices which influenced the structure of poems by Donne, Herbert, and Crashaw had the same function as occultism did for Yeats. ". . . An ancient underground current of Neoplatonic thought . . . is thus affiliated with more orthodox ways of achieving spiritual progress. . . ." Like the *Spiritual Exercises* of St. Ignatius Loyola or the *Spiritual Combat* of Laurence Scupoli occult methods foster "intense, imaginative meditation that brings together the senses, the emotions, and the intellectual faculties of man; brings them together in a moment of dramatic creative experience." Yet the occult practices Yeats followed in the Golden Dawn made him "seek alone to hear the strange things said/By God to the bright hearts of those long dead" and made him ignore "the field-mouse running by me in the grass,/And heavy mortal hopes that toil and pass" ["To the Rose upon the Rood of Time"]. The course of Yeats's thought from his occult interests to *A Vision*, and the course of his life as man and poet, can perhaps be summed up as a movement — like the movement of his alternating gyres and cones — from a condition in which the world seeks the Self to a condition in which the found Self seeks the world. Because of the command that found Self has over the world, we admire the great poetry of Yeats's mature period.

W. B. Yeats and the Tarot

GWLADYS V. DOWNES

ON THE LAST PAGE of Paul Foster Case's analysis of the greater trumps, *The Tarot, a Key to the Wisdom of the Ages*, there is a diagram of the Ten Sephiroth, or Emanations from God, which forms with its circles and paths an image of the soul's journey from the material world to the spiritual. In Rosicrucian terms, the adept passes from Malkuth to Kether, from Kingdom to Crown, through the ten grades of initiation from Zelator to Ipsissimus. The last three stages, in severely conducted circles, are post-mortem ones.

Study of the diagram reveals also the twenty-two letters of the Hebrew alphabet, and the corresponding trumps of the Tarot pack, with all their spiritual significance for the Rosicrucian initiate who meditates on these relationships as part of his training.

As Virginia Moore has so ably demonstrated in *The Unicorn*, Yeats's association with the mystical Rosicrucian Society, the Hermetic Order of the Golden Dawn, was of long duration and immense importance in his spiritual development. He was enrolled as an initiate (6:30 p.m., Friday, March 7, 1890) at the Isis-Urania Temple in London. By 1916 he had progressed through the outer grades to those of the inner order, when he was accepted as Adeptus Exemptus, the highest grade to be attained in the visible world before death. So for twenty-five years he was deeply and seriously involved with images of the universe accepted and taught by the Order.

In his first stage as an initiate, he had to learn about the four suits of the Tarot pack, which represent earth, air, fire and water. Just what is the Tarot? It is a pack made up of fifty-six ordinary cards and twenty-two extraordinary ones called the greater trumps; our modern packs of fifty-two cards are generally accepted as a stylized version of the original Tarot (there is an extra court card, the Knight, in the early pack). The Tarot has been known in Europe since the beginning of the fourteenth century. Case states that an occult tradition places its invention at Fez about 1200 A.D., and that the "invention" means simply a new way of conveying, by pictorial symbols, the esoteric teachings of the Kabala and the secret schools of China, Tibet, and India.

As might be expected, the original images on the cards were gradually changed, distorted, and debased during the next six hundred years. There is, in fact, an exoteric and an esoteric Tarot. The former is represented by a French pack where the important figure of the Fool is simply a mediæval jester; the latter, according to Case, has never been published in its entirety, although it is the basis for A. E. Waite's version, known as the Rider pack. Waite was a member of the Golden Dawn who had access to occult manuscripts relating to the Tarot, and he tried to present a purified version which would be true to the philosophical basis on which it rests. The actual drawing of the cards was done under his direction by Pamela Colman Smith, who was also a member of the Order and a friend of Yeats.

Yeats's own pack, which is still in Mrs. Yeats's possession, is this version prepared by Waite. Its main difference from the exoteric Tarot is the addition of pictorial images to the cards of the four suits (from two to ten in each case), additions which follow very carefully the astrological significance of each suit as it is influenced by different zodiacal signs. Yeats used the pack for divination, for querying the Masters about the future. What, he asked once, would be the fate of the Golden Dawn fellowship during the next two years? It is tempting to speculate about the actual method used — was it the ancient Celtic method recommended by Waite which is so simple and effective (ten cards plus a "significator")? The Continental systems connected with the cards are extremely elaborate affairs. Where did Waite get his ancient Celtic method — in Ireland? from Yeats?

It seems surprising that Yeats's long involvement with Tarot symbolism produced so few definite references to it. Both the images themselves, and their names, are full of magic, vividly alive for the poetic mind — the King of Cups, the Queen of Wands, the Wheel of Fortune, the Hanged Man, the High Priestess, the Hierophant, the Tower, the Fool. It is true that towers meant much to Yeats, that the Fool became an important figure in his mythology, and that the Hermit is probably the basis for the Saint. There are a few lines which recall significant Tarot cards, but not many. I suspect that "What's water but the generated soul?" refers to Key 17, the Star, and that the dancer in "Among School Children" is an echo of Key 21, the Eternal Dancer. This is how she is described by Case,

The dancer represents the merging of self-consciousness with sub-consciousness, and the blending of the two with superconsciousness. . . . The Dancer is the All-Father and the All-Mother. She is the Bride, but she is also the Bridegroom. She is the Kingdom and the King, even as Malkuth, the Kingdom, is by Qabalists called the Bride, but has also the Divine name ADMI MLK, Adonai Melek, Lord King.

Since the Tarot was only part of the organized training of the Rosicrucian initiate, rather than a study in itself, it was possibly overshadowed by the very richness and complexity of the picture of the universe presented by the Order. The Tree of Life, the six-pointed star, the Cosmic Egg, the ritual burial in the tomb (cf. Key 20), alchemy and astrology, all these were part of Yeats's systematic studies, outward and visible symbols of the inward grace he was, as an adept, striving to obtain. I find too, that Celtic imagery, and the country sights and sounds which were so vivid to him, cannot have mixed well with the specific, organized symbolism of the Tarot. It is rare even to find a poem like "The Mountain Tomb," inspired by the founder of the Rosicrucian movement. Where Yeats and the Tarot meet is rather on the level of the archetypal image — earth, air, fire, water, the sun, the moon, the stars, death and resurrection. He took what he needed — a Fool, a Saint, an Emperor — and let the rest go. So it was Eliot, not Yeats, who annotated his Hanged Man and brought the Tarot to the attention of the literary world.

Part Two

CREATIONS

"The Heroic Discipline of the Looking-Glass": W. B. Yeats's Search for Dramatic Design

ANN SADDLEMYER

What attracts me to drama is that it is ... what all the arts are upon a last analysis. A farce and a tragedy are alike in this, that they are a moment of intense life. An action is taken out of all other actions; it is reduced to its simple form. ... The characters that are involved in it are freed from everything that is not a part of that action; and whether it is, as in the less important kinds of drama, a mere bodily activity ... or as it is in the more important kinds, an activity of the souls of the characters, it is an energy, an eddy of life purified from everything but itself. The dramatist must picture life in action, with an unpreoccupied mind, as the musician pictures her in sound and the sculptor in form.

WITH THESE WORDS in *Samhain* 1904 Yeats attempts to analyse his own dramatic method. He had by this time written over a dozen plays for the stage and drawing-room, and established his own theatre. But Yeats's interest in the dramatic form is evident long before 1904. Early in 1889 he wrote enthusiastically to Katharine Tynan about *The Countess Cathleen*,

This new poem of mine promises to be my most interesting poem and in all ways quite dramatic, I think. I shall try and get it acted by amateurs (if possible in Dublin) and afterwards try it perhaps on some stage manager or actor. It is in five scenes and full of action and very Irish.

Nor can it be mere coincidence that in 1892 one of the plans for publicizing the National Literary Society's projected lending library scheme (suggested by Yeats) was a small travelling theatre which would perform plays on patriotic subjects. Two years later Florence Farr, with Miss Horniman acting as "angel," produced *The Land*

of Heart's Desire on the same bill with Shaw's *Arms and the Man*.
Two years later still came his famous encounter with Lady Gregory,
where the talk "turned on plays." From 1896 until his open letter to
Lady Gregory in 1917, more of Yeats's energy than he later cared
to admit was spent on his dream of a theatre which could at the
same time satisfy his craving for the dramatic form and "the seem-
ing needs of my fool-driven land."

As Richard Ellmann points out,[1] both *The Countess Cathleen*
and *The Land of Heart's Desire* are in Yeats's sense "miracle plays,"
a form he had also suggested to Katharine Tynan and Fiona Macleod as early as 1890. It is not difficult to accept Ellmann's theory
that Yeats's first plans for the Irish Literary Theatre were, unknown
to his colleagues, part of his larger plan for a Celtic Mystical Order.
However, although the dramatic form would naturally appeal to
one impressed by ritual as a "manifestation of the invisible world,"
as he defended his pursuit in a letter to Miss Tynan, this does not
explain his choice of the dramatic medium in the first place. For
long before his plans for the foundation of the theatre, mystically
based or not, and even before his serious study of the occult, Yeats
was writing plays with production in mind. "To me the dramatic
form is far the pleasantest poetic form," he confided to the same
correspondent in 1889. While still at art school, he and AE were
writing poetic dramas (about magicians in Asia) in rivalry; about
1886 AE wrote of Yeats to a friend, "His great drama, *The Equa-
tor of Olives*, is finished. The episode of the Sculptor's Garden is in
it." But by that time Yeats had already written five other poetic
dramas, two of them, *Time and the Witch Vivien* and *The Island
of Statues*, for an early love to act, though the latter play, he admitted, "soon grew beyond the scope of drawing-room acting."

Of these early poetic dramas Yeats recalls, "I had begun to write
poetry in imitation of Shelley and of Edmund Spenser, play after
play — for my father exalted dramatic poetry above all other
kinds — and I invented fantastic and incoherent plots." One fable,
Love and Death (dated April 1884), suggested to him by one of his
father's early designs, indicates not only the "Gemini myth" which
was to haunt Yeats's poetry throughout his life but also his basic
theme of the attraction and mingling of opposites. All centred about
the magical and the struggle between this and another world, with
the other world triumphant. All, too, have the "Shelleyan" Arcadian

[1] *Yeats: The Man and the Masks* (London: Faber & Faber, 1961), 130-133.

note, relieved however by a sharp dramatic twist foreshadowing his later theatrical ability. In 1902, defending his choice of subject and implicitly at the same time his choice of form, he was to write,

Drama is a picture of the soul of man, and not of his exterior life. . . . Drama describes the adventures of men's souls among the thoughts that are most interesting to the dramatist, and therefore, probably most interesting to his time. . . . We are interested in religion and in private morals and personal emotion, and so it is precisely out of the rushing journey of the soul that Ibsen and Wagner got the tumult that is drama.[2]

And although he was to make many experiments within the dramatic convention before he was satisfied, his concept and demand of the dramatic form varied little:

Some of my friends, and it is always for a few friends one writes, do not understand why I have not been content with lyric writing. But one can only do what one wants to do, and to me drama — and I think it has been the same with other writers — has been the search for more of manful energy, more of cheerful acceptance of whatever arises out of the logic of events, and for clean outline, instead of those outlines of lyric poetry that are blurred with desire and vague regret. All art is in the last analysis an endeavour to condense as out of the flying vapour of the world an image of human perfection, and for its own and not for the art's sake.[3]

Except for one brief excursion with Lady Gregory into the "less important kind of drama" (*The Pot of Broth*, 1902), Yeats left the "popular" aspect of the theatre to others, and concentrated on the "activity of the souls of the characters," and more specifically, "the rushing journey of the soul" through religion, private morals, and personal emotion as he himself viewed them in conflict with the modern world. And as time went on, he discovered his own achievement of the ideal in the co-operation of both musician and sculptor to "picture life in action." In 1938 he commented in *On the Boiler*, "Masterpieces, whether of the stage or study, excel in their action, their visibility."

Yeats's aesthetic theory was relevant to the dramatic form in many ways. From Pater and Wilde he had learned the importance of style, and now he observed the relationship "between discipline and the theatrical sense." "Active virtue as distinguished from the

[2] "The Freedom of the Theatre," *United Irishman*, November 1, 1902, 5.
[3] Preface to *Poems 1899-1905* (London: A. H. Bullen, 1906), xii-xiii.

passive acceptance of a current code is therefore theatrical, consciously dramatic, the wearing of a mask," he wrote in *Autobiographies*. "A wise theatre" might, in fact, "make a training in strong
and beautiful life the fashion, teaching before all else the heroic
discipline of the looking-glass." [4] In his personal life Yeats consciously
strove for this discipline; now he applied it to the theatre as well.
"Life in itself is a war of forces," he advised Lady Gregory during
a time of crisis.[5] Might not art then, founded as it is upon personal
vision, clarify and extend this discipline? "In the shaping of an
agate, whether in the cutting or in the making of the design, one
discovers . . . thoughts that seem important and principles that may
be applied to life itself." [6] And so we find the proud hero, no matter
what his guise — Seanchan, Cuchulain, Deirdre, Naisi, Conchubar
or Congal — actively striving with his own opposite and finally
achieving success with the acceptance of his own defeat. (At one
time he contemplated a play about Judas, whose betrayal he saw as
necessary to the fulfilment of Christ.) Occasionally success itself is
an activating quality: Dectora becomes queen, and the poet's
creation in turn creates.

The doctrine of the mask, therefore, the struggle of the self for
the self, became one of the essential themes in Yeats's plays. So, too,
Yeats discovered that this theme bred another which was in itself
dramatic, "the war of spiritual with natural order," as he describes
it in his dedication of *The Secret Rose* to AE. In a letter to the
United Irishman in 1905 Yeats had adopted as his motto Blake's
dictum "without contraries there is no progression"; not only by
overcoming one's self, then, but by overcoming one's opposite can
one find truth. In *Where There is Nothing* (1903) Paul Ruttledge
battles against conventional society, which prevents the soaring of
the personality, and conventional religion, which forbids the laughter of the soul, and comes at last to the truth that "where there is
nothing, there is God." The wise sceptic of *The Hour-Glass* (1903)
gains insight through the eyes of the fool: "One sinks in on God;
we do not see the truth; God sees the truth in us." Cuchulain's soul

---

4 "Discoveries" (1907), *Essays and Introductions* (London: Macmillan, 1961),
270.
5 Unpublished letter dated May 18, 1905 in the possession of Mrs. Yeats. In
a letter dated a few days later, he relates this to himself: "I am always so
afraid of the sensitiveness, created by imaginative culture, making one over-
yielding that I perhaps push things the other way."
6 Preface to *The Cutting of an Agate, Essays and Introductions*, 219.

seeks its first "soft, feathery shape," freed by a blind man's desire for twelve pennies: "And is not that a strange shape for the soul / Of a great fighting-man?" And Congal, "That wise, victorious, voluble, unlucky / Blasphemous, famous, infamous man," dies at the hand of a fool — himself. Perhaps, after all, the lost cause is the best cause. The importance of style and the drama inherent in the doctrine of the mask lead inevitably to an awareness of the dramatic potential of ritual and the symbolic significance of the actor in a theatre which is a temple to the soul of man. The actor becomes a symbol, a puppet, in fact, his speech and gestures carrying him and the audience to the world of the spirit evoked by the poet's words.

In an early unpublished draft of *The Player Queen* the palace servants, waiting for the play to begin, discuss the joys and hazards of the actor's life, these people who, like "mortar that never hardens," take on many shapes in a lifetime. Sufficiently divorced from reality by the protective masks of the parts in which they are cast, these player-puppets live only in the poet-juggler's words. They are, in fact, the "bridge" between reality and the dream. An old servant quotes "Aristotle of the books or another":

to know your own true shape that's what a wise man has to do and what he's here to do and when he's found it he's free of the Court.

Free, that is, of reality. "If you would have obedience," the Chancellor advises the Queen, "you must seem to be all the greatness your people dream of being and have not might of soul to be, all that their shivering heart denies them."

Here we see Yeats's concept of the poet as a magus who through his imagination creates the myth by which characters and audience achieve spiritual truth. If the actor is in a sense his created image, then he is the master puppeteer, a combination of the arch-priest and the cultivated whole man. It is through the artist, who uses the world of reality as material for the spiritual world, that unity of being can be achieved. (And for Yeats, "unity of being" implied both spiritual perfection in the theosophical-Cabalistic sense and worldly *savoir-faire* in the Edwardian sense.) He creates the dream, and, paradoxically, like Blake's "spiritual leader," can give that dream reality. As a dramatist, then, Yeats was in turn able to dramatize himself: the magician-poet-creator, his world the spiritual, his audience, which in turn provided material for his pen, Ireland.

In another early draft of *The Player Queen* he gives this ambition of the artist-creator to his heroine:

PLAYER QUEEN: Let me become all your dreams. I will make them walk about the world in solid bone and flesh. People looking at them will become all fire themselves and they will change, there will be a last judgment on their souls, a burning and dissolving. Perhaps the whole age may change, perhaps the whole age may learn. It is only by continual struggle, by continual violence, we force the gates of heaven, that no one is worthy of art, worthy of love whose [*sic*] not always like great kings and queens in soul and body like a runner, like a racer. . . .

YELLOW MARTIN [the poet]: We shall become like Tom the Fiddler. He would sing no song that did not please him.

PLAYER QUEEN: Yes, like Tom the Fiddler, that's what I want.[7]

In order to heighten the role of his puppet-image, Yeats early experimented with the use of masks, thus further ensuring the dramatization of qualities rather than characteristics. For by putting his players into masks, he established further control over them, eliminated any possibility of facial expression detracting from the words, and restricted the character portrayals to the essentially narrow reflection of the images they were to represent. Furthermore, the static nature of the mask gave to the player the quality Yeats was attempting to achieve in his verse:

A mask will enable me to substitute for the face of some commonplace player, or for that face repainted to suit his own vulgar fancy, the fine invention of a sculptor, and to bring the audience close enough to the play to hear every inflection of the voice. A mask never seems but a dirty face, and no matter how close you go is yet a work of art.[8]

By dehumanizing the player, it increased the dignity and power of the words. Then, too, a mask in itself is dramatic, not only because it represents the principle of opposition so dear to Yeats, but because it symbolizes eternal rather than temporal qualities. Once again he found himself moving towards ritual. "Perhaps in the end," he wrote in his preface to *Four Plays for Dancers*, "one could write plays for certain masks." Finally, in *The Only Jealousy of Emer* the character changes masks — thereby changing personality — on stage.

---

7 Unpublished manuscript of *The Player Queen* (before 1915), now in National Library of Ireland, reproduced by permission of Mrs. W. B. Yeats.

8 "Certain Noble Plays of Japan," *Essays and Introductions*, 226.

"I always feel that my work is not drama but the ritual of a lost faith," Yeats once wrote to Sturge Moore. And in order to make credible the "strange events, elaborate words" of that ritual, he required sufficient distance from, rather than involvement in, life. There must be distance from the prosaic everyday reality; at the same time, however, there must be precision and truth. "Tragic drama must be carved out of speech as a statue is out of stone." In order to achieve this sculptural quality Yeats turned his attention to costume and setting as well. The actors, he felt, should form a tableau against a "symbolic and decorative setting" which would in no way detract the attention from the speakers. "One should design a scene which would be an accompaniment not a reflection of the text," he advised Fiona Macleod, making "pictures with robes that contrasted with great masses of colour in the back-cloth and such severe or decorative forms of hills and trees and houses as would not overwhelm, as our naturalistic scenery does, the idealistic art of the poet." [9] "The great thing in literature, above all in drama, is rhythm and movement," he wrote to Frank Fay in 1905. "The picture belongs to another art." Realism of setting and costume should be limited as much as possible, colour, form and light taking its place. A wood, for example, he expounded in a letter to the *United Irishman*,

should be little more than a pattern made with painted boughs. It should not try to make one believe that the actors are in a real wood, for the imagination will do that far better, but it should decorate the stage. It should be a mass of deep colour, in harmony with the colours in the costumes of the players.

Sometimes perhaps a shadowy background would be sufficient, but for many years he could not agree with George Moore's temporary enthusiasm for no scenery at all; one needs "enough of scenery to make it unnecessary to look at the programme to find out whether the persons on the stage have met indoors or out of doors, in a cottage or in a palace." [10] But although scenery should be there, it must remain "little more than a suggestion — a pattern with recurring boughs and leaves of gold for a wood, a great green curtain with a red stencil upon it to carry the eye upward for a palace, and so

9 "At Stratford-on-Avon" (1901), *Essays and Introductions*, 100.
10 Letter to the Editor, *The Daily Chronicle*, January 27, 1899. *cf.* a lecture to the National Literary Society, May 6, 1899, on "Dramatic Ideals and the Irish Literary Theatre," reported by the Dublin *Daily Express*.

on." As the *Westminster Gazette* observed, "in a word, Mr. Yeats would have in his proposed theatre more nature and less realism."

Perhaps because of his own early interest in painting, Yeats tended to emphasize and depend upon colour schemes in his plays. Nearly all of his plays contain explicit directions as to the colours used both in costume and background. A letter to Sturge Moore in 1903 states his principles:

1. A background which does not insist on itself and which is so homogeneous in colour that it is always a good background to an actor wherever he stand. . . .
2. Two predominant colours in remote fanciful plays. One colour predominant in actors, one in backcloth. This principle for the present at any rate until we have got our people to understand simplicity.

The Hour-Glass was staged with a monotonous green background, the chief actor wearing a purple garment; the Fool was dressed in red-brown, the colour repeated in the furniture. (In his diary Charles Ricketts quotes Florence Farr on her role as Aleel in *The Countess Cathleen*: "You see, Yeats had insisted on my wearing mauve — such a trying colour — a mauve tunic just below the knees, you know, and over that a great common purple cloak.") *On Baile's Strand* was mounted with amber-coloured hangings and handpainted medallions on the walls, a great golden spiral playing across the front, blending the more colourful costumes of the kings into the paler background.[11] Occasionally Yeats deliberately aimed at startling effects with the use of a pronounced colour scheme, as in *The Green Helmet*: "I have noticed that the more obviously decorative is the scene and costuming of any play, the more it is lifted out of time and place, and the nearer to fairyland do we carry it." But for the most part he insisted upon the "strange grey dreamlike effect" he sought in the setting for *The Shadowy Waters* and describes in detail in the printed text:

The deck of an ancient ship. At the right of the stage is the mast, with a large square sail hiding a great deal of the sky and sea on that side. The tiller is at the left of the stage; it is a long oar coming through an opening in the bulwark. The deck rises in a series of steps behind the tiller, and the stern of the ship curves overhead. All the woodwork is of dark green; and the sail is dark green, with a blue pattern upon it,

11 Maire Nic Shiubhlaigh and Edward Kenny, *The Splendid Years* (Dublin: James Duffy, 1955), 59; "The Acting at the Abbey Theatre," *United Irishman*, January 7, 1905; letter to Lady Gregory, December 28, 1904, quoted in *Our Irish Theatre* (London: Putnam's, 1913), 45.

having a little copper colour here and there. The sky and sea are dark blue. All the persons of the play are dressed in various tints of green and blue, the men with helmets and swords of copper, the woman with copper ornaments upon her dress.

The effect is one of Pre-Raphaelite, dream-like beauty, with Morris and Burne-Jones colouring, the scenery "thought out not as one thinks out a landscape, but as if it were the background of a portrait." Yeats zealously guarded the colour schemes to his plays, once refusing a play to Florence Farr because she would not agree to his suggestions.[12]

Costumes, in Yeats's mind, were simply a part of the scenery, and he dreamed of a theatre where like the masks the costumes could become part of the imagery also. "Let them have one suit of clothes for a king, another for a queen, another for a fighting-man, another for a messenger, and so on, and if these clothes are loose enough to fit different people, they can perform any romantic play that comes without new cost," he advised in *Samhain*, 1904. "The audience would soon get used to this way of symbolizing, as it were, the different ranks and classes of men."

Fortunately for the Abbey players, his own company did not have to resort to this device of sharing costumes, but in his theatre Yeats was restricted in other ways. He was very impressed by lighting effects, especially the "free and delicate use of light and shadow." "No breadth of treatment gives monotony when there is movement and change of lighting," he emphasized in his notes to *Plays for an Irish Theatre*. But the Abbey Theatre had limited lighting equipment only, and Yeats eventually was forced to give up his dreams of diffuse and reflected lighting.

From the beginning, Yeats was controlled in his theories of staging by the theatre he worked in. Economy was essential, but his demand for simplicity was aided rather than deterred by this factor. He was fortunate too in the style of acting developed by the Fays' company of actors, where movement was subordinated to the voice until even the natural clumsiness of the actors contributed to the total effect of simplicity and stillness. He was fortunate too in having designers such as Robert Gregory, Anne Yeats, Jack Yeats, Sturge Moore, Pamela Colman Smith, Charles Ricketts, and Gordon Craig, but even then the ideas when executed were not always successful because of the theatre's limitations. The small realistic peasant set-

12 Letter to Lady Gregory, May 1905, in the possession of Mrs. Yeats.

ting at which W. G. Fay (and later Lennox Robinson) excelled, was much more within their grasp, and so young dramatists preferred to write in a style they could more readily attain. This in turn resulted in a proficiency for the actors and producers in a style directly opposing Yeats's own ambitions. "The necessities of the builders have torn from us, all unwilling as we were, the apron," Yeats wrote of the first compromise in the building itself. "We would have preferred to be able to return occasionally to the old stage of statue-making, of gesture." The necessities of the players and producers led to further compromise which eventually forced him to turn reluctantly away from the theatre he had founded to other experiments, and finally out of the regular theatre altogether.

"*The Player Queen* is the only work of mine, not mere personal expression, written during these last twenty years, which is not avowedly Irish in its subject matter being all transacted in some No-Man's-Land," Yeats wrote in 1922 in his preface to *Plays in Prose and Verse*. Looking back, Yeats explains this as one of the many debts to Gordon Craig, who designed a set of screens for the Abbey in 1910: "if it is gayer than my wont it is that I tried to find words and events that would seem well placed under a beam of light reflected from the ivory-coloured surface of the screens," "where every line must suggest some mathematical proportion, where all is phantastic, incredible, and luminous." [13] So too, he claims, the players have no nationality, in keeping with the fantasy of the architecture.

The influence of Gordon Craig on Yeats's theories can hardly be over-estimated but has frequently been ignored. Not only did he provide the screens which so excited Yeats (although Craig himself insists that the Abbey never did understand the principle behind them; "hovering, hiding, advancing, retreating," they were to create the impression of timelessness and motion in space[14]), but he contributed designs for *Deirdre*, *The Hour-Glass*, and *On Baile's Strand*. Further, he designed a model stage for Yeats, where the playwright could "produce" his plays as he wrote them, moving the figures

[13] Note to *The Player Queen*, 1922. A contemporary review (*Irish Times*, December 10, 1919) suggests that the Abbey production bears these aims out, the costumes being "more elaborate than usual for the Abbey Theatre — might suggest anything from a mediaeval masquerade to a modern lunatic asylum." An early draft sets the play in "the country of Surrico" with a "suggestion of a Spanish street in the architecture but nothing very definite."

[14] Letter to the writer, February 27, 1960.

about as one would the men in a game of chess, from this sketching the blocking for each scene or tableau. It was Craig, too, who first introduced him to the use of masks. In a letter to Lady Gregory Yeats enthusiastically describes the masks Craig had designed for the Fool and the Angel of *The Hour Glass*:

I am very much excited by the thought of putting the fool into a mask and rather amused at the idea of an angel in a golden domino. I should have to write some words into the play. "They fear to meet the eyes of men being too pure for mortal gaze" or the like. If the masks work right I would put the fool and the blind man in *Baile's Strand* into masks. It would give a wildness and extravagance that would be fine.

Craig's early experiments in lighting also impressed Yeats, who wrote in his preface to *Plays for an Irish Theatre*, "he has banished a whole world that wearied me and was undignified and given me forms and lights upon which I can play as upon some stringed instrument." And in 1903, at a lecture on "The Reform of the Theatre," Craig's comments on stage lighting and design, illustrated by his model theatre, also impressed W. G. Fay:

It was a simple horizon cloth with some rock and trees in the fore-ground, painted in monochrome, but lit in three different colours. For the first time it produced a feeling of atmosphere in stage lighting.[15]

But Craig's influence began long before the foundation of the Abbey Theatre, and important as his designs and model stage were to Yeats's knowledge of structure and effect, it is as theorist that he excited Yeats most. Son of the famous actress Ellen Terry, he did not enter the theatre from the stalls as Yeats did; he began as an actor, his early training under Henry Irving clarifying many of the physical problems of the stage which remained an enigma to Yeats. "I acted and produced long before I dreamed of enunciating any theory — even to myself," Craig insists. But most important to Yeats was Craig's devotion to the "Theatre of Beauty". And here his frequent pronouncements echo Yeats's own concern for style and gesture. "I don't want to imitate man or Nature or anything else on the boards of a theatre," he claimed. "I want to create a new world there — not to copy the real world imperfectly." "Do not forget that there is such a thing as *noble* artificiality."

[15] W. G. Fay, "The Poet and the Actor," *Scattering Branches*, ed. Stephen L. Gwynn (London: Macmillan, 1940), 133-34.

Like Yeats, Craig was concerned with unity of effect, based essentially on the balance and proportion of line, space, light, shade, and colour. Although he made no effort to create realism of detail, he insisted upon stage design which would create the illusion of depth and proportion that were essential to his plan. In his productions, although he depended upon simplicity and proportion to gain this desired atmosphere, he demanded first a three-dimensional rather than the standard two-dimensional scenery, and second, an authentic richness of material and substance. The first requirement led him to the invention of his screens which could replace the conventional scenery; the second led to experiments with lighting and colour materials. Here at last was the artist in the theatre who could create the "new and distinct art" Yeats sought, staging which "cannot even be separated from the figures that move before it." And the "severe, beautiful, simple effects of colour" which Craig achieved through his materials and lighting left the imagination "free to follow all the suggestions of the play." [16]

But Craig's influence on Yeats extended even further, for in his desire for simplicity he eventually saw in the mask and dance the theatre he could not create with the average actor on the ordinary stage. Like Yeats too he found the ineptitude of the average modern actor almost insurmountable:

There is hardly any action which is right, there is hardly any which is natural. Action is a way of spoiling something, says Rimbaud. . . . The actor as he is today, must ultimately disappear and be merged in something else if works of art are to be seen in our kingdom of the theatre. [17]

In his celebrated but frequently misunderstood essay, "The Actor and the Über-Marionette," he pleads for "a new form of acting, consisting for the main part in symbolical gesture. Today they *impersonate* and interpret; tomorrow they must *represent* and interpret; and the third day they must create."

The aim of the theatre as a whole is to restore its art and it should commence by banishing from the theatre this idea of impersonation, this idea of reproducing nature; for while impersonation is in the theatre, the theatre can never become free.

[16] Letter to the Editor of *The Saturday Review*, March 5, 1902; "At Stratford-on-Avon," *Essays and Introductions*, 100-101.
[17] "The Artists of the Theatre of the Future," *The Mask* I (1908), 58 and 65.

Like Maeterlinck (who also wrote "plays for marionettes"), William Poel (who also campaigned for the return of poetry to the theatre), and Yeats, Craig envisaged a drama of repose, which would lead to stylized gesture and tableaux. He was in fact more akin to Maeterlinck than even Yeats, in many ways sounding a note to be picked up later by such modern playwrights as Harold Pinter:

I lean towards the drama of silence just because I believe in and long for a durable drama. And I cannot help but still believe that the most durable drama will be one of silence.

Like Maeterlinck, Craig envisaged a type of acting which would have as its basis the art of the marionette. As the puppet is "a model of man in motion," so the actor should depersonalize himself: "the actor plus fire, minus egotism; the fire of the gods and demons, without the smoke and steam of mortality." [18] The actor in himself was mortal, his art temporary and variable; the mask could make permanent the fleeting art of the actor:

The advantage of a mask over a face is that it is always repeating unerringly the poetic fancy, repeating on Monday in 1912 exactly what it said on Saturday in 1909 and what it will say on Wednesday in 1999. Durability was the dominant idea in Egyptian art. The theatre must learn that lesson. . . . Let us again cover his face with a mask in order that his expression — the visualized expression of the Poetic spirit — shall be everlasting. [19]

"Every actor should wear a mask my dear man," he wrote to Yeats in 1910: "— every actor — just as every gentleman and thief should wear breeches." [20] With his designs for the Fool and Blind Man of Yeats's plays, Craig introduced a technique which had far-reaching effects on Yeats's development as an artist. As an example he contributed even more, for in his pioneer work Gordon Craig, more than any other artist in the contemporary theatre, proved that a theatre of beauty is possible.

There were other influences. "When we studied his art we studied our double," Yeats said of Charles Ricketts in 1936. "We, too, thought always that style should be proud of its ancestry, of its tra-

[18] New preface to *On the Art of the Theatre*, 1924.

[19] Quoted by Janet Leeper in *Edward Gordon Craig: Designs for the Theatre* (King Penguin, 1948), 46.

[20] Quoted by Brigit Bjersby, *The Interpretation of the Cuchulain Legend in the Works of W. B. Yeats* (Dublin: Hodges and Figgis, 1950), 36.

ditional high breeding, that an ostentatious originality was out of place whether in the arts or in good manners." (It is not surprising to find that among Ricketts' admirers was not only Yeats but Oscar Wilde.) "My education in so many things": as man and artist Ricketts rivalled not only Craig but William Morris in Yeats's hierarchy. Like Yeats, Ricketts approached the stage with the eye of the painter rather than the actor; the delicate details he appreciated in his book designs, illustrations, and paintings were brought to his work for the theatre, often causing him to concentrate on details which would never carry across the footlights. "A work of art is a whole in which each portion is exquisite in itself yet co-ordinate," he claimed in his Bibliography of the Vale Press, and this philosophy followed him into the theatre. In this sense he was a more "personal" artist than Craig, emphasizing costume, scenery and minute details in his efforts to create a stage picture, whereas Craig worked from the general design to the particular. Yeats described Ricketts as "one of the greatest connoisseurs of any age, an artist whose woodcuts prolonged the inspiration of Rossetti, whose paintings mirrored the rich colouring of Delacroix." And here is perhaps the secret of his influence and his theory. For Ricketts was a traditionalist rather than an experimenter, concentrating on achieving an atmosphere of beauty and delicacy of effect within the conventional methods of the time. (Here, too, is perhaps the secret of his successful partnership with Bernard Shaw.) If simplicity is required in stage-decoration, "it should be a beautiful simplicity," Ricketts claimed in *Pages on Art*; but he suggested "concentration" as the essential quality of decoration, creating order and focus by emphasis rather than by too much elimination.

Although not a revolutionary like Craig, Ricketts was also a practical man of the theatre, and many of his recommendations and designs were adopted by Yeats. In particular, Yeats appreciated Ricketts' eye for detail in stage effect and costume, which was as practical as it was imaginative. His letters to Yeats and Lady Gregory abound in sketches for costumes, including the suggestion of "doubling" on costumes from other plays, details concerning the best inexpensive material for background and dresses, advice concerning seamstresses and estimates of expenditure. Frequently his imaginative designs had the effect of giving new life to the players also. Writing of the new costumes Ricketts designed for *The King's Threshold* in 1914, Yeats comments,

The Company never did the play so well, and such is the effect of costume that whole scenes got a new intensity, and passages or actions that had seemed commonplace became powerful and moving.

On occasion too a suggestion from Ricketts gave Yeats a new idea for his revisions. Nor did Ricketts' influence stop at the stage dressing; he was an acute critic of Yeats's theory of verse-speaking, and did not hesitate to offer his advice concerning the actual performances of the actors.

Ricketts' stage designs were not limited to the Abbey Theatre, however. From 1905 to 1928 he was active designing productions in London also and his influence extended in other ways. Sturge Moore, who dressed some of Yeats's plays, followed Ricketts' style and manner, and Ricketts was also involved with Moore in the designs of Yeats's books. At one time, also, he proposed raising the funds for a production of *The Countess Cathleen*, to be staged by Craig. In 1903 he was involved with Yeats, Moore, Symons, Edith Craig (Gordon's sister), Walter Crane and Pamela Colman Smith in the formation of "The Masquers," whose object as stated in its Prospectus was

... to give performances of plays, masques, ballets, and ceremonies; and to produce only those works which convey a sentiment of beauty. One of its chief endeavours will be to bring the stage back again to that beauty of appropriate simplicity in the presentation of a play which will liberate the attention of an audience for the words of a writer and the movements of an actor.

And when the Masquers' scheme collapsed, Yeats hoped to appoint Ricketts officially to the Abbey Theatre company. Even after Yeats turned away from the conventional stage to the "two trestles and a board" and the designs and music of Edmund Dulac for his Noh plays, the influence of Ricketts, who in Bernard Shaw's words "always dealt *en grand seigneur*," remained. Like Gordon Craig, William Blake and William Morris, Charles Ricketts represented one of "the great myth-makers and mask-makers, the men of aristocratic mind" in Yeats's kingdom of art.

"It takes a lifetime to master dramatic form," Yeats wrote to his father in 1918. What he could not have foreseen was that when he finally did "discover" the form he had been seeking all his life he would arrive back at a position not far from where he started. His first attempt to dramatize "the soul of man," *The Shadowy Waters*, he rejected in 1904 as too remote and impersonal in its theme, where

... one should lose the persons in the general picture. ... It is legitimate art however though a kind that may I should think by this time
prove itself the worst sort possible for our theatre. The whole picture
as it were moves together — sky and sea and land are as it were actors.
It is almost religious, it is more a ritual than a human story. It is
deliberately without human characters.

But now, after experiments which led him to the foundation of a
theatre and a company rapidly gaining world fame, he turned back
once again to a remote and impersonal art which could do without
scenery or setting, or even a stage, and came very close to eliminating the actor as well. For although he was willing to accept the art
of his fellow-dramatists, an art which involved "a study of the common people" and a preservation of the national characteristics they
represented, he himself turned to the art which required sufficient
distance from everyday life to transcend those same characteristics,
plays which required a convention as strict in its way as the deliberately dehumanized Greek chorus, or, at the other extreme, the
rigidly defined stage management of a Gilbert and Sullivan operetta.
In 1919 he wrote to Lady Gregory,

I desire a mysterious art, always reminding and half-reminding those
who understand it of dearly loved things, doing its work by suggestion,
not by direct statement, a complexity of rhythm, colour, gesture, not
space-pervading like the intellect but a memory and a prophecy.

Gradually gesture gave way to the stately dance just as conversation had given way to the dignified chorus and facial expression
to the gravity of the mask. "I promise a dance. I wanted a dance
because where there are no words there is less to spoil," says the
Old Man in *The Death of Cuchulain*. Artificiality in turn gives way
to artificiality. "I had thought to have had those heads carved, but
no, if the dancer can dance properly no wood-carving can look as
well as a parallelogram of painted wood." Reality twice removed
once more leads to the pure abstraction of the image. Years earlier
Yeats had been astonished at Lady Gregory's experiments with casts
of only two or three characters; now he in turn continued the experiment, restricting himself to musician and dancer. Dissatisfied
with *The King of the Great Clock Tower* ("there are three characters ... and that is a character too many"), he rewrote it as *A
Full Moon in March*, "reduced to the essentials" of Dancer-Queen
and Singer-Stroller. He had criticized Wilde's Salomé for being only

"a soulless doll" but now he found himself creating a dance play which echoed Wilde's technique as much as his efforts towards an artificial style echoed Wilde's theory. And in 1929 he rewrote *The Only Jealousy of Emer* as another dance play, *Fighting the Waves*.

"What matter if people prefer another art, I have had my fill," Yeats wrote in *On the Boiler* of his experiments in choric dance. Yet for the "distinguished, indirect, and symbolic . . . aristocratic form" he finally developed he once again sought historical justification, and found it in Ezra Pound's recent work on the Noh plays of Japan. Here at last, he felt, was the form he had been seeking, a drama "which may delight the best minds of my time" and once more return heroic ecstacy to the stage. Yet the very qualities of stylization and ritual that he appreciated in the Noh he had been seeking in the dramatic form from the beginning; it is significant that he first contemplated translating Sophocles during the early years of the Abbey Theatre, for the poetry he finally developed, passion frozen in form, the endistancement of the personal, has perhaps even stronger resemblances to the classical theatre of Greece. In seeking the simplicity and ritual of poetry which divines its heroic ecstasy as much from the philosophy of passion as from the passion itself, Yeats might just as well have turned for his poetic rationalization to the tragedy of Sophocles. "A table of values, heroic joy always, intellectual curiosity and so on — and a public theme." He had at last captured all in the perfected form.

Yeats wrote of his dance plays,

In writing these little plays I knew that I was creating something which could only fully succeed in a civilization very unlike ours. I think they should be written for some country where all classes share in a half-mythological, half-philosophical folk-belief which the writer and his small audience lift into a new subtlety. All my life I have longed for such a country, and always found it quite impossible to write without having as much belief in its real existence as a child has in that of the wooden birds, beasts, and persons of his toy Noah's ark. I have now found all the mythology and philosophy I need.

It might be said that Yeats never really left the drawing-room any more than Eliot left the cathedral. "The heroic discipline of the looking-glass" requires no public stage.

"Worn Out With Dreams": Dublin's Abbey Theatre

It will take a generation, and perhaps generations, to restore the Theatre of Art... (*Beltaine*, 1899).

We should keep before our minds the final object which is to create in this country a National Theatre something after the continental pattern. (Yeats in a Memorandum, December 1906).

THE HISTORY of the Abbey Theatre has been frequently and well told by players, playwrights, audience, and critics: how Yeats and Martyn brought George Moore back to Ireland and were joined first by Lady Gregory, later by the Fay brothers; how the generous but single-minded English heiress Annie Horniman endowed a theatre to her fellow-theosophist's muse and six years later resigned both friend and building to a nationalism she could not tolerate; how Yeats "discovered" their first playwright in a Paris attic, and twenty years later Lady Gregory nurtured the second in a Dublin slum; and how during the period between Synge and O'Casey the Abbey became a symbol not only of the "Celtic Renaissance" but of a specific tradition in playwriting, producing, and acting. Many too have offered suggestions, criticisms, commentaries and explanations concerning its apparent downfall. But the Abbey still lives. At this moment a new theatre is being completed; new plays are in rehearsal; bookings are heavy. It is significant, however, that its most famous triumvirate dealt in their own work with the absorbing conflict between the dream and the reality. For the reality of the theatre they founded, though at its best an admirable example of a limited tradition in playwriting and acting, is not the theatre of which they dreamed. While still a success, the Abbey Theatre is a failure. Perhaps the failure lies in the dream.

From the beginning, the Irish Literary Theatre, as the first experiment was called, had struggled with a divided image: art and nationalism. Their first manifesto, in the autumn of 1897, read:

We propose to have performed in Dublin, in the spring of every year certain Celtic and Irish plays, which whatever be their degree of excellence will be written with a high ambition, and so to build up a Celtic and Irish school of dramatic literature. We hope to find in Ireland an uncorrupted and imaginative audience trained to listen by its passion for oratory, and believe that our desire to bring upon the stage the deeper thoughts and emotions of Ireland will ensure for us a tolerant welcome, and that freedom to experiment which is not found in theatres of England, and without which no new movement in art or literature can succeed. We will show that Ireland is not the home of buffoonery and of easy sentiment, as it has been represented, but the home of an ancient idealism. We are confident of the support of all Irish people, who are weary of misrepresentation, in carrying out a work that is outside all the political questions that divide us.

It was signed by Augusta Gregory, Edward Martyn, and William Butler Yeats.

New movements were almost an everyday occurrence in the nineties, but this one persisted, eventually becoming a limited company. Seven years later it had acquired its own building, thereby becoming, as its own magazine boasted, "the first endowed Theatre in any English-speaking country." And again first principles were expounded, signed this time by Yeats, Lady Gregory, and John Millington Synge:

First. Our plays must be literature or written in the spirit of literature. . . .
Second. If we are to make a drama of energy, of extravagance, of phantasy, of musical and noble speech, we shall need an appropriate stage-management. . . .
Third. We must have a new kind of scenic art. . . .

These principles differed little from those of the 1897 manifesto, but the word "compromise" was introduced for the first time:

The experiments of the Irish National Theatre Society will have of necessity to be for a long time few and timid, and we must often, having no money and not a great deal of leisure, accept for a while compromises, and much even that we know to be irredeemably bad. One can only perfect an art very gradually; and good playwriting, good speaking, and good acting are the first necessity.

Fifteen more years pass. The movement is of age, and has been received into the most conservative theatres of London and America. It has been praised and on occasion martyred. Books have been written about it; schools have been founded after it. And once more an open letter appears, this time signed by only one director, W. B. Yeats, and addressed, through the public, to the other founder-director, Lady Gregory. The note of hopeful planning has been replaced by a tone of discouraged renunciation:

The Abbey Theatre can never do all we had hoped. . . . We have been the first to create a true "People's Theatre," and we have succeeded because it is not an exploitation of local colour, or of a limited form of drama possessing a temporary novelty, but the first doing of something for which the world is ripe, something that will be done all over the world and done more and more perfectly: the making articulate of all the dumb classes each with its own knowledge of the world, its own dignity, but all objective with the objectivity of the office and the workshop, of the newspaper and the street, of mechanism and of politics. Yet we did not set out to create this sort of theatre, and its success has been to me a discouragement and a defeat.

And so the movement's prime mover leaves the national stage to seek elsewhere his own ambition, "not a theatre but the theatre's anti-self." Irrevocably, the Theatre dreamed of had become a different Theatre, with its own traditions and national ambition:

You and I and Synge, not understanding the clock, set out to bring again the Theatre of Shakespeare or rather perhaps of Sophocles. . . . but the modern world is more powerful than any Propaganda or even than any special circumstance, and our success has been that we have made a theatre of the head, and persuaded Dublin playgoers to think about their own trade or profession or class and their life within it, so long as the stage curtain is up, in relation to Ireland as a whole.

When one considers Yeats's own ambition in the drama, "an unpopular theatre and an audience like a secret society where admission is by favour and never to many," the failure of his personal dream is not surprising; an audience, especially an Irish one, would hardly tolerate for long an autocratic insistence that it support an organization which promised in return little love and less tolerance. And Yeats was not the only dictator of taste. "I don't care a rap" was Synge's public disclaimer at the height of *The Playboy* row; even the devoutly patriotic Lady Gregory described their policy in no less dictatorial terms: "We gave what we thought good until it became popular." But not without a struggle, which occasionally burst out of the small theatre on Lower Abbey Street into the offices of *The Daily Express*, the Church, and even on occasion the Castle. But the story of the Abbey Theatre is a story not of one struggle only, but of a series of struggles. Nor was this a simple battle between playhouse and public; the theatre itself was founded on a paradox which forced not only the directors but playwrights and players to take sides. From the beginning Yeats, Martyn, and Lady Gregory sought an uneasy "union of hearts"; the Irish Literary Theatre was to be not only national in design but cosmopolitan in theory, not only educational in aim but aesthetic in practice.

Yeats's plan for a literary theatre began much earlier than 1899 or even than 1896 when he first met Lady Gregory and their talk "turned on plays." In March 1888 Yeats made his first visit to the Southwark Irish Literary Club in London. In 1891 he helped found the Irish Literary Society of London, and in the same year met Edward Martyn through Arthur Symons. The following year he travelled to Dublin to found the National Literary Society, but returned to London to discuss with Florence Farr a "small theatre in the suburbs." In April 1894, *The Land of Heart's Desire* was performed at the Avenue Theatre in London, under Miss Farr's management and with Miss Horniman's funds; several months later he met George Moore. His early letters to Katharine Tynan indicate his desire to have his plays produced, a desire perhaps strengthened by John Todhunter's work in the Bedford Park playhouse, which Yeats had reviewed for *The Boston Pilot*. In 1896 he met both Lady Gregory and Synge and visited the Aran Islands. He was still suggesting projects for the National Literary Society and writing plays. Then in January 1897, he wrote to Fiona Macleod from Paris:

Our Irish Literary and Political literary organizations are pretty complete (I am trying to start a Young Ireland Society, among the Irish here in Paris at the moment) and I think it would be very possible to get up Celtic plays through these Societies. They would be far more effective than lectures and might do more than anything else we can do to make the Irish, Scotch and other Celts recognise their solidarity. My own plays are too elaborate, I think, for a start, and have also the disadvantage that I cannot urge my own work in committee. If we have one or two short direct prose plays, of (say) a mythological and folklore kind, by you and by some writer (I may be able to move O'Grady, I have already spoken to him about it urgently) I feel sure we could get the Irish Literary Society to make a start.

He was already distinguishing between plays by others for the sake
of the nation, and plays by himself for the sake of art. "The people,
after generations of politics, read nothing but the newspapers, but
they would listen (to what interminable speeches had they listened)
and they would listen to plays." Until now, Yeats had managed
to keep his nationalism and his literary work separate, the two con-
verging only in his vague desire to be considered an Irish rather
than an English writer. But during the summer of 1897 he visited
Lady Gregory at Coole, and for the first time a union of interests
seemed possible. That winter work began, and Yeats wrote from
London of a meeting arranged with Barry O'Brien, the President
of the Irish Literary Society, to discuss "the Celtic Theatre."

In his turn, Edward Martyn had already written two plays which
had been rejected by London managers, and was deeply engrossed
in his admiration of Ibsen and interest in the Irish language. He too
sought a union of aims. During the summer of 1898 their request
for subscriptions amounting to three hundred pounds was circulated,
and with the help of W. E. H. Lecky the law was altered to allow
the granting of "an occasional license for the performance of any
stage play or other dramatic entertainment in any theatre, room, or
building where the profits arising therefrom are to be applied for
charitable purpose or in aid of the funds of any society instituted
for the purpose of science, literature, or the fine arts exclusively."
Lady Gregory acted as provisional Honorary Secretary, and in
January 1899 the Irish Literary Theatre was founded under the
auspices of the National Literary Society, with Miss Florence Farr
as General Manager and Martyn as Treasurer. Martyn promptly
offered to finance the first year's venture. The movement was gaining strength.

As soon as the Irish Literary Theatre was assured of a nationalist
backing, it started to dissociate itself from any political aim, and
the long struggle with the public began. On the one hand, support
was required to achieve the avowed aim of establishing "a kind
of racial festival" with the Theatre at the core; on the other, the
founders claimed their right to ignore all propaganda "but that of
good art." For their model they looked to the continental municipal
theatres and especially to the encouraging example offered by Nor-
way; for their material they turned to "the imagination and speech
of the country, all that poetical tradition descended from the Middle
Ages." Their work must be for "the countryman and the artisan";

yet they appealed to "the imaginative minority and not to the majority which is content with the theatre of commerce." But they believed that both minority and majority (once educated), their "moral nature" aroused by political sacrifices and their imagination by "a political preoccupation" with their own destiny, were ready to be moved by the "profound thoughts" a popular literary theatre could provide. "It is only at the awakening — as in ancient Greece, or in Elizabethan England, or in contemporary Scandinavia — that great numbers of men understand that a right understanding of life and of destiny is more important than amusement." Ireland was on the verge of awakening, and Yeats, Martyn and Moore had something "which it is our pleasure and our duty to say"; Lady Gregory was determined that they should have the opportunity to say it.

"National life and national feeling — these had always been the basis of admirable literature," Yeats declared at an early lecture. However, as the first theatre programme clearly indicates, equal emphasis was placed on their desire to create a *literary* theatre as well as a national one:

By the word "literary" is meant production which, however much it may fall short of its aim, will at least be inspired by artistic ideas, uninfluenced by the purpose which under present conditions governs the production of plays on the regular stage — that of achieving immediate commercial success. The Irish Literary Theatre will appeal rather to the intellect and spirit than to the senses. It will eventually, it is hoped, furnish a vehicle for the literary expression of the national thought and ideals of Ireland such as has not hitherto been in existence. In this object it hopes for the support of Irish people of all sections who desire to aid in serving the higher intellectual and artistic interests of the country.

In order to further their aesthetic aims, they insisted that "in all or almost all cases the plays must be published before they are acted, and no play will be published which could not hope to succeed as a book."

In these first three years of experiment, therefore, the principles were established and the dual aim acknowledged: the theatre would be national, but first it must be art. In 1900 Yeats had felt sufficiently encouraged to write,

We have brought the "literary drama" to Ireland, and it has become a reality. . . . In Ireland, we had among our audience almost everybody who is making opinion in Ireland, who is a part of his time, and numbers went out of the playhouse thinking a little differently of that Ireland which their work is shaping: some went away angry, some delighted, but all had seen that upon the stage at which they could not look altogether unmoved.... On the whole, therefore, I have a good hope that our three years of experiment, which is all we proposed to ourselves at the outset, will make literary drama permanent in Ireland during our time, and give the Irish nation a new method of expression.

But already in 1901, the final year of the Irish Literary Theatre, the emphasis was more national than literary. *Diarmuid and Grania*, an uneasy attempt at modernizing folk drama, proved beyond the capacities of the English company; and Douglas Hyde's *Casadh an Tsúgáin*, the first Gaelic play produced in a theatre, was acted by amateurs, members of the Keating Branch of the Gaelic League, under the direction of W. G. Fay. Present in the audience were Frank Fay and John Millington Synge. So far as the venture had been "an experimental movement to test whether Irish plays could be acted by professional actors," the results were negative. Actors as well as audience would have to be trained. And so the first experiment ended, sufficiently successful as far as audience and playwrights were concerned; not so promising when it came to theatrical conditions. The Directors retired, intending to return to their "proper work," which, Yeats strongly affirmed, "did not include theatrical management." Martyn and Moore turned their attention elsewhere; Lady Gregory sat back and waited.

But the experiment had been more successful than the Directors at first realized, for the next move came from within, and this time the impetus was almost entirely national. In 1899 Willie and Frank Fay, who had for some time been prominent entertainers in the clubrooms and "Coffee Palaces" of Dublin, had organized a small group of amateur actors called the Ormonde Dramatic Society. Both had watched with interest the efforts of the Irish Literary Theatre, Frank reviewing the productions for *United Irishman* and frequently writing long articles on the necessity of Irish actors for Irish plays. They had recently been asked by Maud Gonne's *Inghinidhe na hEireann*, the Daughters of Erin, to produce some tableaux of Irish historical subjects. In August 1901 in the Antient Concert Rooms, which two years earlier had sheltered the Irish Literary Theatre, they presented Alice Milligan's *Deliverance of Red Hugh* to an appreciative audience which included Yeats, Lady Gregory, and AE. All were impressed, Yeats complimenting Frank Fay on "the grave acting" of his company. Encouraged by this success the company reassembled as W. G. Fay's Irish National Dramatic Society. The challenge of the Irish Literary Society had been accepted.

In the meantime *Samhain* appeared, indicating that the Irish Literary Theatre had completed its experiment but was looking about for a successor. The Fays were not to wear the mantle yet, for the Directors made it clear that two paths lay open, one representing the cosmopolitan ideal advocated by Martyn and Moore, the other reflecting the narrower aims of the more fervent nationalists. Both groups recognized the need to train actors, raise funds, and tour Ireland. However, one group advocated working from without in, suggesting help from leading actors (preferably Irish, probably English) and local endowment; the other group insisted that endowment would eventually lead to compromise and English actors to English plays. Yeats himself publicly indicated a desire to withdraw from active participation, at the same time shrewdly refraining from commitment to either viewpoint:

I do not know what Lady Gregory or Mr. Moore thinks of these projects. I am not going to say what I think. I have spent much of my time and more of my thought these last ten years on Irish organisation, and now that the Irish Literary Theatre has completed the plan I had in my head ten years ago, and that others may have had in their heads for all I know, I want to get back to primary ideas. I want to put old stories into verse, and if I put them into dramatic verse it will matter less to me henceforward who plays them than what they play, and how they play it.

In a letter to Lady Gregory he remarked privately but less astutely,

How Moore lives in the present! If the National Theatre is ever started, what he is and what I am will be weighed and very little what we have said or done. A phrase more or less matters little. When he has got more experience of public life he will know how little these things matter — yet I suppose we would both be more popular if I could keep from saying what I think and he from saying what he does not think. You may tell him that the wisest of men does not know what is expedient, but that we can all get a very good idea as to what is our own particular truth.

Lady Gregory was also biding her time, and replied to Yeats,

If all breaks up, we must try and settle something with Fay, possibly a week of the little plays he has been doing through the spring. I have a sketch in my head that might do for Hyde to work on. I will see if it is too slight when I have noted it down, and if not, will send it to you.

At this point the Fays themselves stepped in. The second act of AE's *Deirdre* appeared in the *New Ireland Review* in November, and Frank Fay asked for a final act with permission to produce the play. AE suggested they approach Yeats, who gave them *Kathleen-ni-Houlihan*. Maud Gonne agreed to act in the title role of Yeats's play, and the company included Maire Quinn, Maire Nic Shiubhlaigh (Walker), Dudley Digges, P. J. Kelly, Padraic Colum, James Cousins, and Fred Ryan, all fervent nationalists who would later contribute to the Abbey Theatre. The plays were a success, with Edward Martyn's the only dissenting voice. The Fays and the nationalist group from which they drew their support were growing stronger. Again Yeats was approached, this time for a little comedy "about a man who made soup out of a stone." The remainder of the programme came from the company and their supporters: James Cousins supplied *The Sleep of the King* and *The Racing Lug*, Fred Ryan *The Laying of the Foundations*, Father P. T. McGinley their second play in Irish, *Eilís agus an bhean déirce* (Ellis and the Beggarman). Once more the little amateur company changed its name, officially amalgamating with the earlier more ambitious scheme represented by Yeats and Lady Gregory (Martyn and Moore had long since withdrawn). Yeats became President of the Irish National Theatre Society, with Maud Gonne, AE and Douglas Hyde as Vice-Presidents, and W. G. Fay as Stage Manager. Before he had an opportunity of leaving it, Yeats was once more involved in "Theatre business, management of men." He wrote *On Baile's Strand, The Hour-Glass*, and *The King's Threshold* with the Fays in mind, and gave them *The Shadowy Waters*. More important for the future of the theatre, he introduced J. M. Synge.

Although from the beginning of the second movement Yeats was considered one of the leaders, the balance of power for several years was an uneasy one, Yeats, Lady Gregory and eventually Synge on the side of the Fays, AE and the nationalists in effective opposition. Most of the actors, drawn from the various nationalist groups in Dublin, looked upon membership in the theatre as a part of their political activities. They had at first wanted AE as President because he was more sympathetic to their feelings; but AE retired in favour of Yeats. Yeats took an active part in determining policy and publicizing the movement's aims and theories not only in Ireland but in England. However, AE's voice carried as much weight. Each member of the society had an equal vote, and as the actors outnumbered the playwrights and producers, much "lobbying" was necessary if Yeats and the Fays were to get their way. With the acceptance of *In the Shadow of the Glen*, shortly after their successful first visit to London, feelings ran high, and the first open split occurred; Maud Gonne, Dudley Digges, and Maire Quinn, whose disapproval of *The Land of Heart's Desire* as an insult to their religion had prevented its production, now resigned at the further "insult to Irish womanhood" implied by *In the Shadow of the Glen*. Yeats was relieved, and in a letter to Frank Fay indicated that this defection of the strongest national element would make it easier "to keep a pure artistic ideal." Differences between the two leaders finally came to a head during the winter of 1903-04, while Yeats was lecturing in America and AE was left in charge. There was further rebellion in the ranks, this time, AE reported to Yeats, the actors objecting to "the way in which plays were accepted or rejected without their consent." But the solution AE offered, "some definite rules on a democratic principle," further limited the powers of President and Vice-Presidents, and left the majority of actors in control.[1] Controversy had also arisen over the question of touring. The Society was invited to take part in the International Exposition at St. Louis, Missouri; AE objected on principle, but a few more actors left to join Dudley Digges, taking with them permission to produce AE's *Deirdre*. AE replied in full to a violent objection from Yeats, at the same time clearly stating his own ambitions for the Irish National Theatre Society:

[1] Among the papers in the possession of Mrs. Yeats there is an unsigned, undated page containing two amendments, III and IV, which appear to belong to this time and seem from AE's letters to Yeats to be the rules he refers to. Amendment IV reads, "In all cases a copy of the play proposed for production shall be submitted to the President and Vice Presidents, or to such of them as may be unable to be present at the reading, together with the Stage Manager's comment as to any alterations that seem to him desirable for theatrical reasons. This Rule, however, must not be considered as limiting the right of the Stage Manager to suggest to the Author such slight changes as may seem desirable during the rehearsal of the play. The opinion of the President and Vice Presidents (should they desire to express any opinion) shall be read to the Company before the final vote which decides upon the acceptance or rejection of the Play. The President and Vice Presidents can vote by proxy. Every Member of the Society shall have one vote, and at the request of any Member the voting shall be taken by ballot. A three quarters majority of the votes shall be required before any play is accepted. The author shall not be allowed to be present when the decision is taken." The Members of the Society were the President, the Vice Presidents and the Actors.

With regard to the question of a vice-president giving away the rights of one of its plays I have already written to you today, and I, for one, will protest against the company having any right to control my action in regard to my disposal of my work outside Ireland or England. You say that the only chance of the Company making money is by an American tour. If that is so, then I think the Company had better dissolve at once for I would lose all interest if it were only to live for America by America. I have no interest in its work outside Ireland and if it is hopeless to expect success by working in Ireland with occasional tours in England then it is in my opinion useless to continue taking any interest in it. With this I think the company would agree. They have refused, rightly I think, to go to the States because it would injure their work here. I am sorry Digges and his people went also because I would like to have seen two or three Irish companies in Ireland. . . . I have quite as much interest in the Company as you have, and in my own way have worked quite as much as you have to preserve it here, settling to the best of my ability the rows which threatened its existence, but if they were to assume the right to control my disposal of what I write outside these Islands I would withdraw from them at once. . . . You and the Company will only be known by what you do over here by personal work here, and I think the company realise this well enough.

A few days later he resigned, again explaining in full his position to Yeats:

. . . I feel that as your views and mine about the spirit in which the Society should work are so different, and as the future success of the Society must be to a great extent bound up with your future work, whereas I in all probability will never write again in the dramatic form, it would be unfitting that I should retain an official position in the Society with which your name is associated and which depends almost altogether on your work for its success.[2]

In the struggle between nation and art, Yeats had once more won.

But as AE left new complications were to enter which though increasing Yeats's power in the movement were to cause further crises and to force Yeats once more to decide between nationalism and art. Writing in his *Autobiographies* many years later, he remarks, "Two events brought us victory: a friend gave us a theatre, and we found a strange man of genius, John Synge." Miss Horniman and Synge arrived in the same year, 1903, and made their debuts at the same performance, Synge with *In the Shadow of the Glen*, Miss Horniman with the costume designs for *The King's*

[2] *Passages from the Letters of AE to W. B. Yeats* (Dublin: Cuala Press, 1936), 46-50.

Threshold. Miss Horniman had known Yeats for at least ten years both as a fellow theosophist and as the generous backer of his artistic enterprises. In an article written for *John O'London's Weekly* twelve years after her withdrawal from the scheme she helped finance, she recounts her own version of the origin of the Abbey Theatre:

> I sat alone here in my flat making the costumes for the Irish Players to wear in "The King's Threshold." I was thinking about the hard conditions in which they were working, and the idea struck me that if and when enough money were to turn up, I would spend it on hiring or building a little hall where they could rehearse and perform in fair comfort. I wrote at once to W. B. Yeats, who was then in Ireland. He was not very enthusiastic on the subject. Time went on, and being in Dublin I searched to see if there were any possible places there. Some money came to me quite unexpectedly — enough for me to hire the hall of a derelict Mechanics' Institute in Marlborough Street. There was no space for a vestibule, but the deserted Morgue of the City of Dublin was adjoining, so I hired that from the Corporation. The building eventually was called the Abbey Theatre.

Since 1901 Frank Fay had been advocating that the Irish Literary Theatre build a hall of their own, but help finally came not from Ireland, but from England, not for nationalist reasons but for cosmopolitan ideals, and not to the society itself but to W. B. Yeats. In her formal letter offering the use of the theatre to the Irish National Theatre Society, Miss Horniman stressed the *Samhain* principles advertised by Yeats; in her personal letters to the Directors she made even more clear her own high ambitions and intense dislikes: "The theatre is a means for carrying out a certain theatrical scheme and as long as you continue in the same path, the theatre is at the disposal of you and your friends under whatever title you may choose to use," she wrote to Yeats on the formation of the Limited Society in January 1906. During the same week she wrote to Synge: "The theatre was given for the carrying out of Mr. Yeats's artistic dramatic schemes and for no other reason. These patriots are all jealous of Art, they want to keep the standard down so as to shine themselves." Yet she also stressed that her main interest was art, not Yeats: "I wanted to make the nucleus of an *Art* theatre, not for your work in particular, but a theatre where such work would be done and other good work too of all kinds." The Dublin theatre was to be "the nucleus — the factory — the school — for an international theatre." The fact that the Abbey Theatre happened to be situated in Ireland was purely incidental ("extrinsic to my scheme itself"); Irish plays and players would be accepted if they conformed to her demands for art. Neither nation nor individual could be considered apart from this ideal.[3]

In December 1904 the Abbey Theatre opened with Yeats's *On Baile's Strand* and Lady Gregory's *Spreading the News*. The company now included Sara Allgood, and Willie Fay was on full salary as stage manager and general overseer. The patent had been granted in Lady Gregory's name, as Miss Horniman was not resident in Ireland. The venture first suggested by the Irish Literary Theatre and taken up by the Fays had gained considerably both in artistic and practical strength. The following year it became apparent that the group could not continue under its democratic and rather chaotic conditions. Plans were made to make the society a professional theatre, and Miss Horniman offered a subsidy of £800. Again AE stepped in to help with the constitution, but this time he sided with Yeats and the Fays; and now Synge was also an important voice. After much consultation between the dramatists and producers, the Articles of Association were passed making the Irish National Theatre Society a limited company carrying on the objects of the Society of 1903, but managed by a Board of Directors who were empowered to "appoint and remove stage manager, business manager and all other employees, fix their salaries and arrange their duties." Yeats, Lady Gregory, and Synge were appointed Directors. Shareholders included the Fay brothers, Sara Allgood, Udolphus Wright, Vera Esposito.[4] Yeats had again won, but without their yet realizing it, the Fays had lost power, and the theatre was more than ever a literary theatre created for dramatists. Still more actors left the society, again for political reasons. The remaining nationalists, led by Maire Nic Shiubhlaigh, felt that the Society was moving too far from the aims of a national theatre; after much discussion they seceded and formed their own group, taking Padraic Colum with them.[5] Frank Fay was granted an additional ten shil-

3 Letters from Miss Horniman to Yeats, Synge, and Lady Gregory, and from Miss Darragh to Yeats, in the possession of Mrs. Yeats.

4 Rules of the National Theatre Society Limited, in the possession of Mrs. Yeats. Also in the possession of Mrs. Yeats are letters between Yeats and Lady Gregory discussing the proposed Articles and their plans for carrying the scheme through.

5 Among the Yeats papers are letters from W. G. Fay to Yeats clearly stating his own position in the company, and insisting upon a formal business arrangement: "Without my brother and myself there would never have existed any

lings a week to train the remaining actors in verse-speaking. Maire O'Neill (Sara Allgood's sister) joined the company. The Theatre continued.

Now that the demands of the extreme nationalists could no longer hamper them, the Directors were free to develop the theatre along their own lines. But here again trouble started, for each Director was finding his own path, discovering his individual method, and demanding special response from the company. All remained constant in their emphasis upon a literary theatre, but it soon became clear that more than one interpretation was involved. Yeats's dream was still of a poetic drama concentrating on romantic and historical plays, a dream shared and encouraged by Miss Horniman. Synge and Lady Gregory on the other hand, although both might experiment with historical drama, required a different treatment for their peasant plays. Lady Gregory visualized a theatre "with a base of realism, with an apex of beauty." New playwrights such as William Boyle, Padraic Colum, Lennox Robinson, T. C. Murray, Frederick Ryan, Rutherford Mayne and Seumas O'Kelly appeared, writing mainly of the towns and requiring an interpretation more in the naturalist tradition. The movement which Yeats had visualized as "a return to the people" was itself becoming restricted, and although his sympathies extended to the plays produced by his fellow directors, he saw the apex of poetry receding in the distance.

However, *Samhain* of 1906 still sounded optimistic:

Our work has developed more quickly upon one side, and more slowly upon another, than I had foreseen. We have done little, though we have done something, to find music that would not obscure the meaning and the rhythm of words, and we have done nothing for the story-tellers, but now that our country comedies, with their abundant and vivid speech, are well played and well spoken, we may try out the whole adventure.

---

acting society to produce these plays and if these people that we have made don't think we are competent we are both ready to leave them to do as they like when they can elect and vote and play round till further notice." Gerard Fay, *The Abbey Theatre* (Dublin: Clonmore and Reynolds, 1958), 100-101 quotes excerpts from this letter. In January 1906 Lady Gregory drafted a long statement to the seceding players concerning use of the theatre, division of funds, and the preservation of Miss Horniman's rights in the Patent, again emphasizing that "the theatre was given to carry out Mr. Yeats' dramatic projects. No one not acting in association with him, least of all anyone who is in revolt against those projects, has any moral right to expect the theatre free." According to Holloway's diary for that year, Colum withdrew his plays, but gave back *The Land* in August 1907.

He comforted himself by assuring others that "the building up of a theatre like ours [is] the work of years," and in *The Arrow* of 1906 spoke of the even more distant future:

We are now fairly satisfied with the representation of peasant life, and we can afford to give the greater part of our attention to other expressions of our art and of our life. Our romantic work and poetical work once reasonably good, we can, if but the dramatist arrive, take up the life of our drawing-rooms, and see if there is something characteristic there, something which our nationality may enable us to express better than others, and so create plays of that life and means to play them as beautiful as a play of Hauptmann's or of Ibsen's upon the German or Scandinavian stage. I am not myself interested in this kind of work, and do not believe it to be as important as contemporary critics think it is, but a theatre such as we project should give a reasonably complete expression to the imaginative interests of its country. In any case it was easier, and therefore wiser, to begin where our art is most unlike that of others, with the representation of country life.

(It is ironical that perhaps the greatest mistakes the directors made were in their dealings with the drama of the drawing-room and the town.)

Miss Horniman was not as sanguine; it was difficult to stand by and see one's money devoted to a scheme which seemed to depart in every way from the original project. Moreover, she was not being given either the courtesy or acknowledgement that was her due; suggestions made by her in good faith were shrugged off by the hot-tempered, overworked Willie Fay; Synge, always immersed in his art and private emotions, tried to ignore her frequent and on the whole justifiable tirades. However, she still had faith in Yeats and Lady Gregory, and in their dream. During the summer of 1906, with her usual generosity and solid sense, she resigned any rights she might have had in the theatre policy and announced "Home Rule" at the Abbey. But she still handled the purse strings, and was determined to try once more to salvage "that part of the cargo which is of real importance," Yeats's plays. The plan she suggested coincided with Yeats's own dissatisfaction with the direction in which the theatre appeared to be heading: the engagement of a managing director ("who should be fairly young, of good manners, and such a temper as will make the position possible for him") who would take over the stage management and production of all but peasant plays, thereby building up that side of the repertoire which at the moment was being neglected. All of the officers had long been troubled by the amount of time demanded by the business side of the theatre, and in August 1906, in an effort to ease the load, they had appointed W. A. Henderson, secretary of the National Literary Society, as business secretary. Clearly, however, this was not enough; in December Yeats addressed a lengthy memorandum to his fellow directors, elaborating the problem and suggesting a solution. The popularity of the theatre at the moment depended, he felt, on Lady Gregory and William Boyle, who would eventually tire the audience or create a school of bad imitators. On the other hand, no second verse writer had appeared, and his own work would not draw large audiences for a considerable time. Actors, audience, and future dramatists would therefore have to be trained, and this would require enlarging the capacities of the present company, increasing the number and types of plays available for performance, and if necessary bringing in both players and teachers. "We should keep before our minds," he warned, "the final object which is to create in this country a National Theatre something after the continental pattern."

... To be artistically noble it will have to be the acknowledged centre for some kind of art which no other theatre in the world has in the same perfection. ... Such a Theatre must however if it is to do the educational work of a National Theatre be prepared to perform even though others can perform them better representative plays of all great schools.

The ideal solution would be, he suggested, the addition of more capital in order to engage actors "whose imaginations will express themselves in other forms of work with the same ease and abundance with which W. Fay's imagination expresses itself in comedy"; to employ a teacher who could develop this necessary aspect of the theatre; to become a true repertory theatre, playing continuously; and to engage a managing director to correlate all these activities. This was an ideal, and at the moment highly improbable. But a smaller scheme which could gradually develop these conditions was possible: Willie Fay must be freed from the business and non-artistic side of the theatre in order that his talent for comedy might have the opportunity of improving; a verse teacher should be brought over once a year; Yeats, as the only writer of verse drama, should have the right to bring in players when necessary for the proper production of his own work; and foreign masterpieces should be produced. (In a memorandum of 1915 Yeats was still reserving the right to bring in actors for his verse dramas.)

His fellow Directors' reactions were not surprising, but unexpectedly violent. Synge's reply ran to three typed pages: the unique value of their theatre was, he believed, the fact that the movement was entirely creative, producing "a new dramatic literature in which the interest is in the novelty and power of the new work rather than the quality of the execution"; to turn this now into an executive movement "in which the interest lies in the fine and careful interpretation of works that are already received as classics" would be disastrous for the movement and for Ireland. Rather than copying the continental repertory movement, they should do their best to avoid it for the next ten years; "national dramas have never been created by such a theatre." Continuous playing should be avoided as well, and the company kept small so that it could remain occupied by the small store of native plays at present available. As for the suggestion of bringing in a business manager or "foreign" actor,

I object to giving Miss Horniman any control over the company whatever. If she is given power it ceases to be an Irish movement worked by Irish people to carry out their ideas, so that if any such arrangement becomes necessary I shall withdraw — my plays of course might remain if they were wanted. I object to Miss Horniman's control not because she is English, but because I have no confidence in her ideals.

Yeats would clearly get no encouragement from that quarter.

Meanwhile Miss Horniman renewed her offer to hire a new man to replace the "incapable" Willie Fay, describing the theatre as nothing but "an Irish toy." Lady Gregory was not in favour of the proposals either; she did not want the Fays "shoved out either by force or gentler means," and saw this final secession an inevitable result. She wrote to Synge, "I think as Yeats and Fay represent the extreme right and left, we who are the moderate centre are best out of it, leaving the rearrangement to them." But she also enclosed two proposals, one "more logical and spirited," the other "easier," adding, "We can take Miss Horniman's letter seriously or not, as suits us best." The spirited second proposal doubtless reflected Lady Gregory's own feelings:

We cannot with self respect, and looking at the list of plays produced and the notices of them, accept Miss Horniman's statement that we are "in the public eye an Irish toy." We cannot accept her statement that our stage manager having had "his chance to carry out what he could" has "proved his absolute incapacity." To accept the new man would be to accept these statements. We claim six months in which to work in our own way. We claim the right of taking our work to London and elsewhere before the end of that time, that "the public eye" may judge what we can do while still working by ourselves. At the end of six months, should Miss Horniman renew her offer, we should hold a meeting of authors and actors and make our decision.

But the "easier" proposal was finally offered for Yeats's consideration. Synge and Lady Gregory would accept the new man subject to certain conditions: that W. G. Fay's wages be raised by a hundred pounds a year and that he be given a written contract defining his duties as producer of dialect plays; that the authors be free to withdraw their plays at the end of six months; that Synge's suggestions concerning the necessity for a national theatre be agreed upon; and that the new man be "a thorough theatrical business man, if possible an Irishman."

The new man was Ben Iden Payne, who arrived in January 1907, produced Lady Gregory's translation of Maeterlinck's *L'Intérieur* and Wilfred Scawen Blunt's *Fand,* and left in June. Yeats and Miss Horniman had lost by winning. But as usual many of Miss Horniman's points, although exaggerated, were accurate. "At this moment Fay in the form of Mr. Synge points one way, and I and your interest point in the other," she had written to Yeats on one occasion; on another, "I feel as if whatever we do will be frittered away unless Fay comes to the conclusion that the Directors must direct." Here she struck at the root of the problem. Synge, like Lady Gregory and Yeats, believed in a literary theatre first, a national theatre second; concerning their first London visit in 1903 he had written to Frank Fay,

Archer seems to criticise — at least our prose plays — as dramas first and literature afterwards. The whole interest of our movement is that our little plays try to be literature first — *i.e.*, to be personal, sincere and beautiful — and drama afterwards ... *strong* and good dramas only will bring us people who are interested in the drama, and they are, after all, the people we must have.

But plays must be performed, and in the Fays both Synge and Lady Gregory had discovered actors who in their art employed the same method of heightened realism found in the plays. The Fays belonged to the theatre each desired; but to them the Fays were actors first, producers second. The Fays in turn believed in a national theatre, in an artistic rather than a political sense; they had founded the Ormonde Dramatic Society and then sought Irish plays suitable for their Irish actors. "*The Abbey Theatre was first and foremost a theatrical not a literary movement,*" Willie Fay insisted. "What brought us together was enthusiasm for the art of acting." And as such, in accordance with general theatrical tradition, the Stage Manager should reign supreme. This basic conflict was inevitable and had shown itself as early as 1902 when Yeats and Fay had argued over the work of James Cousins. It finally reached a climax in the year of *The Playboy*, when Fay objected to the Directors' direct interference with actors and insisted on the right to choose the plays. If the Directors were to grant his request, they would be renouncing the *Samhain* principles on which their entire work, peasant and poetry, was based; by refusing, they rejected not only the Fays but their last opportunity to join the traditional theatre.

One more schism was to come however, it too inevitable, and again involving two opposing but equally valid views of art. Miss Horniman had finally had enough; the repertory theatre she and Yeats had planned had not materialized, and she saw the poet whose art she admired spending his energies on "business of men." In July 1908 she indicated that she would not be prepared to renew her subsidy at the expiration of the patent in 1910. By this time she had established her repertory theatre in Manchester (which in turn became the model for the Old Vic), and invited Yeats to join her:

I hope that when you have quite got rid of the remains of my old interference that you personally will see that I did my best to carry out the original scheme and that you will accept the fact that there is no place for you in it. Mr. Boyle would be much more useful, suitable and profitable in every way; if not Mr. Boyle, then some other man of like capacity. The very commonnesses in his work which you tried to get rid of are what are wanted, what are required in the natural development of a real theatre in Dublin for Dublin people. You and I tried to make it an Art theatre and we had not the living material to do it with. Your genius and my money together were helpless. We must both keep our promises uprightly, but we must not waste our gifts, we have no right to do so.

Yeats was obviously not happy with the Abbey, as his memorandum of two years earlier had indicated. At first he felt that the Fays would win, and wrote to Synge in August 1907:

You know of old that I don't believe that Fay is a very competent man to run a theatre, that in fact I think him particularly unfitted for it, but Miss Horniman has definitely announced that she will do nothing more for us at the end of two years. In all probability Fay may survive us, and at the end of that time may carry on some sort of touring company with our good will and what he wants of our plays. I wanted somebody in control over Fay, but now that plan has failed. . . . The theatre is now a desperate enterprise and we must take desperate measures.

If we think back to the two projects suggested in *Samhain* 1901, it appears that the first course had been tried and found wanting, that the second was inevitable. Yeats's dream of a theatre modelled upon the continental repertory theatres had failed to materialize, and the theatre evolving was one which had little room for his work. In the 1904 *Samhain* he had threatened the nationalists with the statement that literature "has an unlucky craving for reality" and would seek it where it might be found. The following year he had rapped the same knuckles, claiming that "so long as I have any control over the National Theatre Society it will be carried on in this spirit, call it art for art's sake if you will." Now was an opportunity to retire honourably for the same reasons he had first joined; the Abbey had not become the nationally centred cosmopolitan theatre he had dreamed of; perhaps that dream was impossible in Ireland. But Yeats refused:

I have thought carefully over your proposal of yesterday and have decided that it is impossible so far as I am concerned. I am not young enough to change my nationality — it would really amount to that. Though I wish for a universal audience in playwriting there is always an immediate audience also. If I were to try to find this immediate audience in England I would fail through lack of understanding on my part perhaps through lack of sympathy. I understand my own race and in all my work, lyric or dramatic I have thought of it. If the theatre fails I may or may not write plays, — there is always lyric poetry to return to — but I shall write for my own people — whether in love or hate of them matters little — probably I shall not know which it is. Nor can I make any permanent allocation of my plays while the Irish theatre may at any moment need my help. At any moment I may have to appeal to friends for funds with a whole mass of plays for a bait.[6]

6 Rough draft in the possession of Mrs. Yeats. Wade, *Letters of W. B. Yeats* (New York: Macmillan, 1955), 500, dates this as early 1908. It is likely that the offer was actually made in the autumn of 1907 while Yeats was in London. *Cf.* his letter to the Editor of the New York *Gael*, December 1899, *Letters*, 328: "I have always written as an Irish writer and with Ireland in my mind."

However, the only new play by Yeats produced at the Abbey between 1908 and 1919 was *The Golden Helmet* (and its revision,
The Green Helmet); when *The Player Queen* was finally produced
late in 1919 it had already received its première by the Stage Society
in London. The Abbey instead became a business, and Yeats was
determined to make it succeed. "I have often failed as a poet but
not yet as a businessman," he wrote to Olivia Shakespear towards the end of his life. The Abbey in its later form owes its life
as much to that determination shared by Yeats and Lady Gregory,
long after it ceased to be the personal venture they had planned,
as to the playwrights who carried it off on another path. *Samhain*
of 1908 announced new plans; before the patent expired they hoped
"to have made the theatre either self-supporting or nearly so, and
to be able to hand it over to some management that will work it
as a business, while keeping its artistic aim." In his diary for 1909
Yeats commented, "If at all possible I will now keep at the Theatre
till I have seen produced a mass of fine work." A small pamphlet
marked *Paragraphs from Samhain: 1909*, "Private and Confiden-
tial," and signed by the two remaining Directors, had the same
familiar ring: the problem of acquiring more money; and the
desire to add more translations, enlarging the experience of the
players in order to keep the theatre "intellectual and courageous."
It is significant that in 1910, during a course of lectures attempting
to raise the necessary capital, Yeats pleaded not for his own drama,
but for the younger "Cork realists" who would be "driven into
exile like Ibsen" if the Abbey found it necessary to close. For his
own work he already had other plans.

Lady Gregory and Yeats continued to act in accordance with the
Beltaine and *Samhain* principles, desiring to broaden the repertoire
to include "masterpieces from every school . . . even though the public be slow to like that old stern art." They approached Ricketts
and Craig with requests to join their forces in Dublin, but although
both designers gave willingly of their advice and talents, both also
preferred to remain free. In 1911, finding that the Abbey players
had all too clearly become a company of "folk actors," the Directors
founded a school of acting under the leadership of Nugent Monck,
whose first productions were medieval mystery plays. In 1937, two
years before Yeats's death, the Peacock, an experimental theatre, was
opened under the direction of Miss Ria Mooney, still a producer
at the Abbey Theatre. Lady Gregory had translated Molière, Suder-

mann and Maeterlinck; Yeats translated Sophocles. But the Abbey itself remained essentially a "people's" theatre; Yeats continued to experiment on his own, and even Lady Gregory moved away from "the Abbey method."

The conflict between art and the nation was apparent in other ways, too, involving other groups. "All true arts, as distinguished from their commercial and mechanical imitations, are a festival where it is the fiddler who calls the tune," Yeats wrote in the 1906 *Samhain*. Unfortunately, here too the directors were hampered by their dual purpose, for more and more frequently they were being forced to distinguish between their requirements for their own plays and the business of training dramatists to keep the theatre going. And it was becoming increasingly apparent that not only was the tendency towards realism but towards realism in its most limited form, that "kitchen comedy" which has since become an Abbey trademark. And here too the Directors had mainly themselves to blame.

In 1899 Yeats had written concerning the Irish Literary Theatre,

Our plays will all be about Irish subjects; and, if we can find enough writers, and I have little doubt we will find them, who will write with some depth and simplicity about legends associated with the rivers and mountains of Ireland, or about Irish historic personages and events, or about modern Irish life, an increasing number of persons will desire to hear a message that will so often illustrate the circumstances of their lives.

Later they distributed a printed form which advised playwrights of the difference between Abbey plays and those suitable for the commercial theatre:

A play to be suitable for performance at the Abbey should contain some criticism of life, founded on the experience or personal observation of the writer, or some vision of life, of Irish life by preference, important from its beauty or from some excellence of style; and this intellectual quality is not more necessary to tragedy than to the gayest comedy.

Careful attention should be paid to dialogue, which must be true to the author without falling into "the base idioms of the newspapers." All plays were given careful reading individually by each Director before a decision was made, and if the author showed promise he received a letter with full comments even though the play might be rejected. Dramatists were encouraged to write out of their own personal emotions rather than conforming to type, as Yeats states in a letter to Miss Winifred Letts, whose play *The Eyes of the Blind* had a brief unhappy production in 1907:

If you would found your work as much as possible on real life you would find it at once easier to write and more powerful in structure. I mean if you would take the class of people you know most of and invent stories not to amuse or startle but to express the truths of their life. Probably you allow yourself to read authors who keep on the surface. If one writes one can hardly ever afford to read anything but old and simple books, or if modern books only the greatest. . . . Those fantastic plots, a product of the contemporary stage, make sincerity almost impossible. A good play must have truth of atmosphere as in poetic writing — a truth of fact or truth of idea (as with Shaw who overflows with theoretical energy) and truth of fact is generally the best to aim for at the start with most writers for the stage. . . . Take any life you know and express its reality as your own eyes have seen that reality. To know what one has seen is the greater part of the labour of literature.[7]

But too frequently the dramatists did not appear, and those who did exhibited an increasing penchant for modern Irish life at the expense of the legendary and historical material the Directors also recommended. As Yeats explained in a letter to Florence Farr in 1905, few could "stand above their subject and play with it, . . . their writing . . . a victory as well as a creation." As time went on fewer still showed any strong personal feeling; in later years Yeats sadly reflected that "the old idealistic tradition" seemed to have disappeared "from great spaces of the public mind." But that single conviction of its founders, "Not what you want but what we want," remained; despite controversy, the theatre remained free while the Directors retained control. In the last year of his life Yeats could boast in *On the Boiler*,

The moment any dramatist has some dramatic sense and applies it to our Irish theme he is played. We may help him with his technique or to clear his mind of the second-hand or the second-rate in their cruder forms, but beyond that we can do nothing. He must find himself and mould his dramatic form to his nature after his own fashion, and that is why we have produced some of the best plays of modern times, and a far greater number of the worst.

However, two exceptions to Yeats's claim stand out, and both raise the question, might the schism between art and the nation

7 Reprinted by Winifred Letts, "The Fays of the Abbey Theatre," *The Fortnightly*, June 1948, 420-423.

have been bridged? The first can be explained only by saying that the Directors had business elsewhere; the second, paradoxically, by believing that the Directors made the plays in question too much their business. In both cases the Abbey Theatre lost a powerful playwright.

Nineteen hundred and seven, the year of *The Playboy*, brought another dramatist to the Abbey who for a short time appeared to reconcile the new school of realists which had grown up around Colum and Boyle with the first movement. George Fitzmaurice's first play, *The Country Dressmaker*, owed much to Synge both in spirit and structure, and was received with mixed feelings by the audience and players alike. Fitzmaurice came from Kerry, and his characters spoke with the richness formerly heard only from Synge. His realism was blended with the colourful fantasy of Synge's and Lady Gregory's world. Yet in all of his plays the dream is mingled with a reality harsher than that of his forerunners; the romance tends to disappear, leaving only the bitter ashes of a cold world. *The Pie-Dish*, produced six months later, was received with some bewilderment by both actors and audience who could not apparently grasp the Faustian fable of the artist's unachieved dream sketched within one act. His next play, *The Magic Glasses*, was not produced until 1913, and with this early experiment in expressionism Fitzmaurice's connection with the Abbey Theatre ended. His fantasy *The Dandy Dolls* was never produced; publication of later plays has gone unnoticed.

The harshness of Fitzmaurice's world is reflected in his comedy, his characters, and their language. Laughter is rough in a peasant world blackly etched in strong passions and words. Powerful personalities are crudely drawn, in keeping with the stark tragi-comic situations through which they stride. Set against his "heroes" are the peasants, whose lives are narrowed by fear of priest, neighbour, and the supernatural. Neither group can enter the world of the dreamer, and even the dream is suspect. All speak a language strongly regional, gratingly poetic. The action, like the language, presses solidly and swiftly forward, a strange choric repetition of key phrases reflecting the relentless, certain, realistically fantastic fate of the characters. In his portrayal of separate worlds, each man forbidden communication with his fellow, and the mingling of naturalist method with fearful fantasy, Fitzmaurice foreshadowed the works of Pinter, Mortimer, and Ionesco.

"We hadn't the genius of Synge, his genius of combining poetry of speech with humdrum facts, and, of course, we hadn't the poetry of Yeats," Lennox Robinson has written of that first Abbey school. Yet in the strange, original genius of George Fitzmaurice they struck and ignored a vein of rich fantasy which might have yielded greater treasure. From a distance of almost fifty years it is as difficult to assign praise or blame as it is to prophesy with certainty what might have been. That Fitzmaurice's originality was recognized is obvious. Yeats wrote of *The Country Dressmaker*: "A harsh, strong, ugly comedy. It really gives a much worse view of the people than *The Playboy*. Even I rather dislike it, though I admire its sincerity." But it is equally clear that he was given neither the opportunity of William Boyle nor the encouragement of Padraic Colum. However, his fate appears to have been the result of ill-timing rather than any personal antagonism or deliberate oversight. *The Country Dressmaker* was produced in October 1907, when the company was going through one of the most difficult periods of the first decade: *The Playboy* riots had occurred in January; Ben Iden Payne, the English manager brought over by Miss Horniman, had arrived in February and after a rather unpleasant six months had returned to England; in June Synge's play had been taken to Oxford and London; the Fays were to resign in December. *The Pie-Dish* appeared in March of the following year as a curtain-raiser to *The Golden Helmet*, and partly because of its unheroic subject, partly because of the contrast with Yeats's heroic farce, the audience greeted it as a comedy. *The Magic Glasses* again struck troubled times, during a period devoted to productions of Hauptmann, Strindberg, and Tagore by the "second company" while the Abbey toured the United States. But by then Fitzmaurice had lost faith as well. Overshadowed by Synge's greatness and the battle of *The Playboy* from the beginning, he had never succeeded in breaking through the barrier of misunderstanding to the sympathetic involvement required by the strange new form of his bitter fantasy-realism. Without realizing it, Yeats had lost a valuable ally in his losing battle against the "Abbey traditionalists"; the dream at last became a divided image.

The rejection of Sean O'Casey on the other hand seems a different kind of paradox. Why should Yeats and Lady Gregory reject *The Silver Tassie*, while at the same time allowing plays of a much inferior calibre to be produced? It could hardly have been the unconcern shown Fitzmaurice, for *The Shadow of a Gunman* and

Juno and the "Paycock" had received acclaim, and the first night of *The Plough and the Stars* had been the occasion of another of Yeats's famous diatribes against his audience. However, if we consider the history of their management, the paradox simplifies; through the years, out of necessity in keeping the theatre open and fulfilling its function as an educational institution, the Abbey had been forced to accept plays of a style and subject matter which the Directors would not tolerate in their own work. For the sake of the theatre they had early learned to compromise; but in their own art they would tolerate no lowering of standards. The Abbey Theatre had produced O'Casey's earlier plays. Not since the discovery of Synge had the theatre revived to such genius. But then came *The Silver Tassie* which, rightly or wrongly, the Directors did not feel worthy of O'Casey's standard. The young dramatist whose fame they felt responsible for, as they had felt responsible for Synge's twenty years earlier, was given the advice they would have given each other.[8] And so once more the Abbey lost a playwright; once more in an apparent victory for art, the nation had lost.

The dream of the founders for a Theatre of Beauty has today merged completely into the Theatre of Realism which, ironically, Edward Martyn had hoped then despaired of founding. That the Abbey Theatre exists at all is a tribute then not only to the determination of its early Directors but to the stubbornness of an audience which also refused to give in. And in the battle between playwrights and public can be seen the final manifestation of this paradoxical dream.

Although Yeats desired an audience which would approve of and understand his nationalist aestheticism, his work appealed to a limited group only. Looking back many years later he remarked to Lady Gregory, "I have never made a play in sympathy with my audience except *Kathleen ni Houlihan*, and that was you and a dream." Rarely did he stir the audience to violent praise or blame; early controversy over *The Countess Cathleen* was deliberately fostered by a political enemy who published a pamphlet entitled "Souls for Gold"; although for years the actors refused to perform in *The Land of Heart's Desire*, on its production in 1911 there was no outcry from the public. Lady Gregory, concerned more with the pit than the stalls, was more successful in attaining rapport with

8 O'Casey published the entire correspondence in *The Irish Statesman* for June 9, 1928.

her audience (although there was some slight doubt whether any nationalist play should show a policeman in as favourable a light as does *The Rising of the Moon*). Occasional murmurs of complaint were heard over individual plays by other dramatists. Yeats's and Moore's *Diarmuid and Grania* and AE's *Deirdre* had roused some objections; Norreys Connell's *The Piper* disturbed the nationalists in 1908; Shaw's *The Shewing-up of Blanco Posnet*, produced in Ireland because the censor had banned it in England, harried the Castle in 1909. But the public reserved its brightest fireworks in the early years for the plays of Synge. *In the Shadow of the Glen* was denounced by those who had earlier attacked *The Countess Cathleen*; *The Tinker's Wedding* was never performed in Ireland because considered "too dangerous"; *The Well of the Saints* almost emptied the theatre; *The Playboy of the Western World* caused a week's rioting in Dublin and a court case in the United States.

The controversy over *The Playboy* illustrates most clearly both the attitude of the public to its would-be educators and a fundamental truth about the theatre movement as a whole. In 1905 Yeats wrote to John Quinn,

We will have a hard fight in Ireland before we get the right for every man to see the world in his own way admitted. Synge is invaluable to us because he has that kind of intense narrow personality which necessarily raises the whole issue. . . . It will be a fight like that over the first realistic plays of Ibsen.

His comments were prophetic, for the battles raged over *The Playboy* evoked the same hysterical denial and exaggerated claims from both camps. The causes were many, but could be considered under the general categories of art, religion, and politics. In the first place Synge, like Ibsen, wrote out of himself and his vision of the world; the heightened symbolic realism achieved by both caught the audience off guard; emotions became involved and the audience was roused to self-identification. Clumsy satires on their countrymen, written with broad humour and accepted "types," could be accepted, for both audience and author remained superior to the characters on stage. This was not so with Synge's Nora or Pegeen; they expressed the universal desires of mankind, and in doing so commented on the general faults of the nation. "They object to Synge," commented Yeats, "because he is profound, distinguished, individual. They hate the presence of a mind that is superior to their own, and so invent and even believe the cry of immorality and slander." What they objected to even more was Synge's refusal to allow his audience or himself to dissociate themselves from his art. While at the same time hysterically denying the truth of his image, they denounced him for eavesdropping through cracks in the floor.

Synge recognized the contradictions in their attitude, and further realized that he was being categorized by the contemporary popular reaction to naturalism. Hence his violent objections to the Ibsenite drama, his desire not to be linked with the "decadent drama" of France, and his refusal to explain his plays to the public. He wished to remain an individual writer, writing out of his own material: "I don't care a rap" was his immediate reaction to criticism, while at the same time he insisted that he wrote for that audience only.

Synge concerned himself only with his desire to create his work; Lady Gregory and Yeats on the other hand were more involved in the principle behind the riots. "We gave what we thought good until it became popular," Lady Gregory had commented. In their determination to create a national drama which would fulfill their aesthetic aims, they tended almost to encourage the rioting over *The Playboy*. In his speech to the audience, Yeats insisted,

We have put this play before you to be heard and to be judged, as every play should be heard and judged. Every man has a right to hear it and condemn it if he pleases, but no man has a right to interfere with another man hearing a play and judging for himself. The country that condescends either to bully or to permit itself to be bullied soon ceases to have any fine qualities, and I promise you that if there is any small section in this theatre that wish to deny the right of others to hear what they themselves don't want to hear we will play on, and our patience shall last longer than their patience.

Both recognized Synge's genius and the right he had to be heard; yet Lady Gregory personally disliked the play, and Yeats's ideal of drama differed greatly from Synge's. But *The Playboy* had become a principle; it was the answer to the political and religious partisans who had plagued them for almost ten years. It was "the true Ireland fighting the false," the artist arrogantly asserting his right, Seanchan rebelling against the king. Here in Synge's masterpiece was the culmination at last of all the *Samhain* principles, the fusion of aesthetic and national ideals:

We must name and number the passions and motives of men. . . . There is no laughter too bitter, no irony too harsh for utterance, no passion too terrible to be set before the minds of men.

In her speech at the Abbey's twenty-first birthday in 1925, Lady Gregory said, "In the Theatre we have the three A's, interdependent, inseparable — Author, Actor, Audience. We are necessary to one another." But the author must remain supreme. Less than a year later the artist once again asserted his right to be heard, and again Yeats scolded his unruly children for rebelling. Storming on to the stage on the first night of *The Plough and the Stars* in 1926, he shouted,

You have disgraced yourselves again. Is this to be an ever-recurring celebration of the arrival of Irish genius? Once more you have rocked the cradle of genius. The news of what is happening here will go from country to country. You have once more rocked the cradle of reputation. The fame of O'Casey is born tonight.

The tone of his words and the subdued reaction of the audience indicate most clearly of all the peculiar and personal relationship between the Abbey Theatre and its nation. And, in turn, they vividly illustrate the reason for the failure of a dream, and the success of a theatre.

A Literary Theatre:
A Note on English Poetic Drama
in the Time of Yeats

ROBIN SKELTON

Much of the poetic drama written in England during Yeats's lifetime was unsatisfactory and has been dismissed by critics. Nevertheless a great deal was written and it sheds much light upon the problems Yeats had to face as a poet in the theatre.

Of the members of the Rhymers' Club, John Davidson was the only one who attempted poetic drama to any considerable extent. (Dowson's one Masque is insignificant.) Davidson's six early plays, *Bruce* (1886), *Smith* (1888), *An Unhistorical Pastoral* (1889), *A Romantic Farce* (1889), *Scaramouch in Naxos* (1889), and *Godfrida* (1898), though attempting to deal with contemporary problems, were all written in a pseudo-Shakespearian style quite at variance with the language of his later poetic *Testaments*. Shakespearean clichés, Elizabethan diction, and elaborately metaphorical rhetoric combine oddly in *Smith*, with references to the England of the eighties. This play, however, is much more bearable than the others which are filled with such passages of pastiche as:

> But call me slave in any mincing term;
> And let the tyrant's frowns be smiles of love;
> The chains, less galling than a lady's arms;
> The labour, just my pleasure's ministry. . . .
> *(Bruce)*

Or even the more outrageous

> I have no father, and I have no king
> Save thee, my Cinthio, and my dearest love.
> I see her heart is almost split in twain;
> But if they rive my body from thine arms,
> My heart entire will stay there: I shall die.
> *(An Unhistorical Pastoral)*

Smith moves uneasily between a diction of this kind and a brusquer colloquialism:

> I've led a dog's life; done dog's duty too;
> And been as happy as a faithful dog:
> And all to save my daughter from the taint
> That taints me, taints the world, and taints the best:
> I've no fine names for it; I know it's there.
> I've taught her everything — professors, books:
> Made her a — what's the word? — a paragon.

This owes something to Browning, but the play as a whole has a formal coherence which Browning's dramas never quite achieved.

Davidson's drama indicates the problem of poetic drama at this time. How can one marry colloquial vigour to the traditional rhetorics of dramatic blank verse? How can one achieve a heroic theme without the use of fustian?

Stephen Phillips' most successful play was *Paola and Francesca* (1900), but it did little to clarify the problem or solve it. Tennysonian rather than Browningesque, it discarded elaborate rhetoric for a syntactical simplicity which occasionally resulted in a moving speech. Paolo says at the close of the second act:

> One path there is, a straight path to the dark.
> There, in the ground, I can betray no more,
> And there forever am I pure and cold.
> The means! No dagger blow, nor violence shown
> Upon my body to distress her eyes.
> Under some potion gently will I die;
> And they that find me dead shall lay me down
> Beautiful as a sleeper at her feet.

This, in its use of monosyllables and falling cadences and in its emotional idealism, is not dissimilar to the earlier dramatic language of Yeats, though Phillips never achieved that particularity of reference which gives the language of Yeats its immediacy.

The turn of the century brought a change in English poetic drama. Lascelles Abercrombie, John Masefield and Wilfrid Gibson turned towards regionalism and peasant drama. Masefield's early plays, *The Campden Wonder, Mrs. Harrison, The Sweeps of Ninety Eight,* and *The Locked Chest* (all written in 1905 and 1906), and *The Tragedy of Nan* (1907) were in prose. *The Locked Chest* was based on Nordic legend, and *The Sweeps of Ninety Eight* referred to the events in Ireland of that year. In all these we can see the influence of Synge; we can also, however, see a desire by an English writer to make use of folk material and of the heroic past of myth, in the way that Irish writers were also using such material. The same impulse towards peasant material is shown by Wilfrid Gibson, whose earlier dramatic poems, like those of his friend Robert Frost, verge upon theatre, but are really extensions of the dramatic monologue method. His later work, notably *Krindlesyke* (1922), is brutally realistic, and as fascinated by the basic emotions of lust, greed, and the fear of death as Masefield's. The language often moves with colloquial ease, but occasionally becomes cluttered with dialect words as in

> Ay, the braw birkie of that gairishon
> Of menseless slubberdegullions: and I trusted
> My eyes, and other people's tongues, in those days:
> And you'd a tongue to glaver a guff of a girl,
> The devil's own. . . .

The vision, however, is more acceptable, and bears some resemblance to that of Hardy whose panoramic *Dynasts* (1903-1908) seems to stand aside from the mainstream of poetic drama in this period, though his novels, oddly enough, are influential.

In Gibson, as in the later and passionately didactic drama of Davidson, [*The Theatrocrat* (1905), *The Triumph of Mammon* (1907), *Mammon and his Message* (1908)], there is an attempt at a new vigour of language and a new radicalism of theme. Davidson's later drama, however, becomes simply a dramatic presentation of his philosophy and shrilly hectic, and thus a dead end for poetic drama. Another dead end was discovered by Charles M. Doughty. His *Adam Cast Forth* (1908) indulges itself in Miltonic pastiche to such an extent that his drama becomes sluggish. *The Titans* (1916) is even more complex syntactically, and uses archaisms with disconcerting assurance. In *Dawn in Britain* (1906), an attempt at epic rather than drama, he showed his own interest in taking material from the heroic past, but unfortunately used the alliterative techniques as well as the stories of Anglo-Saxon times, and the result, though intermittently brilliant, is as a whole unreadable.

Violence broods over much of the poetic drama of this period, and it is even present in the work of Lascelles Abercrombie who was also part of the Frost-Gibson-Edward Thomas circle. In his *Interludes and Poems* (1908), along with several romantically philosophical playlets which explain Rupert Brooke's reference to him as a successor to the Elizabethans, he included *Blind*. This is a story of a mother and her son, both tramps, meeting an old man. The mother has inflamed her son against his father who deserted her and this old man turns out to be he. Though the woman discovers a renewed tenderness for her husband, the son obeys her teachings and kills him. The theme of child killing parent, of parent killing child, of brother slaughtering brother, occurs in many plays of this period, notably in Brooke's *Lithuania* (1915), in Yeats's *On Baile's Strand* (1903), and (to different effect) in Synge's *Playboy of the Western World* (1907). Abercrombie's play, however, in its setting, in its economy of persons, in its themes of heredity and revenge, and in its sense of the inevitable working out of fate, reminds one sharply of Yeats's *Purgatory* (1939). The language and the philosophical attitudes of the two plays are, however, very different. The impulse behind this, as behind the later plays, even those with historical or biblical themes such as *Phoenix* (1923), or *The Sale of St. Thomas* (1911), is towards the portrayal of character rather than the presentation of symbolic truth, and the language is always discursive, explanatory, in a way quite alien to Yeats whose characters rarely explain themselves, and whose blank verse is concise to the point of being enigmatic. Nor are there, in Abercrombie's plays, any indications of a wish to depart from conventional stagecraft.

The later verse plays of Masefield are more original, in that they mingle metres and make use of lyrical interludes. *Philip the King* (1914) suffers to some extent from this lyricism as the songs hold up the action without much intensifying its significance. *Good Friday* (1914) is closer to Yeats's later drama, and in its combination of colloquial verse spoken by the uncomprehending spectators of the great event with highly symbolist lyrics, anticipates Yeats's *Resurrection* (1927). Moreover, just as in *Resurrection* the play is closed by a lyrical comment by the Musicians, so in *Good Friday* the curtain is brought down by the Madman commenting upon the action in an equally privileged manner.

> Only a penny, a penny,
> Lilies brighter than any,
> Lilies whiter than snow....
> Beautiful lilies grow
> Wherever the truth so sweet
> Has trodden with bloody feet,
> Has stood with a bloody brow.

> Friend, it is over now,
> The passion, the sweat, the pains,
> Only the truth remains. . . .

In addition, just as the Musicians interpose a song in *Resurrection* at the critical moment of the action, so does the Madman in Masefield's play. He, however, is much more involved in the action than the Musicians in Yeats's work, and his words concern themselves more explicitly with the events of the drama. Masefield's plays after 1914 are on the whole less effective than either *Good Friday* or *The Tragedy of Nan*, which stand out in his work both for their powerful construction and their use of archetypal symbolism.

The movement of English poetic drama away from naturalism and towards symbolism and a more experimental use of the theatre is well illustrated by *Good Friday*, but appears even more clearly in the work of Thomas Sturge Moore and Gordon Bottomley. Sturge Moore was a lifelong friend of Yeats. He made designs for many of Yeats's books, and their correspondence contains much discussion of symbolism. The great majority of his poetic dramas, however, are pretentious, prolix, and tiresome. There is a great straining after heroic power and symbolic intensity which forces the plays into an absurd theatricality very far from the economy of ritual and the heroic simplicities to be found in the work of Yeats. Nevertheless there is a similar attempt at the presentation of heroic myth and supernatural truth, though the myths are for the most part Greek or biblical. Yeats, of course, admired Moore's classical knowledge and sympathy, as well as much of his verse, and was fond of declaiming "The Swan" from *The Vine Dresser and Other Poems* (1899), Moore's first collection.

Yeats's influence on Moore is considerable. Apart from their exploration of mutual themes, there is the case of *Medea*, which is written in the Yeatsian manner, with the use of the folding and unfolding of the cloth, at Yeats's own suggestion. The difference between Sturge Moore's manner of using this device and Yeats's is easily seen from the very first. The first words of the Curtain Bearer are

> You doubt of ghost and angel, god and jinn?
> You think those bodied like you, the sole speakers
> Who put a show of wisdom into words
> Here on this planet piebald with pale seas?
> Well, those less hood-winked with to-day, still hear
> Voices in chancelled grove and panelled room. . . .

When the moment comes for the unfolding of the curtain, its Bearer says

> Grief dwells with life,
> Joy's limping and wry-necked shadow,
> So the old live with the young:
> Courage has pain for wife,
> And he dies a fool with these words on his tongue
> "In an instant I shall have done with pain,
> And never wish to be dead again."

This is pedestrian, and over-explanatory. Sturge Moore, like the majority of English verse dramatists, places little trust in the communicative power of symbolism unaccompanied by discursive analysis. Moreover, the images throughout *Medea*, as throughout all Sturge Moore's dramas, tend to be arbitrary and picturesque merely, rather than fundamentally connected with the themes of the drama or the mental attitudes of the characters.

Gordon Bottomley is of all the late nineteenth- and early twentieth-century verse dramatists the most efficient. He was a close friend of Charles Ricketts and Sturge Moore, who both influenced and were influenced by Yeats. His earliest plays, *The Crier by Night* (1900), *The Riding to Lithend* (1909), and *King Lear's Wife* (1915), are all violent and depend for their power upon sympathy with ancient myths and the presentation of barbaric superstition. *Riding to Lithend* is Icelandic in setting, but the majority of Bottomley's plays have a Celtic background, though he makes use of Scotland rather than Ireland. After *Gruach* (1921) he turned to the No Play formula, and to somewhat spiritualist themes. Wilson Knight in his masterly *The Golden Labyrinth* (1962) says of Bottomley:

Like Yeats, Bottomley took inspiration from the Japanese No plays, but he developed the formal elements with a stronger understanding of their Dionysian potentialities, the words of his choric introducers suffusing the action with mesmeric force.

He says further:

Through Bottomley's power we are attuned to a ghostly nature, to sense of old actions clinging pitilessly to their localities and to the undying witness of the dead. We are gripped by emotions of iron, by phantasmal presences, and by an eternity transmuting pain.

This second passage could well be applied to much of Yeats's later drama, and indeed Bottomley owes a considerable debt to Yeats, which he acknowledges generously in his notes to *Scenes and Plays* (1929), referring particularly to Yeats's *Four Plays for Dancers* (1921). Like Abercrombie's *Blind* and *The Staircase*, Bottomley's *Towie Castle* presents a ruined place haunted by the memories and presences of the dead, who return, in one way or another, to expiate and explain their lives. This theme, used by Yeats in several plays, particularly in *The Dreaming of the Bones* (1919) and in *Purgatory*, is worked out with real economy and tension. The last speech of Adam Gordon before the curtain is folded and unfolded at the end of the play bears witness to a strong similarity in the viewpoint of both Yeats and Bottomley.

> Whatever is seen and heard, she does not need
> Regret or anything that I can give:
> So there's no joy in pardon. Even this ruin
> Rejects me: I did what I would with it
> Briefly, and now I have not any part
> In this its still completion. Let us go.

The last speech of all reads

> Long and long and long ago,
> Between the Deveron and the Don
> Men lived eagerly, men lived fiercely,
> And the world went on no worse for them.
> Life was everywhere, life at the flow,
> Life like a fire that leapt up and shone,
> Life that could hurt, that could break us harshly —
> Stripping the blossom, leaving the stem.
> O, happy time when the desolations
> That man would make were swiftly healed,
> As the old year's ruin the year renews
> Abundantly, indifferently:
> For now are made barren his ancient stations,
> County by county, mountain and field;
> Strangers forbid to their sons their use,
> They are civilised by vacancy.
> 'Twere better that Towie should burn again
> With its old reverberations of pain,
> And century by century
> Pity arise, deep life flow on
> By Dee, by Deveron, and by Don —
> By Don; By Don; By Don, Don, Deveron;
> Don, Don, Deveron; Don, Don, Dee.

This, in its concluding mouth music, as in its references to the past, is similar to Yeats's thought and tone. Bottomley's version of the

Deirdre story, his *Deirdire* (1944), was his last full length drama. He presented it in Gaelic and in English, and it was an adaptation of Alexander Carmichael's version of the story. This is in prose, but its prose owes much not only to Yeats but also to Synge. Bottomley, indeed, is in many ways as much a part of the Celtic movement as any Irish poet.

Bottomley is the last poetic dramatist we need to consider. When the thirties brought work by Eliot, Auden, Spender, and others, they brought work in a different and more European tradition. The work of Davidson, Doughty, Phillips, Masefield, Gibson, Abercrombie, Sturge Moore, and Bottomley, however, as well as the lesser work of Bridges, Binyon, Flecker, and Drinkwater, belongs to a movement in English poetic drama which has much in common with the Irish drama of the same period. In both England and Ireland there were attempts to use heroic legend in a high style, attempts to probe the possibilities of realistic peasant drama, and, finally, attempts to escape the shackles both of post-Shelleyan romanticism and of naturalism, and to develop a more ritualistic and symbolist theatre. Of all these writers, however, only Bottomley and Masefield reach a mastery of form and symbolism that places them anywhere near Yeats, Synge, or O'Casey. Gibson's often savage realism is more passionate and powerful than that of the majority of Abbey Theatre realists, but it lacks flexibility of tone, and, being in blank verse, often falls into stock linguistic attitudes.

Nevertheless, it is important to realize that the poetic drama of Yeats does relate to more than the work of his fellow Irishmen, and that many of the impulses of Lady Gregory, Synge, O'Casey, and Yeats were shared by poets across the water. It is also, perhaps, valuable to realize that this whole movement was quite different from those of the European *avant-garde*, and that it was not until after the second world war that English and Irish playwrights, poetic or otherwise, really became part of the general European scene.

The Dun Emer and the Cuala Press

LIAM MILLER

THE DUN EMER PRESS was one of the most important European members of the private press movement at the beginning of this century, but the primary significance of the achievement of this press does not rest on this fact. The technical and artistic developments of other presses were perhaps greater, although few of them functioned over so great a span of years, or maintained such a consistency in the quality of their publication.

The real mark which the Dun Emer press made on its time developed from the fact that this was primarily a writer's press, guided editorially by William Butler Yeats who, in a period in which there was a dearth of Irish publishing, developed a list dedicated to the publication of new Irish writing and commenced a movement which led to the re-establishment of Dublin as a noteworthy centre of publishing.

Emer, Cuchulain's beautiful wife, was renowned in the old Irish heroic tales for, among other things, her skill in needlework and the domestic arts, and thus it seems fitting that Evelyn Gleeson when she returned to Ireland from London in 1902 with the purpose of founding a group of industries for the education and employment of Irish girls, should choose as patroness for the scheme the Lady Emer, and that she should rename "Runnymede," the large house she had purchased in the village of Dundrum outside Dublin to house the venture, "Dun Emer" or Emer's fort.

A brochure describing the Industries and printed at the press describes the scope and aims of the venture: "a wish to find work for Irish hands in the making of beautiful things was the beginning of Dun Emer . . ." and goes on

... the idea is to make beautiful things; this of course, means materials honest and true and the application to them of deftness of hand, brightness of colour and cleverness of design. Everything as far as possible is Irish, the paper of the books, the linen of the embroidery and the wool of the tapestry and carpets. Designs are also of the spirit and tradition of the country. The education of the work-girls is also part of the idea; they are taught to paint and their brains and fingers are made more active and understanding. Some of them, we hope, will become teachers to others, so that similar industries may spread through the land.

Evelyn Gleeson, founder of the Industries, was the daughter of an Irish-born doctor, Edward Moloney Gleeson whose family residence was near Nenagh in County Tipperary, and who, at the time of his daughter's birth in 1855, was practising medicine at Knutsford in Cheshire. Dr. Gleeson later gave up his medical practice and returned to Ireland to found the Athlone Woollen Mills in which flourishing industrial concern he was succeeded by his son Gerald. Evelyn studied painting in London and developed a lively interest in the arts and crafts movement, particularly in the crafts of weaving and tapestry. Her friends in London belonged to the Irish artistic circle which at that time included the Yeats family (John Butler Yeats, the painter; W. B. and Jack B., his sons; and their sisters, Elizabeth and Lily). The Irish Literary Society attracted Evelyn Gleeson, who found in the Yeats sisters a common interest in craft work, combined with an urge to contribute in some practical way to the Irish revival.

The Irish revival of the 1890's combined with her interest in craft work and the movement for the emancipation of women, were factors in the development of Evelyn Gleeson's plan to found an establishment in Ireland for the training and employment of girls. The Yeats sisters were invited to assist the project with their special skills and, with the plan for her industries formulated, Evelyn Gleeson moved to Dublin in the summer of 1902 to find premises. Dun Emer was a large, old-fashioned house standing in spacious and well-arranged grounds, with a glazed entrance porch and, on the south aspect, windows with green slatted shutters facing towards the Dublin mountains. The house was approached through the entrance gates with the name inscribed in Irish characters and along an avenue lined with trees and shrubs. Inside, on the ground floor, the drawing-room had moss green walls and the library which was furnished in oak contained Miss Gleeson's collection of pictures and books. Across the hall, the dining room was decorated in dull gold and furnished in carved oak. The wide staircase rose between peacock blue walls to the work rooms on the first floor. The embroidery room, which also in the beginning housed the weaving and tapestry workers, was a very large, sunny room on the south side of the house. The printing room was a large room on the first floor where, on the end wall, AE had executed a mural in pastels. Here Elizabeth Yeats worked with two girls, Esther Ryan, who joined the staff, aged fifteen, on January 3, 1903, and whose entire life until her death in 1961 was to be spent in the service of the Press; and Beatrice Cassidy, another Dundrum girl, who came to work on February 23 of the same year. The names of Esther Ryan and Beatrice Cassidy first figure in the colophon of the tenth book issued from the press, Katharine Tynan's *Twenty-One Poems*, in 1907. Later, other girls were to join the press, among them Padraic Colum's sister, Eileen, and Maire Nic Shiublaigh (Maire Walker), the Abbey actress.

On the advice of Emery Walker, who acted as typographical adviser to the press, Elizabeth Yeats took a month's course at the Women's Printing Society in London. This formed the basic training for her part in the Dun Emer Industries. Elizabeth did not join the Industries in Dublin until the autumn of 1902. Her father had come back to Dublin earlier in the year and took a house at Dundrum which he named Gurteen Dhas. Elizabeth started work at the press immediately after her return to Dublin.

The establishment of the press was more complex than the establishment of the other Industries. Unlike other private presses of the period, which concentrated on beautiful reprints, Elizabeth Yeats's aim was to produce the new literature of Ireland in worthy editions. With this in mind she recruited her brother, who was by then one of the most prominent figures in the Irish literary revival, as editor of the books she was to publish. Yeats had worked with John O'Leary on the editing of *Poems and Ballads of Young Ireland* in 1888, at which time he was writing his own *Wanderings of Oisin*, and he later edited *Fairy and Folk Tales of the Irish Peasantry*. The involvement with Irish tradition shown by these titles is reflected in his editorial work for his sisters' press, as was his work in planning the ill-fated New Irish Library, commenced by Unwin in London but discontinued after a short time.

Yeats was very much concerned with the setting up of his sisters' press and his letters indicate the passage of the first book through the various stages of its production. Writing to Lady Gregory on December 4, 1902, he admires the first proof sheets of the book and on December 16 he writes about the final revisions to his Cuchulain play *On Baile's Strand*, which forms the concluding section of *In the Seven Woods*. A letter, also to Lady Gregory, on January 3, 1903, shows him still at work on the book: "I hope in a couple more days to have got *Cuchulain* finally right and sent to my sisters. Then ... I propose to put certain parts of *The Hour-Glass* into verse.... The play will then go to enlarge my sister's book."

The Hour-Glass did not in fact form part of *In the Seven Woods* and was not printed at the press until the privately issued Cuala Press edition of the revised play in January 1914.

Three days later Yeats wrote again to Lady Gregory:

After sending you that letter about the play I recollected how stupid I was. There was no reason in the world why including it in my sister's book should exclude it from the book of plays. However, I will not include it in my sister's book, if you still greatly object. My reasons for wishing to do so are these. They are going to charge ten shillings for the book and as an artistic press like theirs is forbidden to adopt the usual methods of padding out the poems, the Cuchulain play and all will come to about forty or fifty pages. This may be long enough. It will depend to some extent on the general look of the book.... My sister's book is merely a specially beautiful and expensive first edition of certain of my best things. I have been thinking of putting a note at the end explaining why I have called the book by the name of one of the shortest poems *In the Seven Woods*.

Later, Yeats is in correspondence with Sydney Cockerell about various aspects of book production — binding details for the Bullen edition of *Ideas Good and Evil* in which the future Dun Emer binding style is foreshadowed: "I should like to have it [*Ideas of Good and Evil*] bound in boards, grey or blue, a white back, bound round with real cords, like one of the examples you showed me." And, in a letter dated March 22, specific details of the forthcoming Dun Emer Press book are discussed:

My dear Cockerell ... I return proof of colophon, for which many thanks. It is charming, but I rather agree with you that it would be better somewhat larger. I don't quite know to what extent my sisters are in a hurry but Mr. Walker probably knows this. I only saw them amid a whirl of people in Dublin and shall not be able to go into details with them for another week or more when I shall be in Dublin again.

W. B. Yeats. Portrait by Augustus John.

When Helen Lived

We have cried in our despair
That men desert,
For some trivial affair
Or noisy, insolent, sport,
Beauty that we have won
From bitterest hours;
Yet we, had we walked within
Those topless towers
Where Helen walked with her boy,
Had given but as the rest
Of the men and women of Troy,
A word and a jest.

WB Yeats,

Holograph Manuscript of W. B. Yeats's "When Helen Lived" signed by the Author.
(Beals Deposit, University of Washington Library.)

W. B. Yeats, *The Secret Rose* (1897), with Cover Design by Althea Gyles.

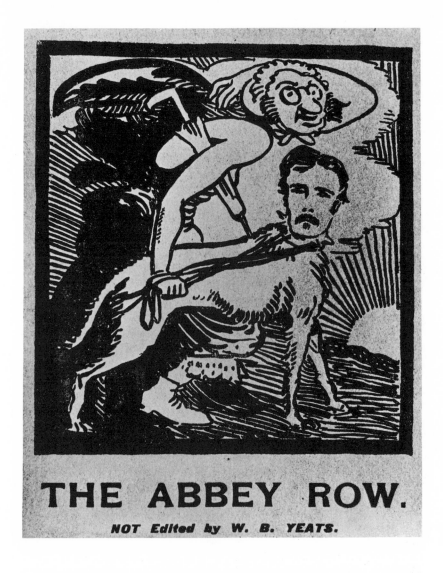

THE ABBEY ROW.

NOT Edited by W. B. YEATS.

J. M. Synge. Portrait by Jack Yeats.

Inscriptions by members of the Abbey Theatre Players in a copy of
Synge's *Riders to the Sea*.

Early cast of Synge's *Riders to the Sea*: Brigit O'Dempsey, Sara Allgood and Maire O'Neill.

THE PITY OF LOVE

A PITY
BEYOND
ALL TELLING
Is hid in the heart of love :
The folk who are buying & selling:
The clouds on their journey above;
The cold wet winds ever blowing;
And the shadowy hazel grove
Where mouse-gray waters are flowing
Threaten the head that I love.

W·B·YEATS.

Hand-coloured print from the Cuala Press.

Villiers de l'Isle-Adam, *Axel* (1925), with Cover Design by T. Sturge Moore.

À BROAD SHEET

JANUARY, 1902.

FINN.

This sod has bound us
Like brother to brother,
Like son to father.
Let him who breaks it
Be driven from the threshold
Of God-kind and man-kind.

DIARMID.

Let the sea bear witness,
Let the wind bear witness,
Let the earth bear witness,
Let the fire bear witness,
Let the dew bear witness,
Let the stars bear witness!

FINN.

Six that are deathless,
Six holy creatures,
Have witnessed the binding.
The Blood Bond, from
"GRANIA," by George Moore
and W. B. Yeats.

SPINNING SONG.

There are seven that pull the thread.
One lives under the waves,
And one where the winds are wove,
And one in the old gray house
Where the dew is made before dawn;
One lives in the house of the sun,
And one in the house of the moon,
And one lives under the boughs
Of the golden apple tree;
And one spinner is lost.
Holiest, holiest seven,
Put all your power on the thread
I have spun in the house this night!

W. B. Yeats.

THE POOKA!   THE POOKA!

First number of *A Broad Sheet*, edited by Pamela Colman Smith.

Lady Gregory. Portrait by Flora Lion.

"CHIN-ANGLES" — or How the Poets Passed.

The story is told in Dublin that W. B. Yeats and ("Æ") George Russell set out, respectively, from 82 and 84 Merrion Square to see each other . . . and passed at 83! The above shows how it happened.

Caricature by Isa MacNie

The book is a long way yet from the level of the printing but Mr. Walker will know perhaps when they mean to bring out a prospectus and whether the colophon is to be a part of it.

A colophon design was under consideration at this stage and a later letter to Cockerell on May 16 indicated that a block was paid for in May 1903, but this was evidently never used and the press worked without a specific device until 1907 when Elinor Monsell's device "Lady Emer" appears for the first time in *Twenty-One Poems* by Katharine Tynan.

In the summer of 1903 a prospectus was printed announcing the ideals and first books of the press. This gave the titles of six works, of which four eventually were published and two were later abandoned. These two were the prose story by George Bernard Shaw and the book *On Speaking to the Psaltery.* The Shaw story was "The Miraculous Revenge," which had originally been printed in *Time* (London, March 1885), and was obtained from Shaw for the press by W. B. Yeats, who wrote on December 4, 1902, to Lady Gregory:

I think I have arranged that they follow... [*In the Seven Woods*] with a very witty and unknown story of Bernard Shaw's. He offers to correct the proofs entirely for the purpose of making the print look nice. He says Morris never revised for any other reason.

A 1903 letter of Elizabeth Yeats states: "Mr. Bernard Shaw's book is postponed because we decided that the prose story . . . was not suitable." No work of Bernard Shaw's was issued by the press. The Shaw story was later suggested by W. B. Yeats to George Roberts for his periodical *The Shanachie*, in which it appears in the issue for spring 1906.

The book *On Speaking to the Psaltery* was discussed by Yeats in a letter to Sydney Cockerell on May 16, 1903:

I want my sisters to bring out a Primer on the New Art. Dolmetsch is ready to write an Essay and to go through Mrs. Emery's notations. To touch them up here and there and pick the best. I have been discussing with Dolmetsch the problem of music printing. As far as I can make out it will be impossible for my sisters to do this part of the work. What I want to know is, would it be out of the question to have the letterpress printed by my sisters and the musical notations printed by the Chiswick Press (they have a charming musical type) and these notations made up into a little music book and put into a pocket made in the cover of the Primer? If this would be all wrong I must get Bullen to publish the Primer and to print the whole thing at the Chiswick Press.

W. B. Yeats's essay "On Speaking to the Psaltery" appears in his *Ideas of Good and Evil* (Bullen, London 1903). In August 1903 the first book from the press was sent to the subscribers. This was W. B. Yeats's *In the Seven Woods*, which contains an important collection of his poetry and his play *On Baile's Strand*. The book sold out on publication and the book was reprinted in a similar style in New York early in 1904. The typographic style and the standards set in *In the Seven Woods* were adhered to throughout the history of the press, and the press, renamed Cuala after 1908, continued to publish books until 1946.

In the copy of *In the Seven Woods* which was sent to John Quinn in New York, Yeats wrote: "This is the first book of mine that it is a pleasure to look at — a pleasure whether open or shut." Yeats at this time was very closely involved with the affairs of the press, especially the editorial side, as the following letter from AE to John Quinn in May 1903 indicates: "With regard to the Dun Emer Press, Yeats and I fought over one poem and, both being stiff-necked, he suggested that I should make a selection of all my verses instead for his sister, and this I am doing." AE had made some embroidery designs for the Dun Emer workshops and his book, *The Nuts of Knowledge*, was to be the second issued from the Dun Emer Press. Yeats was in America on a lecture tour during the final production stages of *The Nuts of Knowledge* and the edition went smoothly through the press and was issued on December 1, 1903. In this book the first use of decoration in the work of the press occurs. This was a circular device designed by the author and represents the ancient Irish symbol An Claidheamh Soluis [The Sword of Light]. With the publication of *The Nuts of Knowledge* the regular style of binding used by the press was established. This consists of a natural Irish linen spine with coloured paper-covered boards.

A letter to his sister from Yeats in New York, written on Christmas Day, 1903, expresses his pleasure in the book and indicates his continued concern with every aspect of the work. He criticizes the size of the device and discusses the publications of an American press, The Roycrofters. Another letter, written ten days later, shows that he was attempting to get American subscribers for the books, and a letter to Lady Gregory on January 4 shows him sorting out the copyright position in his "Red Hanrahan" stories for later publication.

But in Ireland, early in 1904, the affairs of the press were undergoing a crisis, and during January Lily Yeats wrote to her brother suggesting that he should finance the project. Yeats wrote to Lady Gregory for advice and suggested that the business affairs should be looked into by George Pollexfen. John B. Yeats, in Dublin, was also attempting to solve the difficulties and AE acted successfully as intermediary between Miss Gleeson and the Yeats sisters. By the middle of February all was again well and the third book, Douglas Hyde's translations of *The Love Songs of Connacht*, was finished printing on April 16. By September difficulties had again risen and a scheme was adopted whereby a limited company was formed, Dun Emer Industries Limited, with AE as a committee member, Miss Gleeson as president and Elizabeth Yeats secretary. This company was to pay Miss Gleeson for rent and attendance at her premises and comprised the embroidery and printing sections under the management of the Yeats sisters. This foreshadows the eventual division of 1908. The fourth book, *Twenty-One Poems* by Lionel Johnson, selected by W. B. Yeats, was finished on All Hallow's Eve but was not publicly issued until February of the following year. Meanwhile, Elizabeth Yeats visited Emery Walker in London early in January of 1905 for advice about the future development of the press and a grant towards her expenses was obtained from the government. During her absence Esther Ryan managed the press.

Bookplates were designed and printed at the press from its earliest days and the fourth prospectus issued in April 1904 announces the designing and printing of these. A large range of plates was produced throughout the history of the press, many of them designed by Jack B. Yeats. The fifth prospectus appeared in August 1904 and announced Yeats's "Red Hanrahan" as expected for December, but the sixth prospectus, which is dated January 1905, indicates that "Red Hanrahan" is not yet ready. In fact, *Stories of Red Hanrahan* did not appear until May 16, 1905, although its printing was finished on August 15, 1904. This delay may have been partly due to Elizabeth Yeats's visit to London and to some friction between Miss Gleeson and the Yeats sisters. In any case, no committee meeting was held between January 10 and March 23, 1905, and sales and income from sales were much less than in the first two years of the press. The prospectus quoted of May 1905 indicates that all the early titles with the exception of Lionel Johnson's poems were out of print, but succeeding titles sold much more slowly and the next book, Yeats's *Stories of Red Hanrahan*, was still available from the Cuala Press in January 1913, eight years after publication.

Stories of Red Hanrahan has an illustration by Robert Gregory depicting the four aces from a pack of cards spread over the provinces, or four green fields, of Ireland. This is the first of several designs by Robert Gregory to be used at the press.

The next book also proved to be a slow selling title. *Some Essays and Passages by John Eglinton*, selected by W. B. Yeats, finished printing on April 16, 1905, and was issued on August 25. John Eglinton was the pseudonym of William Kirkpatrick Magee who produced several volumes of essays, memoirs and letters until his death in 1961. He did not quite see eye-to-eye with Yeats's editing of his work and insisted that a note be printed in the book saying:

The writer of the following pages would like to say that he has had no hand in the selection which Mr. Yeats has done him the honour to make for the Dun Emer series and, in particular, that if consulted he would hardly have approved of the inclusion of the last essay written over 12 years ago in which a metaphor is pressed to the point of being recommended as a gospel.

Yeats continued his pursuit of material for his sisters' press and a letter of December 7, 1904 to Mrs. William Allingham about the proposed selection of her husband's poems shows his concern with providing for the press a good list and illustrates his editorial approach:

Dear Madam, I would very much like, if you would give me permission, to make a small selection from your husband's poetry for publication by the Dun Emer Press. These books, which are printed by my sister in a very beautiful old type, have had considerable success. The edition is of course very small, 250 or 300 copies, but we could pay you a small royalty. It would be quite a small book, let us say 25 poems, and could not in any case interfere with the sale of the ordinary editions. Books by AE, by Lionel Johnson, by Douglas Hyde and by myself have already been printed and a book by Lady Gregory will follow the selection from your husband's poems should you give me permission. We are anxious to bring out in this series representative Irish books. I have the greatest possible admiration for Mr. Allingham's poetry. I am sometimes inclined to believe that he was my own master in Irish verse, starting me in the way I have gone whether for good or evil. I believe that I shall be able to make a little volume of his work which will be a great joy to a great many people. Yours sincerely, W. B. Yeats.

The book, *Sixteen Poems by William Allingham*, was finished in September and published on November 27, 1905. The next book was one of the largest done under the Dun Emer imprint and one of the most popular, Lady Gregory's renditions of old Irish legends, entitled *A Book of Saints and Wonders*. The printing was not finished until August 1906, but it was rapidly bound and was published on September 10. The book contains Robert Gregory's second design for the press and the stories have their titles in capitals indented into the text matter. This style was copied in the commercially issued London and New York editions of the work which appeared in the following year. November saw the completion of *By Still Waters*, AE's second Dun Emer Press title, which used the device he had drawn for *The Nuts of Knowledge*. This book had been considered as early as April 1904, as a letter of that date from AE to Yeats shows. The letter refers to it as another work to be done after Lady Gregory's. It did indeed follow Lady Gregory's book but it had taken over two and a half years to reach publication.

Elinor Monsell, who had been responsible for the Queen Maeve with wolf-hound device used by the National Theatre as its emblem, was asked by Yeats to design a press mark for the Dun Emer Press and the result was an elegant engraving on boxwood, 2⅜″ high, showing Lady Emer standing by a tree. This device figures in many of the books printed at the press, the first being the tenth book, *Twenty-One Poems* by Katharine Tynan, finished in March and published in August 1907.

With the publication of *Twenty-One Poems*, many of the regular features of the press books are finally established. The names of the printing staff of the press are included in the colophon for the first time. A specific press mark is used rather than an illustration for the particular book, and the binding is in "Dun Emèr" style.

It was decided in September to send Lily Yeats to the Irish Exhibition in New York in the following January and Ruth Pollexfen was co-opted on the committee to take her place during her absence. The scope of the press was widening and the first hand-coloured prints from drawings by Jack Yeats had appeared. Among these were drawings based on Synge's *Playboy of the Western World*, which had been staged at the Abbey in 1907. From the publication of these prints it was a short step to *A Broadside*. *A Broadside* was inspired by the series of broadsheets with hand-coloured drawings produced by Jack Yeats and Pamela Colman Smith in London in 1902, and by their miscellany, *The Green Sheaf*, in which Jack Yeats's Wren Boys drawing was first printed in 1903 and 1904.

Meanwhile the final book to appear under the Dun Emer imprint, Yeats's volume of essays, *Discoveries*, was completed in September and published in December 1907. *Discoveries* contains the third design of Robert Gregory's to be done for the press and represents one of Yeats's favourite symbols, a charging unicorn.

The final piece issued from Dun Emer was the first number of the first series of *Broadsides*, which was published monthly for a total of 84 parts, the remaining 83 bearing the Cuala imprint. *A Broadside* is among the titles announced in the last prospectus issued from Dun Emer in May 1908. This list shows that of the eleven books issued, eight are out of print and three still available, and it announces three titles in preparation of which two were to appear from Cuala and one, a selection from the poems of Aubrey de Vere and Sir Samuel Ferguson, was to be abandoned.

Each part of *A Broadside* contained two or three drawings by Jack Yeats and traditional and original poetry and ballads, printed in folio format, with usually two out of three drawings hand-coloured. This handsome series was widely praised in the literary and artistic press and was a form of publishing very dear to Yeats, who was to revive the idea in two later series printed at the Cuala Press in 1935 and 1937.

Despite the efforts at expansion, however, conditions at Dun Emer were not happy and, during May of 1908, the Yeats sisters acquired the lease of a cottage at Churchtown, near Dundrum, to house the press and the embroidery workshops. Miss Gleeson insisted on retaining the title Dun Emer and an agreement was reached whereby the press and equipment should be moved to the new address and the Yeats sisters should find another name for their venture. "Cuala" was the old Irish name for the barony in which the Churchtown cottage stood, so it was decided to change the title of the Press to Cuala. Accordingly, at a meeting on July 9, 1908, the resolution to change the title of the press to the Cuala Press, and of the venture at large to Cuala Industries Limited, was passed unanimously. The changeover is reflected in the lapse of time between the dates in the colophons of the last Dun Emer book, *Discoveries*, which was finished on September 12, 1907, and the first Cuala book, *Poetry and Ireland*, essays by Yeats and Lionel Johnson, which was finished on October 8, 1908.

The Dun Emer Industries continued their production of hand-woven tapestries and rugs under the direction of Miss Gleeson and are still working in Dublin under the direction of Miss Gleeson's niece, Miss Katherine MacCormack. Miss MacCormack contributed the following brief account in a letter to the editor of the *Irish Times* which appeared on September 16, 1953.

Sir, I was interested to read in to-day's Irishman's Diary an account of the Dun Emer Press, but I was surprised to see that there was no mention of the woman who made it all possible. In the autumn of 1902 Evelyn Gleeson took a house in Dundrum, changing its name from Runnymede to Dun Emer. Here she started the Dun Emer Industries and superintended the handweaving of rugs, which she herself designed. She had arranged for Lily and Elizabeth Yeats to come from London and work at embroidery and printing, and in this way the Dun Emer Press was founded.

After some time the Industries were separated, the Misses Yeats continuing their work, as the Cuala Industries, in Churchtown; while Miss Gleeson still carried on the weaving at Dun Emer, under the name of the Dun Emer Guild. With fifty years' work behind it, the Dun Emer Guild is still in existence in Dublin. Miss Gleeson died at her home, Dun Emer, Dundrum, in May 1944. . . .

Katherine MacCormack.

Under the new style of Cuala the press continued its work and issued a further sixty-six books in the regular series. The first series of *A Broadside* ran to eighty-four parts in all, finishing in 1915. Two further series were produced, each of twelve numbers, in 1935 and 1937. Some miscellaneous books, not in the regular series, were issued and an extensive range of hand-coloured prints and greetings cards. These latter publications were continued long after the final book, Elizabeth Rivers' *Stranger in Aran*, was issued in 1946. In 1943, the fortieth anniversary of the press, a handlist was printed and bound into the books issued in that year. Over thirty private editions were printed and, in 1939, the press entered the realm of commercial publishing with the issue of W. B. Yeats's *On the Boiler*. This was intended to be the first number of an occasional review, but due to his death no further issues appeared.

"Images That Yet Fresh Images Beget":
A Note on Book-Covers

JOAN COLDWELL

IT IS OBVIOUS that many of the cover designs for the early editions of Yeats's work give visual representation to symbols central to his thought. Rose, cross, hawk, tree, tower and mask — these are some of the motifs recurring in the designs as they do in the verse. Less apparent is the extent to which Yeats himself supervised the conception and execution of the covers and made a significant contribution to the movement towards better book-design.

The designers he commissioned belonged to a small group of artists who in the eighteen-nineties effected a revolution in the appearance of machine-bound books. The invention of publisher's cloth earlier in the century had resulted in the mass production of cheap, second-rate imitations of leather covers; now, with eyes opened by William Morris to the possibility of restoring beauty to everyday objects, designers questioned whether cloth-binding need necessarily be inartistic. Must cloth imitate leather? Were there not designs proper to this material alone? Some who sought answers to these questions had been associated with Kelmscott House and now carried the influence of Morris from the handicraft side of binding to the wider sphere of trade-work. Great impetus to the movement was given by the success of the cloth-bound *Yellow Book* and by the effectiveness of Beardsley's poster style of design in this periodical and for other Bodley Head publications. The guiding principle was that there should be no attempt to achieve effects suited only to leather. Since the material itself was less distinguished, emphasis must be thrown on the stamped or printed design, which might beautify the given space by any means, purely decorative, pictorial or symbolic, so long as it remained harmonious with the contents.

There is no question as to which type of design Yeats preferred for the covers of his books. His occult practices alone convinced him of the power of the visual image and he felt that the cover could be made to work on the reader's imagination, in support of the symbolism of the contents. An objection he makes to a suggested design shows the importance he attached to symbolic value:

. . . it would make a fine design but don't nail the hawk on the board. The hawk is one of my symbols and you might rather crudely upset the subconsciousness. It might mean nightmare or something of the kind for some of us here.[1]

Yeats's active concern with cover-design began with his objection to the "facile meaninglessness" of the cover to his *Poems*, 1895. This was the work of H. Granville Fell, whose designs for the *Book of Job* and the *Song of Solomon* were to be acclaimed as "books of the year" by *The Studio* in its issue devoted to "Modern Bookbindings and their Designers," (Winter 1899-1900). Yeats had admired one of Fell's designs at an earlier exhibition but he felt that the artist's work had deteriorated; in John Quinn's copy of *Poems* Yeats wrote, ". . . Dent had spoilt him with all kinds of jobs & when he did this the spirit had gone out of him. I hate this expressionless angel of his." For the second edition of *Poems*, and for all subsequent editions until that of 1929, Yeats arranged to have the Fell cover replaced by one designed by Althea Gyles, the first of the "symbolic artists" who were to create emblematic cover designs for Yeats's books.

Althea Gyles, a young Irish poet and artist, owed a good deal of her prominence as a designer to Yeats's championship. Her personality intrigued Yeats, who appears to have acted as a somewhat unreliable confidant; letters to Lady Gregory gossip about Althea's disreputable love affairs and practical inefficiency, "She seems to be perfectly mad, but is doing beautiful work." Yeats twice published critical appreciations of her art. He wrote a prefatory note to her contribution to *A Treasury of Irish Poetry*, in which he predicted for her an important place among the group of Irish poets "who seek to express indirectly through myths and symbols, or directly in little lyrics full of prayers and lamentations, the desire of the soul for spiritual happiness." But he felt that it was as an

[1] *W. B. Yeats and T. Sturge Moore, Their Correspondence, 1901-1937*, ed. Ursula Bridge (London, 1953), 38.

artist that she had so far shown most promise: "Her drawings and
book-covers, in which precise symbolism never interferes with beauty
of design, are as yet her most satisfactory expression of herself." An
essay in *The Dome*, December 1898, is devoted to a more thorough
analysis of Althea Gyles' art. Yeats entitled it "A Symbolic Artist
and the Coming of Symbolic Art" and praised a cultural climate in
which "Subject pictures no longer interest us," where symbolic
pattern and rhythm were creating "a new religious art and poetry."
A comparison with Blake and interpretations of the symbols in some
of Miss Gyles' drawings demonstrate the nature of Yeats's fascination with symbolic design and his belief in the sympathy between
this artist's imagination and his own; "her inspiration is a wave of
a hidden tide that is flowing through many minds in many places."

Althea Gyles designed three covers in all for Yeats, of which the
most striking is that for *The Secret Rose*, 1899. So skilfully does this
design weld together images central to Yeats's verse that Richard
Ellmann (*The Identity of Yeats*, London, 1954) has found in it the
one unified picture of the poet's early symbolic structure. In the
centre of the gold-stamped design is the four-petalled rose attached
to a cross which had been the focal point of the *Poems* cover. Now
the rose and cross are embedded in the heart of a serpent-like tree
at whose tip appears a trinity of smaller roses, and beneath these
are the kissing faces of a man and woman.

Rose and Kabbalistic tree appear on later covers designed by the
man who worked longest and most closely with Yeats in this field,
not only for the public press but also for the Cuala. T. Sturge Moore
created twelve covers for Yeats's books between 1916 and 1940,
shaping and modifying his designs according to Yeats's suggestions.
Their friendship was fruitful in other directions too. Sturge Moore,
a founder with Ricketts of the short-lived Literary Theatre Society,
had an active interest in the drama both as writer and designer and
he helped Yeats with suggestions for setting and costumes for *The
Hour-Glass* and *The Shadowy Waters*; both of them were members
of the Masquers society. Their correspondence is full of illuminating
criticism of each other's work; like Althea Gyles, Sturge Moore was
a poet as well as an artist and this perhaps accounts for his successful visual interpretation of Yeats's symbols, his own poetry having
a similar pictorial quality. He had also much of Yeats's intense
passion for symbolic beauty; his most magnificent book-cover, that
for Finberg's translation of Villiers' *Axel* to which Yeats wrote the

preface, involved "fighting hard for every inch of beauty against both publisher and printer."

The letters discussing Sturge Moore's design for *The Winding Stair* demonstrate their method of collaboration. Yeats had chosen a title from among the symbols in one of the poems, the "winding, gyring, spiring treadmill of a stair" in "Blood and the Moon." The most obvious design would be one illustrating the title:

The Winding Stair, as you will see by one of the poems, is the winding stone stair of Ballylee enlarged in a symbol, but you may not think the stair, even when a mere symbol, pictorial. It might be a mere gyre — Blake's design of Jacob's ladder — with figures, little figures. . . . If you cannot get a good design on The Winding Stair idea I might change the name of the book, but prefer not. Of course a suggestion of a stone stair might be possible — a hooded figure coming or going, perhaps just entering, a mere suggestion of stairs.

(September 26, 1930)

"A mere suggestion" of a winding stone stair is at the centre of the final design as it appeared in 1933, but in the meantime Yeats had had ideas of changing the title to *Byzantium* and sent a copy of that poem to Sturge Moore, "hoping that it may suggest symbolism for the cover." He added that the poem had originated from Sturge Moore's criticism of "Sailing to Byzantium" which had shown the need for exposition of the idea in the last stanza.

The artist found "a good number of possible graphic images" in the new poem but was still a little puzzled: "Is your dolphin to be so large that the whole of humanity can ride on its back?" To which Yeats replied, (October 8, 1930), "One dolphin, one man," adding a question which throws interesting light on the evolution of his images, "Do you know Raphael's statue of the Dolphin carrying one of the Holy Innocents to Heaven?" Though the original title was restored, the man "astraddle on the dolphin's mire and blood" remained prominent in the design; Sturge Moore, however, seems to have been unable to resolve to his own satisfaction the images in "Byzantium," for he has added a snout and a tail-fin of further dolphins in the "dolphin-torn" sea! Yeats accepted the compromise and was pleased with the result:

I am grateful to you for that fine cover. It is one of the best you have done. Were it in gold it would, I think, equal that for *The Tower* though I know there are some that prefer blue to gold.

(September 7, 1933)

Yeats not only kept an eye on the symbolism but also recommended changes in the technical execution of Sturge Moore's designs. He proposed alterations to the cover for *Per Amica Silentia Lunae*, 1918:

I suggest that you do it all in the same thin lines, rose and all. This is merely a suggestion — have thick lines for the rose if you will. I have a notion that the rose will look more luminous in the same thin lines as the rest; it is itself a convention that one knows and yet so simple that it could hardly be changed. I think it a fine grave design.[2]

Sturge Moore's is a stylized and multifoliate rose of the same family as Althea Gyles' flower, but it is offset by four sinister thorns upon the stem. Similarly, Moore's Kabbalistic tree, on the cover of *Responsibilities*, 1916, has the serpent-like roots and branches of the Gyles cover but in a more realistic form, and it is pushed into the background by the fierce hawk Yeats considered "such a fine beast."

There is thus a hint of continuity in the symbolism of Yeats's covers, but with those made for him by Charles Ricketts there is a move away from emblematic design towards the purely decorative. (Continuity may be seen in another way, though; Sturge Moore's early covers for Yeats show a good deal of the influence of Ricketts, particularly in the use of the vertical line. At the start of his career, Moore had joined Ricketts at the Vale Press; he edited the Vale Shakespeare and first published his own verse in *The Dial*.)

In November 1922, Macmillan published the first two volumes of a collected edition of Yeats's work, *Later Poems* and *Plays in Prose and Verse*. Ricketts' design, stamped blind on the green cloth cover, emphasizes geometric pattern; the only pictorial motif is that of the small bird with outstretched wings who occupies each corner, and this is rather the delicate Pre-Raphaelite bird of *The Pageant* cover than any "fine beast" in keeping with Yeats's symbolism. At this time, however, there seemed to be a slight alteration in Yeats's attitude towards the function of a book-cover, a feeling that pure decoration might in the long run be more successful than an over-poweringly symbolic design. He thanked Ricketts for having given his work "a decoration of which one will never tire" and was wholly enthusiastic:

Yesterday my wife brought the books up to my study, and not being able to restrain her excitement I heard her cry out before she reached the door 'You have perfect books at last.' Perfect they are — service-

2 *W. B. Yeats and T. Sturge Moore*, 28.

able and perfect. . . . It is a pleasure to me to think that many young men here and elsewhere will never know my work except in this form. My own memory proves to me that at 17 there is an identity between an author's imagination and paper and book-cover one does not find in later life. I still do not quite separate Shelley from the green covers, or Blake from the blue covers and brown reproductions of pictures, of the books in which I first read them. I do not separate Rossetti at all from his covers.[3]

But if obvious symbolism had temporarily disappeared from the covers, it was not altogether dispensed with. An unusual feature of Ricketts' design is the decoration of the end-papers, on both of which is a frame the size of a bookplate enclosing a unicorn and a fountain, set against stars, and, less prominently, a hawk and a moon. The whole subject of bookplates interested Yeats for some time when he engaged Sturge Moore to design personal plates for members of his family. The design for Mrs. Yeats's bookplate incorporated a unicorn, but a much more feminine and romantically curly-horned beast than that devised by Ricketts. Though Yeats was later to authorize Moore to design a bookplate that would conceal the Ricketts end-paper, at first sight he was delighted with the decoration, "The little design of the unicorn is a masterpiece in that difficult kind."

Many of Yeats's books were issued in uniform bindings with the 1922 edition but the poet's wish that all he had done might "gradually be put into this form" was never fulfilled. However, the unicorn design survived; stamped in gold on the spine of the Macmillan *Collected Poems*, 1950, and *Collected Plays*, 1952, is a miniature adaptation of Ricketts' end-paper decoration. The unicorn and the fountain were alone retained, symbols of the search for perfection and of everlasting life. It is appropriate that from all the cover designs Yeats supervised these should be the emblems to reach the widest public, for the concern with book design was a significant, though admittedly small, part of Yeats's work towards a union of all the arts, "the painter painting what the poet has written," together in the "one search for perfection."

3 *The Letters of W. B. Yeats*, ed. Allan Wade (New York, 1955), 691.

Vision and Revision:
Yeats's The Countess Cathleen

DAVID R. CLARK

W. B. YEATS's *The Countess Cathleen* ends with a vision and is progressively revised towards a unity in which everything is subordinated to that vision. First the final scene — the showing forth of the Countess' salvation — is redone. Then the rest of the play is from time to time altered to support that scene. In the process, the quality of the original fable is much changed.

In the revisions of *The Countess Kathleen*[1] Yeats's preoccupation with learning to write drama as it had already been written competed with his attempts to write his own particular kind of drama. To learn dramatic as distinguished from narrative plotting and to make his composition reflect the possibilities and limitations of staging — these were his first problems. If he had rewritten the play many years later, all of this practice work might have disappeared. There would have been one act, set where the devils are bargaining for souls, and centred on Cathleen's transformation. There would have been a moment when she, suffering damnation, has a clear, bitter, yet impenitent knowledge of what her sacrifice has been — that she has refused a heavenly mansion, raging in the dark:

It was not, nor is it now, more than a piece of tapestry. The Countess sells her soul, but she is not transformed. If I were to think out that

---

[1] Spelt thus in the first edition of 1892 only. The principal revisions are in *Poems* (London: T. Fisher Unwin, 1895); *Poems*, 1899; *Poems*, 1901; *The Poetical Works of W. B. Yeats In Two Volumes*, Volume II, *Dramatical Poems* (New York, London: Macmillan, 1907); *The Countess Cathleen* (London: T. Fisher Unwin, 1912).

scene to-day, she would, the moment her hand has signed, burst into loud laughter, mock at all she has held holy, horrify the peasants in the middle of their temptations.[2]

Comparison of the various versions of *The Countess Cathleen* will show both Yeats's progress in dramatic construction and his attempts to represent more completely the unique nature of his vision. It does not show these two movements in complete harmony. A comparison of the final scene of the play in the first published version with a revised version of the same scene will show great advance in dramatic construction but a change, perhaps an at least temporary loss, in Yeats's ability to unite, in one representation, vision and the objective world.

I

The Countess Cathleen uses as its material the convergence of Pagan and Christian Irish tradition. The original fable was included among traditional Irish stories about the devil in Yeats's *Fairy and Folk Tales of the Irish Peasantry*.[3] Demons bring plague and famine to Ireland and then offer the oppressed peasants gold for their souls. The Countess Cathleen O'Shea, who is so good she would be nobility in Heaven as on earth, in desperate pity redeems the other souls with the sale of her own. She dies broken-hearted, but Heaven cancels the bargain; her soul is saved and the demons disappear. Yeats remarks:

I have no doubt of the essential antiquity of what seems to me the most impressive form of one of the supreme parables of the world.

He finds

the sacrifice of Alcestis . . . less overwhelming, less apparently irremediable.[4]

2 *The Autobiography of William Butler Yeats* (New York: Macmillan, 1938), 356.

3 *Fairy and Folk Tales of the Irish Peasantry* (London: Walter Scott, 1888), 232-235. Yeats had found the story "in what professed to be a collection of Irish folklore in an Irish newspaper." *Poems* (1901), 295. By 1895, he had learned that the story was of recent introduction. *Poems* (1895), 282. But not until 1901 was he able to note the source, *Les Matinées de Timothée Trimm by Léo Lespès. Poems* (1901), 295. Yeats never admitted the irony in the fact that his intensely national drama had cosmopolitanism to thank for its genesis.

4 *Poems* (1901), 295.

This redoubtable claim will surprise us less if we reflect that the question "whether a soul may destroy itself for a good end" was of central importance to Yeats. He sought "unity of being" and this search was complicated by the division of his loyalties among art, patriotism, love and religion.

Yeats had written in 1888:

To the greater poets everything they see has its relation to the national life, and through that to the universal and divine life: nothing is an isolated artistic moment; there is a unity everywhere. . . .[5]

Art, which is but a vision of reality, put this easy unity to the test in *The Countess Cathleen*.

In the preface to *Poems* (1901) Yeats discussed the poetic use of the Irish Christian cycle.

Christianity and the old nature faith have lain down side by side in the cottages, and I would proclaim that peace as loudly as I can among the kingdoms of poetry, where there is no peace that is not joyous, no battle that does not give life instead of death; I may even try to persuade others, in more sober prose, that there can be no language more worthy of poetry and of the meditation of the soul than that which has been made, or can be made, out of a subtlety of desire, an emotion of sacrifice, a delight in order, that are perhaps Christian, and myths and images that mirror the energies of woods and streams, and of their wild creatures. Has any part of that majestic heraldry of the poets had a very different fountain? Is it not the ritual of the marriage of heaven and earth?

The convergence of Christianity and the old nature faith is used in this play to show the struggle of two universal ways of life — a spiritual and a materialistic — for control of a particular place — Ireland.

Universal spiritual values are represented by the Christian God and spirits, who are at home everywhere. They struggle with universal material values, represented by Satan and his demons, who, wherever they may go, are foreign exploiters. The plague-smitten land, the starving peasants, and the enslaved Gods of ancient Ireland represent the Irish land and people, individual target of temptation by material values. The land, the peasants, the fairies all fare ill under the domination of foreign demons. The fairies, though pre-

5 *Letters to the New Island* by William Butler Yeats, edited with an introduction by Horace Reynolds (Cambridge, Massachusetts: Harvard University Press, 1934), 174.

Christian, serve the demons unwillingly, and feel gratitude to the kind Countess, who, loving Ireland as well as God, has done them service. The land itself flourishes wherever the influence of the demons has not reached. Food will be purchased with the sale of Cathleen's castles, pastures, and forests. Men are still unspoiled on the mountains, to which the foreign influence has not penetrated. The Herdsman says:

> The vales are famine crazy — I'm right glad
> My home is on the mountain near to God.[6]

Aleel, the man of songs (Kevin in the 1892 version), is a bridge between the old Gods and the people of the present. He sings the ancient Irish myths, but he has given his soul to the Christian Cathleen, and the devils cannot take it from her. Their ultimate defeat is hinted in their difficulty with this figure who stands for an art both spiritual and national.

Cathleen is caught in an apparent quandary, forced to choose love and beauty, or patriotism, or God. But, since the lover Aleel is also a poet of Irish legend, her renouncing him for her country is really a gesture of love and a defense of aesthetic values. Again, she is forced to choose between serving her particular people and serving her universal God. She chooses to serve her people. We learn, however, that to serve her people is to serve her God. What would puzzle abstract thought and conventional morality, she knows through sympathetic intuition. The coming together of the spiritual values indigenous to Ireland with those of universal Christianity resolves the apparent conflict between duties.

The dilemma is to settle the relative claims of art, love, patriotism, and belief; to find a way to uniting these by fusing Irish paganism, traditional Christianity and an aesthetic faith in the occult symbols of artist mystics; and thus to present a united front to materialism. The artist, represented by Aleel, is involved, almost against his will, in the common struggle of love, patriotism, and belief against the dominant new philosophy of the age.

Nationalism provides a drastic and terrible end to the dilemma. Only by being sacrificial to the destiny of a people can art be more than aestheticism, love more than desire, religion more than opiate. In the sacrifice, however, art, love and religion reach their apotheosis. Cathleen's action is beauty, charity, passion, faith.

6 *The Countess Cathleen* (1892), 38.

The Countess Cathleen, like later dramas, concludes where the "gyres" turn into a "sphere," where the antinomies are resolved, where the contradictories through the very intensity of their opposition call upon the unity which transcends them. The play ends at a moment of revelation, of passionate perception, when ordinary human seeing and suffering melt away.

II

The first version of *The Countess Cathleen* is set in the sixteenth century. Poetic drama is perhaps easier to accept for a modern audience if set in the time of its greatest flourishing. At that time, moreover, the Christian belief could still claim universality, the Irish tradition vitality. And the chivalrous tradition was still productive of Petrarchan love-songs and of unhappy courtly loves like that of the Irish bard in this play. The feudal system would allow Yeats's heroine to be a focus of religious, economic, social, and artistic life. She represents the kind of aristocracy in which Yeats believed.

There is no attempt at historicity, however. In later editions the scene is laid simply "in Ireland, and in old times." Already Yeats is moving away from presentation of actuality. He wrote in the first number of *Beltaine* that he had

tried to suggest throughout the play that period, made out of many periods, in which the events in the folk-tales have happened. The play is not historic, but symbolic, and has as little to do with any definite place and time as an *auto* by Calderon. One should look for the Countess Cathleen and the peasants and the demons not in history, but . . . in one's own heart.

Regrettably, they must perhaps have more of a local habitation and name than Yeats gives them before we can find them even in our hearts. The ruined house and bare tree of *Purgatory* are somehow more evocative of the ideas of nation and land than is all the tapestry of *The Countess Cathleen*. And in *Purgatory*'s fusion of symbolism and realism there is a truer marriage of heaven and earth. Yet the continuing validity of the Christian myth, the credibility of the peasants' belief in it, and the traditional form of the fable all lend *The Countess Cathleen* a kind of supra-personal authenticity which later dramas lack.

Yeats's 1892 version is much closer to the narrative form of the story as it appears in *Fairy and Folk Tales* than are the later versions. The division into scenes follows the change of place and time in the story, without the attempts to unify and elaborate the action which are evident later. Yeats has even borrowed dialogue (such as "Their claws were clutched under their gloves of leather").

The conception of the chief characters, both Countess and Demons, is not basically altered — although the parallel between British imperialists and the Demons is suggested. The characters Yeats adds — principally Shemus Rua, keeper of the hostelry; Teig, his son; Mary, his wife; Oona, Cathleen's foster-mother; Kevin, a young bard — are not motivated so as to direct the action significantly.

In later versions there is revision towards unity shown by the progressive reduction of the number of characters; the fusing of characters whose functions may be combined; the growing tendency to portray, not human inconsistency and idiosyncrasy, but passionate types; the growing prominence of Aleel, who is ultimately the second major character and the primary interpreter of the action; the addition of the love scenes between Aleel and the Countess in order to motivate Aleel's centrality and to shift the whole centre of the play from the traditional and outer toward the private and inner; the alteration of the final scene from supernaturalism based on naturalism to an elaborate and vague angelic show in which the objective world dissolves.

In the first version (1892), Scene I, Mary Rua and Teig her son await in their peasant cottage the coming of Shemus Rua, Mary's husband. When he comes, bringing a dead wolf, he is bitter because the famine has reduced them to such straits. In this mood he rails recklessly, and inadvertently calls on demons. They come in the form of two merchants, give Teig and Shemus magic wine, and buy their souls.

In Scene II at Cathleen's castle, Cathleen is seeking peace from her people's troubles by hearing her foster-mother Oona talk and sing to her. They are interrupted by a servant who admits first a gardener and then a herdsman. Both tell of depredations by starving men. Later the servant admits Cathleen's steward. The latter brings with him a peasant who had stolen apples and a peasant who had stolen sheep. They have gained money by selling their souls to the Demons and come to restore what they stole.

In Scene III the Demons rob Cathleen's treasure-room with the aid of spirits — Sheogues, Soulths and Tevishes and the ghosts of the two robbers, who have now killed each other. The Demons deceive Cathleen into thinking that the grain and cattle she has ordered brought from a distance have been delayed. They leave as she is thanking God that she still has the treasure to help her people. Then peasants enter with the discovery that the treasure is gone. The porter reports that Demons have passed his gate.

In Scene IV, at the inn of Shemus Rua, the Merchants buy souls: that of a Middle-aged Man and that of a Young Woman. The bard, Kevin, enters, desperate with sympathy for Cathleen, and tries to give his soul away, but is led off by Shemus and Teig. This is the first appearance of the young minstrel who, as Aleel, is almost as important as Cathleen herself in the final version. An Old Woman sells her soul, and another peasant ludicrously tries to sell half his soul, but even the Demons will have none of him. Then the Countess enters and completes her fatal bargain.

In Scene V, in the castle, Oona and Peasants are disturbed by screeching noises. None of these peasants have appeared previously and yet Yeats takes time to individualize them in this final scene: First Peasant, Second Peasant, Neal (an old peasant), and a Young Peasant who questions Oona about Kevin and the nature of love. After the others leave to investigate the noises, Oona, alone, finds owl feathers on the steps of the oratory in which Cathleen has secluded herself. Thinking some hawk has killed an owl, she enters the oratory, but backs out immediately seeing a vision of angels who carry in Cathleen's body and announce that she is saved. The peasants return and join Oona in mourning.

Skipping the intermediate versions of the play, one may turn to the one in *The Countess Cathleen*, 1912, and observe what has happened. Many characters are eliminated. Aleel has taken on numerous minor functions as well as a major role. He appears in about every scene. Shemus and Teigue have increased in prominence, taking all the functions of the earlier minor characters on the bad side and developing a considerable opposition to Aleel. In Scene I Shemus and Teigue have become blacker characters and Mary whiter. Aleel, the Countess and Oona are introduced momentarily before the Demons come, to serve a number of unifying functions. Shemus and Teigue instead of selling their souls immediately now have to serve the Merchants through the rest of the action.

In Scene II the Steward meets Aleel, Oona and the Countess as they near the castle and tells them all the unfortunate news without the aid of the Servant, the Gardener and the Herdsman. Teigue and Shemus run in and give news of the soul-selling, thus cutting out the scene in which the peasant robbers confess and make the same announcement. Five characters are dropped in these changes. Instead of the servant's pursuit of the peasants in an attempt to buy back their souls with Cathleen's money, we have Aleel's fruitless but brave pursuit of Shemus and Teigue.

In Scene III Aleel comes to the castle to say that he has had a vision and to warn Cathleen that she must leave with him or die there. She recognizes that she is being tempted to find escape in love and beauty (perhaps in Tir-nan-oge) from a patriotic, religious, and human responsibility and refuses to go. She simultaneously intimates her love for Aleel and renounces it. Aleel is enlarged here into a symbol of her spiritual sacrifice. The rest of the scene is the robbery of the treasure and the suggestion to Cathleen by the Demons that her soul is marketable.

Scene IV, done before the curtain to give time for the changing of sets, is not in previous versions. Various peasants cross, talking about gold; the demon merchants follow them, and Aleel tags behind singing "Impetuous heart be still, be still." Scene V, the marketing of souls, is elaborated but not fundamentally changed until Cathleen sells her soul and goes out to distribute the wealth to the peasants. Then Aleel has his elaborate vision of angels warring upon devils and learns that Cathleen is saved. The last scene is almost entirely Aleel's.

III

Let us look in more detail at the most significant change, the change in the ending. Scene V of *The Countess Cathleen* (1892) is completely altered when it appears as the last part of Act III in 1895, and (with no change) in 1899. With few and minor alterations it becomes the last part of Act IV in 1901, but is not essentially changed in 1912.

Scene V (1892) is laid in the castle at dawn. "A number of peasants enter hastily, half-dressed, as though aroused suddenly from sleep." A screeching noise has awaked them and they search for the cause of it. All but Oona and a young peasant go search the northern tower. The young peasant has seen Kevin wandering in the woods:

> They say he hears the sheogues down below
> Nailing four boards.
>
> OONA
> For love has made him crazy,
> And loneliness and famine dwell with him.

The young peasant goes to ask old Neal about love. Oona, now
hearing Cathleen in the oratory, where she has been pacing all night,
goes to the steps and finds them covered with owl feathers. Thinking
some hawk has chased its prey through an open window, Oona goes
into the oratory to investigate. She returns immediately, overcome
by a vision.

> My dear mistress
> Must have dropped off to sleep. All night
> She has been pacing in the chapel there.
>
> [*She goes over to the oratory steps and finds them covered
> with feathers.*]
>
> I know what clamour frighted them — some bird,
> Some hawk or kestrel, chased its prey to this;
> These are owls feathers. I will go and see
> What window has swung open over-night.
>
> [*She goes into the oratory and returns hastily, leaving the
> door open. A bright light streams through the open door.*]
>
> My hour has come, oh blessed queen of heaven,
> I am to die, for I have seen a vision.
> O, they are coming, they are coming, coming.

Spirits carry in the body of Cathleen from the oratory and lay her
head on Oona's knees. They are singing the Pre-Raphaelitish lyric
beginning "All the heavy days are over," and ending

> *She goes down the floor of heaven,*
> *Shining bright as a new lance,*
> *And her guides are angels seven,*
> *While young stars about her dance.*

The spirits report to Oona that God commanded them to save
Cathleen.

> We are angelical.
> She gave away her soul for others — God,
> Who sees the motive and the deed regards not,

> Bade us go down and save her from the demons,
> Who do not know the deed can never bind.
> We came and waited; some score minutes since,
> As mortals measure time, her body died,
> For her heart broke. The demons, as two owls,
> Came sweeping hither, murmuring against God.
> We drove them hence; and half our company
> Bore the bright spirit to the floors of peace,
> And half now give the body to your care.
> Let it have noble burial; build a high
> And ample tomb, for she who died and lives
> Was noble in her life and in her beauty;
> And when men gaze upon the flying dawn,
> We bid them dream of her.

Having honored the body with lines echoing Shakespeare's *Hamlet*, Yeats honors the soul with Dante, or at least with Dante Gabriel Rossetti:

> Farewell! the red rose by the seat of God,
> Which is among the angelic multitude
> What she, whose body lies here, was to men,
> Is brightening in my face, I bear no more
> The heavy burden of your mortal days.

The vision over, Oona is silent for a moment, but then, realizing the Countess is dead, she shrieks and the peasants rush in. Each mourns Cathleen in a simple line, until Oona cries:

> Be silent. Do you dare to keen her? Dare
> To set your grief by mine? Stoop — lift her up;
> Now carry her and lay her on her bed,
> When I have keened I will go be with her,
> I will go die, for I have seen a vision.

And the peasants go out, carrying the body.

In the revision of 1895 the merchants depart to capture Cathleen's soul, and Aleel, who has been thrown to the ground by Shemus and Teig, crawls to the middle of the room. It grows dark and a storm arises. Aleel, as poet and seer, now becomes narrator and raisoneur, describing the supernatural events which form the conclusion. He sees the devils come, and many of them are evil figures from Celtic myth. Balor, Yeats's notes tell us, is "the Irish Chimaera, the leader of the hosts of darkness at the great battle of good and evil. . . ." Barach deceived the great Fergus in order to betray Deirdre and

Naisi. "The Druid Cailitin and his sons warred upon Cuhoollin with magical arts." Concobar or Conhor was the king who pursued Deirdre and her love, finally killing the latter by treachery.

These are specifically Irish demons, who betrayed the best in Irish manhood — Cuhoollin — and in Irish womanhood — Deirdre.

> And all their heads are twisted to one side,
> For when they lived they warred on beauty and peace
> With obstinate, crafty, sidelong bitterness.

Oona enters, searching solicitously for Cathleen who had not told her that she was going to Shemus Rua's to sell her soul. Aleel warns her to "Crouch down . . . out of the blind storm" of demons.

> Cathleen has chosen other friends than us,
> And they are rising through the hollow world.

One of them is the sorceress Orchil, type of the damned beauty, accompanied by carnal sinners. This is the sort of company Cathleen has chosen. Oona prays that her soul, rather than Cathleen's, may be condemned.

As Aleel gazes down through the earth, the peasants carry in Cathleen, who awakes long enough to struggle with the demon host.

> O hold me, and hold me tightly, for the storm
> Is dragging me away.

She gives direction for the division of money after her death.

Two peasant women are given contrasting speeches — one worrying whether Cathleen will leave enough money, the other ready to sacrifice everything to save Cathleen.

After her last beautiful speech, the most remarkable in the play, Cathleen dies.

> Bend down your faces, Oona and Aleel:
> I gaze upon them as the swallow gazes
> Upon the nest under the eave before
> He wander the loud waters: do not weep
> Too great a while, for there is many a candle
> On the high altar though one fall. Aleel,
> Who sang about the people of the raths,
> That know not the hard burden of the world,
> Having but breath in their kind bodies, farewell!
> And farewell Oona, who spun flax with me
> Soft as their sleep when every dance is done:
> The storm is in my hair and I must go.

Oona tests Cathleen's breath with a mirror, as is done in Lear, and half-screams "O, she is dead." Aleel shatters the mirror, since it can no longer show her live face, and tells his heart to die, since

> ... she whose mournful words
> Made you a living spirit has passed away
> And left you but a ball of passionate dust.

He calls for the end of earth, sea, Time, Fate and Change — left empty of value by her death. He then beholds an actual battle of angels and devils. When this is over, the darkness is broken by a visionary light. The peasants seem to be kneeling on a mountain slope. Above them stand angels with drawn swords who have driven off the Demons.

The others fall to the ground, but Aleel, now standing, seizes one of the angels and demands to know the fate of Cathleen. He learns that she is saved, that

> the Light of Lights
> Looks always on the motive, not the deed.
> The Shadow of Shadows on the deed alone.

The play ends with a humble speech of Oona's, asking to be reunited with Cathleen.

If, after reading the 1895 ending, we go back to the 1892 version, it seems most unworkmanly, introducing new characters at the very end — Neal and the Young Peasant — and leaving the last view of Cathleen for the loyal but pedestrian Oona, who acts simply as witness not as interpreter. We are not even in the early version told whether or not Oona knows what happened in the previous scene. Kevin who does know is left wandering around behind the scenes. Cathleen, who has carried the play thus far, appears only as an eloquent corpse. The struggle, in her, of good and evil forces is not represented, nor any of her sorrow and pity at leaving her friends. It is the effect of her action on herself that an audience would be primarily interested in — not merely in the fact of her dead body — and our interest is not satisfied in this version.

It is interesting, however, that the simplicity and concreteness of the symbolism is something Yeats returned to in his later plays. The discovery of owl feathers on the steps as a proof of the defeat of the demons — however clumsily managed in this play — is the sort of thing out of which Yeats built later plays — a well, a heartbeat, an egg, some words cut on a window-pane. Later he would support the concrete symbol with symbolic dance or action so that there would be no pretense of a superficial one-level realism which the play itself would question. A symbolic super-structure carefully worked out, in action, on several levels would go a long way towards convincing one of the concrete reality — on one level — of those owl feathers.

The revised version of 1895 shows much more competent stagemanship, yet is almost pure show. Although reassured by a dim vision of angels that the Demons are defeated, one misses the conviction of owl feathers between the finger tips. The transformation of the usual and concrete into the symbolic or supernatural was the insight which Yeats later found valuable in the Japanese Noh plays which were the models for such plays as *At the Hawk's Well* (published 1917), *The Dreaming of the Bones* (1919), *The Only Jealousy of Emer* (1919), and *Calvary* (1921).[7] The owls have their analogue in the hawk of *At the Hawk's Well*.

In this 1895 version, as in all later versions, instead of using natural *and* supernatural as he did in his last plays, Yeats allows the "real world" to dissolve into the cloudy mist of the Celtic twilight.

> ALEEL
>
> I shatter you in fragments, for the face
> That brimmed you up with beauty is no more:
> And die, dull heart, for she whose mournful words
> Made you a living spirit has passed away
> And left you but a ball of passionate dust.
> And you, proud earth and plumy sea, fade out!
> For you may hear no more her faltering feet,
> But are left lonely amid the clamorous war
> Of angels upon devils.
>
> *(He stands up; almost every one is kneeling, but it has grown so dark that only confused forms can be seen.)*

7 This Noh-like transformation may be found in Yeats's earliest plays: *cf.* the two contrasting appearances of Ebremar in *Mosada* (Dublin: Sealy, Bryers, and Walker, 1886); the discovery that an old peddler is Time in "Time and the Witch Vivien," *The Wanderings of Oisin* (London: Kegan Paul, Trench, 1889), 53-57; the dramatization first of the external and then the internal action of the knight who unknowingly seeks infamy in "The Seeker," *The Wanderings of Oisin*, 136-140; the metamorphosis of Naschina from mortal shepherdess to immortal queen in "The Island of Statues," *The Wanderings of Oisin*, 141-154 (Act II, Scene III. The whole poem appears in *The Dublin University Review*, April, May, June and July 1885).

And I who weep
Call curses on you, Time and Fate and Change,
And have no excellent hope but the great hour
When you shall plunge headlong through bottomless space.

(A flash of lightning followed by immediate thunder.)

A PEASANT WOMAN
Pull him upon his knees before his curses
Have plucked thunder and lightning on our heads.

ALEEL
Angels and devils clash in the middle air,
And brazen swords clang upon brazen helms.

(A flash of lightning followed by immediate thunder.)

Yonder a bright spear, cast out of a sling,
Has torn through Balor's eye, and the dark clans
Fly screaming as they fled Moytura of old.

(Everything is lost in darkness.)

AN OLD MAN
The Almighty wrath at our great weakness and sin
Has blotted out the world and we must die.

(The darkness is broken by a visionary light. The peasants seem to be kneeling upon the rocky slope of a mountain, and vapour full of storm and everchanging light is sweeping above them and behind them. Half in the light, half in the shadow, stand armed angels. Their armour is old and worn, and their drawn swords dim and dinted. They stand as if upon the air in formation of battle and look downwards with stern faces. The peasants cast themselves on the ground.)

It remains to discuss the differences between the alternate endings in the 1912 version.[8] Yeats's note in that edition stated:

Now at last I have made a complete revision to make it suitable for performance at the Abbey Theatre. The first two scenes are almost wholly new, and throughout the play I have added or left out such passages as a stage experience of some years showed me encumbered the action; the play in its first form having been written before I knew anything of the theatre. I have left the old end, however, in the version

[8] An alternate end for the Abbey Theatre is added in an appendix, *The Countess Cathleen* (1912), 124-128.

printed in the body of this book, because the change for dramatic purposes has been made for no better reason than that audiences — even
at the Abbey Theatre — are almost ignorant of Irish mythology — or
because a shallow stage made the elaborate vision of armed angels
upon a mountain-side impossible. The new end is particularly suited
to the Abbey stage, where the stage platform can be brought out in
front of the proscenium and have a flight of steps at one side up which
the Angel comes, crossing towards the back of the stage at the opposite
side. The principal lighting is from two arc lights in the balcony which
throw their lights into the faces of the players, making footlights unnecessary. The room at Shemus Rua's house is suggested by a great
grey curtain — a colour which becomes full of rich tints under the
stream of lights from the arcs.[9]

The Abbey version may be contrasted with the ending quoted above.

> ALEEL
>
> I shatter you in fragments, for the face
> That brimmed you up with beauty is no more;
> And die, dull heart, for you that were a mirror
> Are but a ball of passionate dust again!
> And level earth and plumy sea, rise up!
> And haughty sky, fall down!
>
> A PEASANT WOMAN
> Pull him upon his knees,
> His curses will pluck lightning on our heads.
>
> ALEEL
>
> Angels and devils clash in the middle air,
> And brazen swords clang upon brazen helms.
> Look, look, a spear has gone through Belial's eye!
>
> (A winged ANGEL, carrying a torch and a sword, enters
> from the R. with eyes fixed upon some distant thing. The
> ANGEL is about to pass out to the L. when ALEEL speaks.
> The ANGEL stops a moment and turns.)

Irish ignorance of Celtic mythology has caused Balor, Barach,
the Cailitin, and Concobar to be replaced by the biblical and
Miltonic Asmodel and Belial in Aleel's vision. Orchil and her multitude of alluring women are omitted. The storm of evil which is
dragging Cathleen is not given a concrete physical counterpart in
the Abbey ending. The stage darkens, but directions such as *The
wind roars* and speeches such as

9 *The Countess Cathleen* (1912), 123. By the "old end" Yeats means the
1895 end.

VISION AND REVISION   155

> And while we bore her hither cloudy gusts
> Blackened the world and shook us on our feet;
> Draw the great bolt for no man has beheld
> So black, bitter, blinding and sudden a storm.

are omitted. Did the Abbey not have a wind machine? From Aleel's speeches are pruned not only the rich symbolism of Celtic mythology but all the operatic largeness meant to build up to the vision of the angels on the mountain side.

The remaining lines are the same in both versions except that the Abbey ending drops the final stage direction, the melting away of the vision.

> *(A sound of far-off horns seems to come from the heart of the Light. The vision melts away, and the forms of the kneeling* PEASANTS *appear faintly in the darkness.)*

There would seem to be no reason to quibble with Yeats's judgment that only deficiencies of his theatre and audience made necessary the changes in the alternate ending for the Abbey Theatre.

IV

Yeats was not unsatisfied with the final version of *The Countess Cathleen*. He had vastly improved it in construction, characterization and style. He had begun the play in reaction against Shelley's *The Cenci* and Tennyson's *Becket*. Shelley and Tennyson had been "deliberately oratorical; instead of creating drama in the mood of *The Lotus Eaters* or of *Epipsychidion* they had tried to escape their characteristics, had thought of the theatre as outside the general movement of literature." Yeats, on the other hand, began *The Countess Cathleen*, "avoiding every oratorical phrase and cadence." [10] He was trying to keep within that area — the drama — where theatre and literature overlap, and he was not at first successful. The version produced in 1899 "was ill-constructed, the dialogue turning aside at the lure of word or metaphor. . . ." [11]

Yeats was aiming at organic work, dialogue being inseparable from structure and yet written in verse approaching that of the best romantic poetry — a difficult ideal, involving a careful discipline

[10] *Letters to the New Island*, "Preface," ix.
[11] *Autobiography*, 356.

of each passage in terms of the development of the whole. On these grounds he objected violently to Wilde's *Salomé*:

> The general construction is all right, is even powerful, but the dialogue is empty, sluggish and pretentious. It has nothing of drama of any kind, never working to any climax but always ending as it begun. . . . He thought he was writing beautifully when he had collected beautiful things and thrown them together in a heap.[12]

This passage shows that from the beginning Yeats aimed, not at a dramatic frame of events upholstered in poetry but at what Eliot has called "the perfection of verse drama, . . . a design of human action and of words, such as to present at once the two aspects of dramatic and of musical order."[13]

Yeats's alterations in structure and style brought the play a long way toward this goal. The "first meagre version"[14] — Yeats hoped, after finishing the final version — was "very different . . . from the play as it is to-day after many alterations, every alteration tested by performance."[15] Yeats was satisfied, too, with the improvement in characterization.

> . . . My *Countess Cathleen* . . . was once the moral question, may a soul sacrifice itself for a good end? but gradually philosophy is eliminated until at last the only philosophy audible, if there is even that, is the mere expression of one character or another.

Representing the sacrificial passion of the Countess Cathleen is a different thing from posing a philosophical query. Yet it is a different thing too from painting a realistically individuated person. The characterization goes deeper than individuality. It avoids both abstraction and surface particularity. Cathleen is neither an idea nor an accurately mirrored individual. She is an heroic motive. Yeats's play went through the same process in being written as that by which "in Christianity what was philosophy in Eastern Asia became life, biography and drama."[16] The Countess' own history becomes like the life of Christ, the miraculous incarnation of what was a religious conception.

[12] *W. B. Yeats and T. Sturge Moore, Their Correspondence 1901-1937*, ed. Ursula Bridge (London: Routledge and Kegan Paul, 1953), 8-9.

[13] T. S. Eliot, *Poetry and Drama* (Cambridge, Massachusetts: Harvard University Press, 1951), 43.

[14] *Autobiography*, 172.

[15] *Autobiography*, 356.

[16] *Autobiography*, 399-400.

One should not, however, approve the "triumphant thing" [17] which Yeats has made of the final version, without realizing its limitations. The play does not present the full tragic rhythm from purpose, through passion (or suffering), to perception, accepting the old myth and varying it only in expression, rather than in content or arrangement. The love scene between Aleel and the Countess is not part of the original fable. This addition represents the way a modern journalistic playwright, as opposed to the old masters Yeats admired, would handle a traditional story.

The old playwrights took old subjects, did not even arrange the subject in a new way. They were absorbed in expression, that is to say in what is most near and delicate. The new playwrights invent their subjects and dislike anything customary in the arrangement of the fable, but their expression is as common as the newspapers where they first learned to write. [18]

One is reminded of Eliot's disapprobation of Tennyson for tampering "unscrupulously with the meagre records" in his *Becket*, "introducing Fair Rosamund, and . . . suggesting that Becket had been crossed in love in early youth." [19]

The first version of *The Countess Cathleen*, however meagre, had its values, which Lionel Johnson sympathetically distinguished at the time. The "very absence of all complexity strengthens the power of the poem; it has the moving appeal of nature . . . the entanglement, the estimate of motives, the casuistry, unasserted in the play, are present, as it were, in the minds of God and of His angels." [20] In his revisions Yeats left the narrow path of the traditional fable and was in danger of being lost on the way of the chameleon.

Nor is *The Countess Cathleen*, in any version, a tragedy of vision in a realist sense. Cathleen is not transformed, does not "horrify the peasants in the midst of their temptations," [21] as she might have done in a dance play by the late Yeats. In his "delight in the moment of exaltation, of excitement of dreaming," Yeats worked, through revision, toward an art which diminished "the power of that daily

---

[17] Lennox Robinson, "The Man and the Dramatist," *Scattering Branches*, ed. Stephen Gwynn (New York: Macmillan, 1940), 72.

[18] *Autobiography*, 444.

[19] Eliot, *Poetry and Drama*, 29.

[20] *Autobiography*, 356.

[21] *Autobiography*, 356.

mood," summoning in its place "rhythm, balance, pattern, images that remind us of vast passions, the vagueness of past times, all the chimeras that haunt the edge of trance." [22] That art refined away the real world as others see it and have seen it for centuries replacing it with his own imaginative world. This sort of drama, which he explored more fully in *The Shadowy Waters*, *The King's Threshold* and *Deirdre*, neither retains the full tragic rhythm or achieves, as do his last plays, a new drama of passionate perception, an idealist drama which nevertheless dramatizes the third stage of the tragic rhythm, the moment of revelation, or epiphany, and presents the total rhythm in an essentialized form.

[22] *Essays* (New York: Macmillan, 1924), 300-301.

Part Three

CONTEMPORARIES

Image-Maker for Ireland:
Augusta, Lady Gregory

ANN SADDLEMYER

... but we are "image-makers," and must carry out our dreams.
(Letter to Sir Hugh Lane)

Ups and downs, ups and downs; and we know nothing till all is over. ... I would like my name set in clean letters in the book of the people. (Sarsfield in *The White Cockade*)

THROUGHOUT Lady Gregory's work and constant in her collaborations with Yeats is a delight in what she called "our incorrigible genius for myth-making," and despite the courage with which she struggled to keep the Abbey Theatre going for so many years, it is perhaps as myth-maker and mythologizer that she can best be recognized in "the book of the people." For even in her dream of an Irish theatre, Lady Gregory's main ambition was to restore once again to Ireland her native dignity:

I had had from the beginning a vision of historical plays being sent by us through all the counties of Ireland. For to have a real success and to come into the life of the country, one must touch a real and eternal emotion, and history comes only next to religion in our country. And although the realism of our young writers is taking the place of fantasy and romance in the cities, I still hope to see a little season given up every year to plays on history and in sequence at the Abbey, and I think schools and colleges may ask to have them sent and played in their halls, as a part of the day's lesson.

Her first play, *Colman and Guaire*, was written not with stage production in mind, but as a play in rhyme which "might perhaps be learned and acted by Kiltartan school-children." Consistently she saw the theatre as part of the same movement which had earlier given impetus to the Gaelic League:

It was a movement for keeping the Irish language a spoken one, with, as a chief end, the preserving of our own nationality. That does not sound like the beginning of a revolution, yet it was one. It was the discovery, the disclosure of the folk-learning, the folk-poetry, the folk-tradition. Our Theatre was caught into that current, and it is that current, as I believe, that has brought it on its triumphant way. It is chiefly known now as a folk-theatre. It has not only the great mass of primitive material and legend to draw on, but it has been made a living thing by the excitement of that discovery.

Twenty years after she wrote these passages in *Our Irish Theatre* she was still writing plays that children as well as adults could enjoy. Unlike Yeats's, her dream of an Irish theatre was fulfilled, with her own work playing a far more important part than she had ever dreamed possible. In 1934 Yeats wrote that her plays were "constantly acted, not only in Dublin but by little companies in village halls. Their names are as familiar as old proverbs." [1] A visitor to Ireland will still find her work popular, both in English and in Irish, at the Abbey and in the provinces. Always she wrote for Ireland: writing of her people as she had observed them during her childhood and widowhood in Galway; of Irish history and folklore as she had collected it for her books; for the children and countryfolk of her nation.

Patriotism for Lady Gregory was a simpler ideal, founded on a much smaller scale than the literary nationalism of her colleagues. Descendant of the Persses of Roxborough who arrived in Ireland with Cromwell, and of the O'Gradys of literary and legal fame, until her marriage with Sir William Gregory of Coole she had seen little of Ireland beyond her own county, Galway. But the west of Ireland she did know well; as a young girl she had eagerly observed the great working-estate, and as a young widow she capably managed the Coole property for her son Robert, later for her grandson Richard. Yeats had memories of tales told by Mary Battle in the kitchen at Sligo; Lady Gregory heard tales of the faery — even more stirring, of the rebellion of '98 — from her old nurse Mary Sheridan. Later she herself participated in the foundation of village libraries, visited the cottages on the estate, acted as secretary to the families of American immigrants. Her marriage for some years interrupted her firm relationship with the peasantry but did not dissolve it, and after her husband died she once more picked up the threads of her friendship with those who still hold her memory dear in

[1] *The Irish National Theatre* (Roma: Reale Accademia D'Italia, 1935), 6.

Ireland. "She has been like a serving-maid among us," said an old peasant to Yeats.

Patriotic she had always been, ever since the first Fenian pamphlet she bought as a child in the small village of Loughrea:

> For a romantic love of country had awakened in me, perhaps through the wide beauty of my home . . . or it may be through the half revealed sympathy of my old nurse for the rebels whose cheering she remembered when the French landed at Killala in '98; or perhaps but through the natural breaking of a younger child of the house from the conservatism of her elders.[2]

However, it was not until she found herself turning against England that she became intensely nationalistic. In 1898 her edition of her husband's grandfather's papers was published, and when questioned concerning the Home Rule sentiments that crept into her comments, she replied: "I defy anyone to study Irish History without getting a dislike and distrust of England." (At the unexpected success of Martyn's re-written play, *The Bending of the Bough*, she assured the bewildered authors, "We are not working for Home Rule; we are preparing for it.") It was not, in fact, until after she had become involved with the Irish Literary Theatre that she met John O'Leary and the other political rebels who had influenced Yeats. Through her husband, one-time Member of Parliament and Governor of Ceylon, she had made many friends among English Unionists, but at all times she managed to reconcile, if at times uneasily, the friendships formed during Sir William's work for England and those she herself made in her work for Ireland. In this sense alone, she was invaluable to Yeats; he was willing to accept "the baptism of the gutter" for the sake of his national dream, but she preferred "the baptism of clean water."[3] Involvement in the idea of a national theatre, however, increased her nationalism still more, and where Yeats subordinated his ideals of art to no nation, she avowed her determination to work principally for "the dignity of Ireland." As her interest in art increased, so too did her love for her country. The one inspiration fed on the other.

As she herself sought for the dignity her nationalism demanded for her country, so she also demanded it of others. The patriotic verses in *The Spirit of the Nation* appealed to her because of "a certain dignity, an intensity born of continuity of purpose; they are

---

2 Introduction to *The Kiltartan Poetry Book* (London: Putnam's Sons, 1919), 3-4.

3 *Our Irish Theatre* (London: Putnam's Sons, 1913), 71.

roughly hammered links in a chain of unequal workmanship, but stretching back through the centuries to the Munster poets of the days of Elizabeth." In her own work she strove for this same dignity and "continuity of purpose." (Many years later Yeats was to place her — along with Queen Victoria — in Phase Twenty-four of *A Vision* in which the true mask is self-reliance and organization.) She, like Yeats, was moved by the death of Parnell, not realizing until later, however, that by tearing from the corner of a newspaper Katharine Tynan's lament she had

unwittingly taken note of almost the moment of a new impulse in literature, in poetry. For with that death, the loss of that dominant personality, and in the quarrel that followed, came the disbanding of an army, the unloosing of forces, the setting free of the imagination of Ireland.

Always her nationalism retained this strong desire to win once more the dignity of Ireland, and like Yeats, she believed it possible through the arts. One day while collecting folk tales on Aran, she happened to glance through a volume of *Don Quixote*, and the thought of England's false half-vision of Ireland crossed her mind:

They see in us one part boastful quarrelsome adventurer, one part vulgar rollicking buffoon. . . . But we begin to think after all that truth is best, that we have worn the mask thrust upon us too long, and that we are more likely to win at least respect when we appear in our own form. . . . Poetry and pathos may be granted to us, but when we claim dignity, those who see only the sham fights of Westminster shake their heads. But here, in real Ireland, dignity can live side by side with the strongest political feeling.[4]

The words re-echo through the Irish Literary Theatre's manifesto of 1897: "We will show that Ireland is not the home of buffoonery and easy sentiment . . . but of ancient idealism."

Lady Gregory's nationalism and concern for the historic past of her nation led her, like Yeats, to a study of folklore. "In these days, when so much of the printed history we were taught as children is being cast out by scholars, we must refill the vessel by calling in tradition, or if need·be our own imaginings," she wrote in 1912 concerning her highly individual treatment of King James in *The White Cockade*. And her *Kiltartan History Book* bears the following dedication: "Dedicated and Recommended to the History Classes

4 "Ireland, Real and Ideal," *Nineteenth Century*, November 1898, 769-782.

in the New University." But first came her study of the Irish language, one step further than Yeats had gone.

Even as a child, she relates, she had been eager to learn Irish, but had received nothing but discouragement and mockery from her elders. Later, after her marriage, she bought a grammar and "worked at it for a while with the help of a gardener." But it was not until her own son had shown a like interest in the language that she studied it in earnest. By then Douglas Hyde had founded the Gaelic League, and through the newly-awakened interest in the legends of the past as told by the early poets, she discovered "this disclosure of the folk learning, the folk poetry, the ancient tradition," which was "the small beginning of a weighty change." "It was an upsetting of the table of values, an astonishing excitement. The imagination of Ireland had found a new homing place." And with it her own imagination found roots at last. The excitement of this new revolution led her to a study not only of the folklore of the past, "the call of my own country, Oisin and Finn and Cuchulain," but to a renewed interest in the folklore of the present, and her excitement in collecting stores from the peasantry soon paralleled Yeats's. She writes in her introduction to *Visions and Beliefs in the West of Ireland*,

"The Celtic Twilight" was the first book of Mr. Yeats's that I read, and even before I met him, a little time later, I had begun looking for news of the invisible world; for his stories were of Sligo and I felt jealous for Galway.

The importance of Lady Gregory's study and collection of folklore cannot be overestimated. Referring to *The Canavans* in a note to *The Arrow* in 1906 she explains,

I took my historical atmosphere less from history books than from the tradition of the people, who have not been taught English history in the schools, and so have learned it through tradition or the songs of the wandering poets, of Raftery, or another.

Her contribution was in one sense more objective than Yeats's, for as she admits, "Even when I began to gather these stories I cared less for the evidence given in them than for the beautiful rhythmic sentences in which they were told." Having no theories and nothing to prove, she recorded fully, carefully, and sincerely:

To gather folk-lore one needs, I think, leisure, patience, reverence, and a good memory. I tried not to change or alter anything, but to write down the very words in which the story had been told. . . . I filled many copybooks and came to have a very faithful memory for all sides of folk-lore, stories of saints, of heroes, of giants and enchanters, as well as for these visions.

Her collection was not published until 1920, but in her autobiography she indicates that she had already begun work before the plans for the theatre were initiated; as early as September 1898, she published an article in the *Daily Express* on "Some Folk Stories of Usheen." Her reliability is still praised by the Irish Folklore Commission and has gained her the title "mother of folklore." [5]

Her search led her far afield, "among the imaginative class, the holders of the traditions of Ireland, country people in thatched houses, workers in fields and bogs," and by such a circuitous route she found herself back in the world she had left on her marriage. "My own imagination was aroused," she wrote in *The Kiltartan Poetry Book*:

I was becoming conscious of a world close to me and that I had been ignorant of. It was not now in the corners of newspapers I looked for poetic emotion, nor even to the singers in the streets. It was among farmers and potato diggers and old men in workhouses and beggars at my own door that I found what was beyond these and yet farther beyond that drawingroom poet of my childhood [Thomas Moore] in the expression of love, and grief, and the pain of parting, that are the disclosure of the individual soul.

Yeats was to search for the celebration of the soul in ancient mythology, turning at last to the legends of his own country; Lady Gregory also found the synthesis of her nationalism and her art in the tales at her own back door, from "the men and women . . . in poorhouses and on roadsides or by the hearth who have kept in mind through many years the great wonders done among the children of the Gael." And, like Yeats, she found in "the book of the people" the continuity and re-birth of tradition she was seeking as foundation for her own beliefs and art.

This continuity of the intellectual life of the people was endangered, however, by "the shoving out of the language." No more did minstrel-poets like the blind Raftery celebrated in *Poets and Dreamers* wander the roads, with the power of satires and curses on their tongues. Her studies of folklore led her in turn, therefore,

---

5 *Cf*. Elizabeth Coxhead, *Lady Gregory: A Literary Portrait* (London: Macmillan, 1961), 58.

to a translation of the early myths of Ireland, to the great cycles of the Tuatha de Danaan, the Fianna, and the Warriors of the Red Branch. *Cuchulain of Muirthemne* appeared in 1903, greeted by Yeats as "the most important book that has come out of Ireland in my time." *Gods and Fighting Men* came in 1904, and Lady Gregory was hailed by her admirer as "the Irish Malory." If her method of popularization is referred to, the appellation of an Irish Malory is a fitting one. But scholastically speaking, these two volumes cannot be accepted with the confidence due her folklore collections. Nor did Lady Gregory intend them to be accepted as literal translations. The imagination of the Gael which had first stirred her as she collected folklore among the peasants had moved her in turn to recapture that imagination in a form which would be available to her countrymen. In her dedication to the people of Kiltartan she explains her method and intentions:

When I began to gather these stories together, it is of you I was think-ing, that you would like to have them and to be reading them. For although you have not to go far to get stories of Finn and Goll and Oisin from any old person in the place, there is very little of the history of Cuchulain and his friends left in the memory of the people, but only that they were brave men and good fighters, and that Deirdre was beautiful.

When I went looking for the stories in the old writings, I found that the Irish in them is too hard for any person to read that has not made a long study of it ... and the stories themselves are confused, every one giving a different account from the others in some small thing, the way there is not much pleasure in reading them. It is what I have tried to do, to take the best of the stories, or whatever parts of each will fit best to one another, and in that way to give a fair account of Cuchulain's life and death. I left out a good deal I thought you would not care about for one reason or another, but I put in nothing of my own that could be helped, only a sentence or so now and again to link the different parts together. I have told the whole story in plain and simple words, in the same way my old nurse Mary Sheri-dan used to be telling stories from the Irish long ago, and I a child at Roxborough.

Standish O'Grady, who had himself worked over the same field, sympathized with her attempt to refine and simplify the saga, but criticized what he felt was her timidity:

One of the great stories of the whole World ought to be printed and published in the very words that our ancestors thought fit to use, with

all the barbarism and the very loose morality of the age set down
exactly as those people thought and wrote.[6]

But although she may have been concerned with the sensitive feelings of the drawing-room, as O'Grady and Rolleston implied, her
aim had been to get the sagas into the drawing-room at all, and
there she succeeded. Her two books still remain the source books
for most Irish writers, and Yeats repeatedly acknowledged his great
debt to her work. As long as her books remain, the danger to the
traditions of Ireland is in abeyance. And in turn she herself used
them as source books for her plays.

"I have told the whole story in plain and simple words," Lady
Gregory stated in her Dedication. *Cuchulain of Muirthemne* was
her first extensive use of the Anglo-Irish dialect referred to as "Kil-
tartanese," and which she used herself throughout all her plays. In
1903 Synge was to use a variant of this language in his first plays,
again duly acknowledging Lady Gregory's precedence in the field.
And throughout their work as collaborators, the influence of Lady
Gregory's research into language as well as tradition can be seen
in Yeats's own work.

"I sometimes think my life has been a series of enthusiasms," Lady
Gregory concludes in her journals. An enthusiasm which produced
over forty plays, founded a theatre, battled through twenty years to
keep its doors open, and in turn joined combat with the Castle, the
press, the American courts and the English judiciary, is no slight
one. She kept one poet alive, and gave hope to another playwright.
Perhaps her most fitting epitaph lies in the words of the latter:

Lady Gregory, mother of many books, Daughter of Ireland, daughter
of wise words, of good deeds, of great humour, lover of tree and sweet
herb, of beast and bird, we hail thee still! We do not wish, nor can we
afford, to murmur farewell to thee for a long, long time to come.[7]

6 *The All-Ireland Review*, August 9, 1902, 357-58.
7 Sean O'Casey, Foreword to *Lady Gregory: Selected Plays*, chosen and introduced by Elizabeth Coxhead (London: Putnam, 1962), 9.

"All Art is a Collaboration"?
George Moore and Edward Martyn

ANN SADDLEMYER

We all did something, but none did what he set out to do. Yeats founded a realistic theatre, Edward emptied two churches — he and Palestrina between them — and I wrote *The Untilled Field*.

WITH THESE WORDS George Moore summed up — not for the first time and certainly not for the last — his activities with the new literary movement in Ireland. To a certain extent, as with all of Moore's repartee, the statement is true: Yeats did not publicly recognize his failure in creating "A People's Theatre" until 1919; Moore found writing about his nationalism more appealing than writing for it; Martyn's dedication to his private principles of art, whether in polyphonic church music or "the intellectual theatre" of Ibsen and Wagner, left him always the solitary champion of lonely causes.

Yet although both Edward Martyn and George Moore proved to be embarrassments to the literary movement they helped establish, without their timely encouragement Yeats's literary and national ideals might conceivably have never had a chance in Ireland. Paradoxically also, without Martyn, Moore would have lost not only his best copy but the source of many enthusiasms; and without his irritating cousin, Martyn would have led not only a more peaceful life but a less satisfactory one. "All art is a collaboration," Synge wrote in his preface to *The Playboy of the Western World*. In the collaborations, both deliberate and unintentional, between Yeats, Martyn, and Moore, can be observed a comedy rivalling Synge's play as a medley of irony, satire, richness and malice.

I

Yeats and Lady Gregory sought a union of the peasant with the artist-aristocrat, and in Edward Martyn they found the invaluable combination of Catholic peasant and landlord gentry. Martyn was a neighbour of Lady Gregory in Galway; his father's family descended from one of the "Fourteen Tribes" who had established themselves in Ireland during the period of the early Crusades; his mother came from the wealthy peasant Smyth family (on the occasion of her marriage his mother was presented by her father with her weight in gold). A sincere Catholic to the point of asceticism, Martyn had studied at Oxford under Pater and taken the Grand Tour of Europe under the rather unlikely tutelage of his distant cousin George Moore. Inextricably involved in music, drama, and his country, he represented the three national emotions, religion, patriotism, and the land. But Martyn did not understand or care for the peasants from whom he had sprung, and they in turn had little trust of him.[1] His nationalism, though intense, was private and individual, reflecting his own taste and inclinations rather than any deep concern for or sympathy with his countrymen, whom, he felt, "perverse education and worse government have distorted to the degradation of intellectual savagery."[2] However, he was deeply concerned for Ireland, and devoted his life and his fortune to "a very determined fight for some of the improvements in civilisation" he sought for his country. Towards the end of his life he wrote,

I am one of those who walk the thorny path of the reformer, a path everyone knows is as thorny as that of the venerable female of our rather eccentric patriotic device. Perhaps it is because we have chosen a decrepit old woman as the symbol of our country struggling for her rights, and called those who follow her "wild geese," that we may be more difficult material for the reformer than other people.[3]

Martyn's passion to help his country was equalled by his hatred of England. Lady Gregory records in *Our Irish Theatre* that his

[1] For many of these impresssions of Martyn and his tastes I am indebted to his man-servant, Mr. Owen Linnane, of Tulira Castle, Ardrahan, County Galway.

[2] Martyn, "Wagner's Parsifal, or the Cult of Liturgical Aestheticism," *The Irish Review*, December 1913, 538.

[3] From his unpublished introduction to *Paragraphs for the Perverse*, a collection of his essays which, with all his collected papers, has since disappeared. Quoted by Stephen Gwynn in *Edward Martyn and the Irish Revival* (London: Jonathan Cape, 1930), 31.

conversion to nationalism came about through a reading of W. E. H. Lecky's political survey, *Leaders of Public Opinion in Ireland*, but even during his childhood and school days, Martyn had disliked England. His father and only brother had both died early; his mother, determined to mould him to the required standards of a respected ancient family, had given him the education of an English gentleman. But Martyn resented what he considered the wasted training of his youth:

My earlier days were wasted foolishly in trying to inculcate in me an Englishman's ideas, accent and outlook. . . . After finishing my so-called education I became the owner of an estate and mansion, things I never wanted . . . I had no idea how to manage land nor did I want to.

His dislike of England remained throughout his life. On one occasion he refused to allow the singing of the National Anthem at a concert on his estate, and in 1904 Dublin was regaled with the lawsuit he brought against the Kildare Street Club when, because of his letters objecting to the King's visit, he was asked to resign.

Martyn's dislike of England was, like Yeats's, mainly an aesthetic one. An article in the *Daily Express* in 1898 is reminiscent also of Synge's attitude:

Indeed a fatal deterioration of the Celt would seem to follow from his contact with the Saxon. His incomparable sense of refinement and elegance . . . fades and vanishes before the comparative grossness and materialism of the Saxon touch. . . . That is why in those parts of Ireland which are much affected with English influences we generally remark a certain air of second-hand, shabby England defacing all objects and customs . . . while the inhabitants of the shabby England are often vulgar, the Celtic peasants of the uncontaminated West are naturally refined.

Like Swift, Martyn disliked "Handy Andy," but believed in a national ideal; "We have many clever, brave and constant people, the best I have ever known in any country, but we have not enough of them." Like Yeats, he expressed his own vision of Utopia in his writings. That he lacked the genius of either of his countrymen is obvious, but in temperament and inclination he was more kin to the great Dean than to his fellow-worker.

Martyn's first published work, *Morgante the Lesser: his Notorious Life and Wonderful Deeds* (1890), was in fact a satirical novel in which, embedded in the egoistic Bowel Philosophy with which he crudely satirizes nineteenth-century culture and aestheticism, can be traced his own theories of art and civilization. The influence of Swift and Rabelais mingles with the doctrines of Pater, and Martyn's description of Agathopolis, "the golden city that sages have yearned to reach, that none may enter with corrupt mind, that chases the unworthy and fades from his sight," owes much to his own vision of Byzantium. The citizens of Martyn's "golden city" bear the calm unsullied expressions of Butler's Erewhonian youths, "indicating at once a character so courageous, and an ideal of life so lofty, that one might well doubt that they were indeed the sons of men." The interests of this spiritual aristocracy are, naturally, the antique tradition of Greek literature ("poetry of the higher and more sublime order" and historical criticism), liturgical music, and the theatre. Appropriate to a creator whose ideal was the cultivated man of letters and whose purse freely opened to the demands of the Irish Literary Theatre, Agathopolis is governed by a benevolent but firm dictator, "a magnificent patron of the arts and of gifted men."

Art for Martyn was a means to an end, therefore. "Founded on some philosophical idea," it must exert a "refining and educational influence upon the artistic and moral character of the nation," as he wrote in *Samhain* in 1901. If his nationalism was cosmopolitan in character and personal in interpretation, his philosophy of art was subject to the higher demands of education and spiritual refinement. His aim remained constant, the remoulding of the nation to which he owed allegiance into the Agathopolis which could with impunity demand that loyalty. Nor did his demands for refinement of the soul stop there: castigation of his own conscience led to the acts of burning his classical poetry and willing his body to science.

In keeping with the rigorous demands of his faith, Martyn advocated classicism in the decorative arts and music, tradition in language, aristocracy in politics. Deploring "the vulgarity of pretension and sham — the vulgarity of the intellect" evident in the "trade architecture" which, he felt, had replaced the simplicity of early Irish art, he encouraged stained-glass artists, sculptors, and painters to return to the style of the early ages. Similarly, he advocated a revival of the Irish language. "Nothing Irish will ever succeed until Ireland shakes off her self-imposed slavery and becomes really Irish again," he claimed; to achieve this, Gaelic must return not only to the schools but to "the Big House" as well. He became a member of the governing board of the Gaelic League and Sinn Fein, of which he was president from 1904 to 1908. But although he early evinced an interest in Irish history and archaeology (George Moore records that he travelled with an archaeological party in the west of Ireland), he himself admits, in an article in *An Claidheamh Soluis*, that his interest in things Irish was brought about in part by his love of things Greek:

... my studies of Irish have convinced me that it is finer and more beautiful than any language I know, except Greek, which will always be to me the most beautiful, the tongue of the highest civilisation the world has ever seen. It was indeed my Hellenism that first led me to the Irish language through the subtle Greek refinements I found in Irish ornamental art.

But his most abiding passions were again a result of his travels and studies away from Ireland. His interest in the sixteenth-century ecclesiastical music of Palestrina led to the impressive foundation of the Palestrina Choir in the Pro-Cathedral of Dublin; his admiration for "the subtle, mighty Norwegian," Ibsen, led to the founding with Yeats, Lady Gregory and Moore of the Irish Literary Theatre. And in the theatre too, aestheticism must be subordinated to asceticism. The drama must be considered "a vehicle for enunciating high and philosophical truths," deriving its glory from "those old, yet ever new springs of emotion in human nature."[4]

From the beginning Martyn was more concerned than Yeats and Lady Gregory with the "drama of ideas" exemplified by Ibsen: "Every great drama, every work worthy to be thought Art, must be founded on some philosophical idea." Although nationalist in politics as we have seen, his ideal in art was avowedly cosmopolitan, as he pleaded in the first issue of *Samhain*:

[to] put before the people of Ireland native works, also translations of the dramatic masterworks of all lands, for it is only by accustoming a public to the highest art that it can be led to appreciate art, and that dramatists may be inspired to work in the great art tradition.

These three aims — "educating the multitude" to an appreciation of good modern drama, establishing a company "that will be more interested in Arts than in Philistinism and personal vanity," and founding a subsidized theatre which would be free to experiment — remained basic to Martyn's work in the theatre throughout his life. The first he was able to fulfil privately, financing the early produc-

4 Martyn, "The Modern Drama in Germany," *Daily Express*, February 11, 1899.

tions of the Irish Literary Theatre, "the most significant action of my life," and in 1914 establishing The Irish Theatre with Thomas MacDonough and Joseph Mary Plunkett. The second aim resulted in a lifelong crusade for his beloved Ibsen, who remained the most profound effect on his own work. The third led to his break with the theatre he had done so much to found and his frequent struggles with amateur actors in Dublin. ("The greatest difficulty with which a reforming dramatist in Ireland has to contend is the kind of people whom he is forced to employ as actors.")

The Heather Field was Martyn's first play and the new movement's first success. In a memorandum written for Horace Plunkett in 1904, Yeats reports that it "proved itself in performance an extremely powerful play." According to contemporary reviews, the audience saw in it an allegory of the state of Ireland. On the one hand, with its "mental drama arising from the clash of the poetic and matter-of-fact temperaments" of the protagonists, the play strongly echoes Ibsen's psychological drama. On the other, the conflict between Carden Tyrell's dream of the "departed joys" of his youth as reflected in the heather field and the reality of the troubled times of the present strikes the note to be sounded more powerfully in the works of Synge and later Irish dramatists. By following his dream, through the heather field, Carden Tyrell recaptures the beauty of "the music of the morning." But Martyn's dreamer seeks a world far different from the call of Synge's vagrant; and the voice of the author can be more clearly heard in the generous but melancholy philosopher, Barry Ussher, who appreciates the music of the morning ("nature's ethereal phonograph") but recognizes the inevitable acceptance of "the pain of loss," a "true idealist . . . in a way so drilled and careful, that he will never let himself go." *The Heather Field* is Martyn's best play, constructed with the clear and logical framework he felt essential to a satisfactory work of art. The patterning and balance are almost extreme in their formalism.

In his review of *The Heather Field and Maeve* in the *Daily Express*, AE commented on "the current of subtle spiritual reverie which is characteristic of the awakening genius of the Gael"; certainly in his second play Martyn is more strongly influenced by the Celtic twilight of his fellow nationalists than by Ibsen's clear cold light of dawn. Again the scene is Ireland, the central figure an idealist who strives to unite the Hellenic beauty of form with the magic of the mythical Celt. But whereas Carden Tyrell's tragedy is the result of a disposition "too eerie, too ethereal, too untamable for good, steady, domestic cultivation" (as is the heather field), Maeve's dream of a love which would not be returned is as unsympathetic as her cold and distant nature. Here Martyn has managed to combine in one characterization the worst qualities of both extreme aestheticism and ardent Celticism. His aim is reflected in his own analysis of Hauptmann's *Hannele*, published in the *Daily Express* the same month that *Maeve* appeared in print:

With what marvellous art this beautiful dream-drama brings before us the dream of life and the life of dream. It is a masterwork of construction, and profoundly original withal, although the first idea may possibly have been suggested by Calderon's "Life and the Dream." It is impossible to give an idea of the perfection of the scenes. Those of the peasants and paupers have a sort of Dutch charm like the genre pieces of Boers by Teniers and Ostade, while the dream visions, with their soft beauty as of the poetic, ingenious designs of Bontet de Montvel, go with simple pathos to the heart.

In Martyn's dramatization of a girl pining to die for a lover who had no existence, set within a realistic framework of peasants in the west of Ireland, he too was attempting to portray a "dream-drama," "the wistful dream of beauty which haunts the heart of the modern Celt as it haunted the heart of the ancient Greek." The fault lies not so much in the idea as in the construction and characterization: the blending of moments of vision with textual dissertations on Irish folklore and archaeology is awkward; the attempt to symbolize English rapacity in the anxious character of Hugh Fitz Walter is crude and unconvincing; the setting is overloaded with ruined abbeys, cairns, round towers, and distant mountains. But in his minor characters Martyn is more successful. The O'Heyne, Prince of Burren, strikes a more authentic note in his peevish reiteration of bad luck and resentment; Finola is the only sympathetic woman character in all of Martyn's work; and in the characterization of Peg Inerny, the sly old vagrant who reigns in the life of dreams as the beautiful Queen Maeve, there is a touch of genius. The play's reception was as mixed as its ingredients: Maeve's continual longing for "the day-ghost" and "the immortal beauty of form" brought unsympathetic titters from the audience and caused Yeats several years later to fear a similar reaction to Synge's verbal repetitions. But the enthusiastic applause to Peg Inerny's final triumphant speech led directly to the creation of Yeats's Kathleen-ni-Houlihan: "You think I am only an old woman; but I tell you that Eire can never be subdued."

Martyn dedicated the first edition of *The Heather Field and Maeve* to Moore, Yeats and Arthur Symons; the most successful scene in *Maeve* is the dream sequence in Act II, which although conceived by Martyn was "polished" for the stage by Symons. He was less successful in his next rather unwilling collaboration, when George Moore, with Yeats's help, revised *The Tale of a Town* as *The Bending of the Bough*. The story of this strange collaboration has been frequently told, first by Moore with elaborations and unkind shafts in *Hail and Farewell*, later by Yeats in his *Autobiographies*, more indirectly by Martyn himself in *The Dream Physician*. Martyn's play as it stands, "a comedy of affairs in five acts," is an unwieldy indictment with symbolic overtones of small-town politics, reminiscent of but not slavishly copying Ibsen's *An Enemy of the People*. Powerful but clumsy in characterization, overtly nationalist in theme and intention, it was the movement's first attempt to portray contemporary town life on the stage and as such its sharply outlined criticism provided a sturdy example for such later playwrights as Padraic Colum and Lennox Robinson. It was also the most original of Martyn's plays, exhibiting both the admirable qualities of *The Heather Field and Maeve* and the defects of all his work. The characters are well contrasted, the "philosophical idea" — again the conflict between compromise and the ideal — probable, the situation appealing to a nationalist audience. But in his portrayal of both character and situation Martyn exhibited the lack of literary tact which was already proving embarrassing to his colleagues. General acrimonious argument around the council table is paralleled by the petty family jealousies around the maiden aunts' tea table, the tangles of both restricting rather than contributing to theatrical interest; Millicent Fell, the young hero's fiancée, is an acid portrait of the qualities Martyn detested in the Oxford "bluestocking," with insufficient sympathy to make her human; there is little distinction between family squabbles and party politics. Furthermore, having little of the poetry of Ibsen or his own *Maeve*, the play moved further still towards the realism Yeats opposed. It is not surprising that the Directors felt that *The Tale of a Town* did not, as Lady Gregory reported in a letter to Padraic Colum, "come up to the required standard."

What is surprising is that they should think Moore's adaptation,

The Bending of the Bough, did come up to that standard. For although Moore deepened the characterization, tightened the construction, and emphasized the political at the expense of the personal element in the play, the result is not much of an improvement over the original version. There is in fact almost as much loss: the bluff outspoken Mrs. Costigan is transformed into the unsuccessful politician Macnee; the play on "union of hearts" is omitted, thereby losing much of the political overtones that phrase implied during the years immediately following the split in the Parnell party; the "blarney" of the original visiting Mayor is dispensed with, thus eliminating any interest this scene did have. The most interesting alteration occurs in the characterization of Jasper Dean, who in the second version paradoxically achieves more of the idealist spirit apparent in Martyn's earlier plays, torn as he is between the call to realism represented by his fiancée, and the material advantages of her position, and the prophetic oratory of Kirwan, who represents not only idealism in politics but "the spiritual destiny of the Celtic race." ("The difficulty in life is the choice, and all the wonder of life is in the choice.") Yeats also had a hand in the revision, his main contribution being Jasper Dean's speech in the first act.

Although the theme of the play, universal in interest and national in significance, had value and in more capable hands has since proved eminently suitable for dramatization, the failure of both Martyn and Moore indicates their limitations as dramatists. On the other hand, the weakness of Lady Gregory and Yeats in accepting the play in either form indicates the first departure from their original aims and prophesies the ultimate failure of their ideal theatre. For neither approved of Moore's version of the play, as Yeats implies in a letter reporting on the progress of the revision:

It is foolish of Martyn to call the play "ugly," for ugly as it is from my point of view and yours, it is beauty itself beside what it was; and as for "commonness" in the writing, neither of them know what style is, but Moore can at least be coherent and sensible.

The play was of value, he felt, as "a splendid and intricate gospel of nationality and may be almost epoch-making in Ireland." This was the attitude Moore himself had towards his adopted child, believing that "it will cause a revolution." As a nationalist piece of propaganda, the play fared well, receiving the same applause Martyn's *Peg Inery* aroused. But *Maeve* had been chosen for its passages of beauty, and the nationalist approval came as a surprise. *The Bending of the Bough* had only its sentiment to recommend it; as Frank Fay commented in his perceptive review of the Irish Literary Theatre experiment, its basic defects were theatrical, not literary ones: "writing for applause and a good curtain."

The Tale of a Town was Martyn's last contribution to the dramatic movement he had helped initiate and sponsor. His next step was a further embarrassment to Yeats, and an indication of the course he was to follow in the pursuit of his ideals for the theatre. In reply to Yeats's request for an article on the Fays' production of AE's *Deirdre*, he wrote a letter extolling the play but damning the actors with faint praise:

> The excellence of AE's play, "Deirdre," I never for a moment doubted. . . . I saw in the reading that the acts were scientifically right in construction; and the performance confirmed my opinion. . . . The charm with which the great story of "Deirdre" is set forth was manifest to all, and the movement and many dramatic situations would have been more manifest under conditions of a more competent acting and stage management. I do not mean to say that the acting was bad. On the contrary, it had some good features in it, notably the all-important feature of being in the right key. It was, however, ineffective and quite wanting in that intensity which is necessary to give life to any strong dramatic situation.

The following year Yeats reports in a letter to John Quinn that Martyn has "taken up another amateur company and is getting them to play his plays. He took a big theatre for them last week and paid them. George Moore did the stage-management, and the company played *The Heather Field* and *A Doll's House*." With this gesture Martyn ended his association with the Irish Literary Theatre; for the rest of his life he gave generously of both time and money to establish his dream of "a society for producing native drama and continental masterpieces," which would deal with "the problems of people more complex and refined" than those of the Abbey Theatre. Finally with the foundation of The Irish Theatre in 1914 "for the production of non-peasant drama by Irishmen, of plays in the Irish Language, and of English translations from European master-works for the theatre," he found what he had been seeking. Perhaps more than either of his co-directors, Martyn remained true to his early ideals of the theatre. Looking back at the end of his life to that first experiment, he could still admit, "But the Abbey plan was intellectually sound, and it triumphed by creating a thinking audience for itself." That it was not his audience, he had learned long before Yeats made the same discovery. It is to Martyn's credit that he withdrew from the venture he had done so much to encourage with more grace than those who remained had shown towards him. His failure as a playwright did not alter either his ideals for the theatre or his faith in his dream. His statement of that faith, as expressed in *The Place-Hunters* (1902), illustrates not only his strength but his devotion to both Art and his Nation:

Gratitude — Of course we don't expect any gratitude! It is only weaklings hanker after gratitude. Nation-builders, in working out their will, think themselves lucky if they even escape assassination.

Martyn died in 1923 at the age of sixty-four, an embittered, lonely and disappointed reformer, confined to his rooms by arthritis and even more by the "pig-headedness" his brilliant cousin found so amusing. The theatre he helped found and then renounced lived to practise the realism he advocated and Yeats denied. "Edward is sorry he didn't build a theatre twenty years ago, and 'put the key in his pocket'," Lady Gregory wrote in her Journal after their last visit together. It is ironical to reflect that if he had done so, the Abbey Theatre today would doubtless be a great deal better.

II

Without Edward Martyn, it would be difficult to find a focal point for that artful collaborator George Moore. Although Moore was also Roman Catholic and a landlord from the west of Ireland, the similarity between the two cousins ends there, unless, as Yeats suggests in *The Cat and the Moon*, they are to be considered the inseparable sides of the same coin. Like all his enthusiasms, Moore's patriotism passed through all the phases between two extremes. "It is one of Mr. Moore's peculiarities," commented Max Beerbohm in the *Saturday Review* on Moore's farewell to England,

that whatever is uppermost in his mind seems to him to be the one thing in the world, and he cannot conceive that there will ever be room for anything else. . . . But even if the Keltic Renascence prove to be the most important movement ever made in Art it will not long enchain him.

Beerbohm was of course right, and the prodigal did return, his disgust of the English being replaced by an even more fervent dislike for the once-praised Irish. But Moore must be allowed the last word, which he takes in *The Untilled Field*, a collection of stories that clearly express his debts to "dear Edward," to Yeats, and to his entire sojourn in Ireland:

"You knew from the beginning that Paris was the source of all art, that everyone here who is more distinguished than the others has been to Paris. We go to Paris with baskets on our backs, and sticks in our hands, and bring back what we can pick up. And having lived immersed in art till you're forty, you return to the Catholic Celt! Your biographer will be puzzled to explain this last episode, and however he may explain it, it will seem a discrepancy."

If Yeats's "Masters" brought him metaphors for his poetry, how much more did Moore's own enthusiasms bring him material for his art.

It might be said that Moore was always Irish, even when most vehemently denouncing his own country (to the extent of embracing Protestantism). And indeed, throughout his work he never really escapes from his past. Like Martyn he had received his education abroad, substituting the coteries and salons of Paris for the more conventional studies of Oxford. Unlike Martyn, he returned to his Irish estates only to disencumber himself of them. The Celtic Renaissance was not, however, his first glance at Ireland for copy; nor, except for a brief flirtation with a tragedy about Martin Luther, was the drama his first love. Having published *A Modern Lover* (1883) and *A Mummer's Wife* (1885), both based on Zola's theory of naturalism and first-hand observation, he wrote *A Drama in Muslin* (1886), a sympathetic portrayal of the "marriage trade" as practised in the upper circles of Dublin society. But his task over, including an amusing exchange with the Castle officials duly publicized by Moore, he once more returned to civilization, leaving as his parting shot an unfortunate diatribe against that town "of miserable vice and hideous decrepitude," that "country of abandoned dreams," with its "damp, flaccid, evil smell of poverty," where dirt and patriotism "are apparently but two words for one and the same thing." Ten years after he had published *Parnell and his Island* he was back, embracing the once-abandoned dreams, acknowledging the patriotism if not the dirt, and advocating for all but himself the Irish language. "That one child should learn Irish interests me far more than the publication of a masterpiece," he wrote to Yeats in 1901. And in 1902 he entertained Dublin (those who attended and those who had not) to a Gaelic lawn party. The same year, under the auspices of the Gaelic League, he published *The Untilled Field*, translated into Irish by a Trinity College student.

But by then his allegiance had switched from Yeats to AE, his connection with the Irish literary movement had ceased, and with it much of his fervent nationalism. "Ireland . . . is no country for an educated man," the artist-hero of *The Untilled Field* exclaims.

Let the Gael disappear. . . . Since Cormac's Chapel he has built nothing but mud cabins. Since the Cross of Cong he has imported virgins from Germany.

Since his nation would not appreciate his art, he could not appreciate the nation. And in 1908, while still living in Dublin, he wrote to his friend Edouard Dujardin in Paris, "Ireland is the cemetery of Catholicism. . . . 'The Celtic Renaissance' . . . does not exist, it is a myth, like a good many other things."

It would, however, be both unfair and dishonest to leave the impression that Moore's sojourn in Ireland was one of "intellectual slapstick" only, as William Gaunt has described it. Near the end of his life he was to quote as his epitaph, "Nature I loved, and next to nature, art," and it was because of this passion for art that he returned to Ireland. Moreover, he involved himself in the Irish Literary movement at the request of Yeats and Martyn, who had had little experience with the theatre at the time, and whose work he respected. A letter written to Yeats in 1898 contains the following passage which indicates much of the characters of both:

I am your best advertiser in all the houses I frequent I cry: I am not the Lord. There is one greater than I, the lachet of whose shoe I am not worthy to tie.

Always a willing collaborator, if at times a difficult one, Moore gave willingly for the enthusiasm of the moment, and his contribution to the dramatic work of both Martyn and Yeats can not be denied. However, Moore was never as unwisely hasty in his judgments as many critics imply, and his attitude towards language in general is proof of this.

Speaking of Swinburne in *Avowals*, Moore commented, "Like everybody else in these islands, he looked upon prose narrative as an entertainment rather than as an art." Narrative to Moore meant a plot in language, and the style was more important to him than the plot. His theories in fact are very similar to the "living speech" Yeats himself advocated, and if we examine his interest in the Irish language we find it an interesting complement to Yeats's own:

A language may be compared to a seed, for a seed is a potential flower, and every language is a potential literature; the beauty of the flower and the literature vary according to the quality of the seed and the language, and the influences they use and when they rise into the upper air.... Style becomes necessary when language becomes corrupt... compel[ling] those who desire a work of art to isolate themselves in some less vulgar speech.... I plead for the preservation of that mysterious background of legends and traditions out of which Ireland has come, and which a hundred years of determined Anglicisation has not altogether blotted out.... In stealing from him [the peasant] the traditions of his race, his songs and legends, you do not give him what is best in England... but the gutter press of London.[5]

Admittedly this is a grafting of Moore's belief in style on to an already burdened branch of Yeatsian dialectic, but through the unwieldy argument one can hear the George Moore of the constant revisions, the incessant search for truth in art, and the struggle to master the tools of that art. And although Moore may have insisted upon carrying on his education in public, as Oscar Wilde once quipped, the technical virtuosity he finally achieved was a result of this interest in a living language which he could mould to his interpretation of life. "George Moore is the best living novelist," writes Virginia Woolf in *The Death of the Moth and Other Essays*, "— and the worst; writes the most beautiful prose of his time — and the feeblest; has a passion for literature which none of those dismal pundits, his contemporaries, shares." And her masterly summing-up concludes with the key to Moore's sympathy for the language of his own country, "and has taught himself an accent, a cadence, indeed a language, for saying it in which, though they are not English, but Irish, will give him his place among the lesser immortals of our tongue." In a letter to John Eglinton in 1914, Moore himself acknowledges his debt, though referring to Eglinton, Richard Best, and AE rather than to Yeats: "You see I didn't know how to write until I went over to Ireland — it was you fellows that taught me."

But although Moore himself struggled for a style which has its roots in the accent of his compatriots and for a time at any rate believed in the Gaelic League, he never agreed with Yeats's belief

5 "A Plea for the Soul of the Irish People," *Nineteenth Century*, February 1901, 285-95.

in the peasant dialect developed by Lady Gregory. "Is it not true that peasant speech limits the range of our ideas?" he asks in *Vale*. "Peasant speech is only adapted to dialogue," and therefore, to Moore, whose abilities were by now obviously not dramatic, useless. Nor, although he would plead for the revival of Gaelic as the only salvation of the peasant, did he ever resign his own aristocratic sympathies. "Art is the direct antithesis to democracy," he declares in his *Confessions*. In the same article that pleaded for the soul of the peasant, he insists on a selected audience. And not many years later he began issuing his own works in limited editions. Eventually his belief in a literary renaissance disappeared as well, and he returned to the London he had abandoned ten years earlier — "Art comes to a country and flourishes in it for a while, and then leaves it, never to return." [6]

A man of many enthusiasms, but as Beerbohm pointed out, only one at a time, Moore gradually moved from apostleship to Zola by way of Antoine's Théâtre-Libre in Paris to apologist for the Independent Theatre of London. As early as 1884 he had severely criticized the decline in dramatic writing in England. After observing a performance of Ibsen's *Ghosts* in Paris in 1890 he embarked on a campaign to bring Ibsen and a cultivated taste to the English public. First of course it would be necessary for that public to endow a national theatre freed from "the thraldom of farcical melodrama and melodramatic farces." This would be a theatre primarily for authors,

a theatre which, by producing some thirty or forty new plays every year, will allow us to say what we have to say, and in the form which is natural and peculiar to us.

He already considers himself one of the playwrights, but feels it necessary to warn his prospective audience,

that it is as imperative for an English as for a French Théâtre-Libre to refuse good conventional plays as bad ones. . . . To get the *fine fleur* of society, literature and art the Théâtre-Libre must offer a supremacy of sensation — the strange, the unknown, the unexpected. The plays need not be great plays — great plays are out of the question — they need only be plays with something in them; even though that something is not always deeper than the charm which we find in a piece of bric-a-brac, or a piece of old china.[7]

[6] Moore, *Conversations in Ebury Street* (London: Heinemann, 1924), 228.

[7] Moore collected these essays and reprinted them with improvements in *Impressions and Opinions* (London: T. Werner Laurie, 1913).

Oddly enough, when the Independent Theatre was finally founded in London, and not by Moore, his contribution came about as the result of a wager. *The Strike at Arlingford*, produced by the Independent Theatre in 1893, had less of the *fine fleur* of France than the realistic problem drama of Ibsen (William Archer compared the play favourably with Shaw's *Widowers' Houses*), but it gave Moore the responsible position of a man of the theatre, and on this basis he was asked to join the relatively inexperienced trio in their efforts to found the Irish Literary Theatre. As a homesick young man Yeats had heard in the sound of a London fountain lake water lapping with low sounds by the shore of a western isle; now Moore too would have his summons:

I walked in a sort of devout collectedness awaiting what was to happen, and very soon, half-way down the road, I heard a voice, not an inner, but an external voice as from somebody close behind me, saying, "Go to Ireland!" [8]

Moore's idea of a theatre was in many ways similar to Martyn's: an endowed theatre which would be free from the dictates of that "filthy cur, feeding upon offal," the general public; a company untouched by the "mummer worship" current in the commercial theatre, thereby once more elevating playwright over actor; a policy cosmopolitan in design, recommending "great dramatic masterpieces of European renown, and plays dealing with our own national life, history, and legend" (which in Moore's temporary support of the Gaelic League included plays in Irish). But from the beginning the partnership was an uneasy one, for Moore shared Martyn's belief that "the modern realistic drama — the literary drama of the present day — is the acting drama" and took Ibsen's "perfect sense of craftsmanship" as his model. Moore's ambition in drama was in fact his concern in the novel, the problem of "conveying an interesting and truthful reflection of life," as he says in a note to *The Strike at Arlingford*. Perhaps this was his main departure from Martyn's creed; he wrote to Dujardin that "the only end of life is life, and the only end of art is to help us to live," and the artist should go no further in his didacticism. In an interview with the *Pall Mall Gazette* in 1893 he stated his creed:

The only two conditions that can be fairly imposed upon a playwright are — firstly, that his work should be a work of art; secondly, that it should interest.

[8] *Ave* (London: Heinemann, 1911), 365.

Further, Moore had a more profound grasp of Ibsen's technical accomplishment, and like him turned to France for his first model, a debt he indicated in conversation with Michael Field, as recorded in *Works and Days*:

We talked much of the construction of plays for the stage: he made me realize the leading fault of our work — its want of rhythmical progression — the haphazard development of plot which has contented us. The firm yet pliant structure of a work is one of the requirements of style. And preparation for events and entrances is the true forethought that gives dramatic art integrity and musical movement.

And so Moore brought with him to Ireland not only a superior knowledge of stagecraft but the emphasis on style and structure which would lead him first into collaboration with his fellow directors and eventually send him once more to the form of art he found more satisfactory, the novel.

Moore's interest in structure and situation was both his strength and his weakness as a playwright. Because of it the dramatic form intrigued him and gave him a clearer grasp of stagecraft than either Yeats or Martyn at that time had. In spite of it, however, he was unable to make the next essential step, development of the situation through dialogue. "The situation was quite perfect, but when I wanted words they would not come," he confessed to Michael Field, and elsewhere he makes the revealing comment, "Plays read to me exactly as they act — only better." Both Martyn and Yeats recognized his "power of inventing a dramatic climax" and consequently were willing to accept his help, as he in turn was willing to accept theirs for the sake of "the beauty of the creation." Indeed, for the sake of the creation, Moore willingly used all suggestions; in a letter to Yeats thanking him for his help in the characterization of Ulick Dean in *Evelyn Innes* he suggests that Yeats should not confide in anyone regarding "this little collaboration." "I am willing to take the credit for work which I have not done without assistance so that the few who are capable of seeing may see its beauty."

But although the part "that headlong, intrepid man" played in the establishment of the Irish Literary Theatre has since been distorted by the accounts and counter-attacks of both Yeats and Moore, his influence as "man of the theatre" and collaborator can hardly be ignored. As he himself reminds us in *Ave*, without his help the first productions might never have reached the stage; Lady Gregory acknowledged his "excellent help in finding actors," and he virtually took charge of rehearsals. He both defended and encouraged the enterprise with his customary energy and publicity, going so far as to have a controversy with William Archer in the *Daily Chronicle*; Yeats in turn admired his efficiency and in the first flush of enthusiasm dubbed him "the Aristophanes of Ireland." Further, he wrote a play with Yeats. For like Martyn, Moore had also breathed the rarified air of the Celtic Twilight, and in his Hall of Fame set beside Ibsen "the genius of W. B. Yeats, being a survival of that of the prophet and the seer of old time," as he acknowledges in his introduction to *The Heather Field and Maeve*. He greatly admired that "divine play," *The Countess Cathleen*, and gave liberally of both his praise and constructive criticism. But Moore could never resist more direct involvement; soon the inevitable suggestion followed, a scenario "which might be of some use," and finally, collaboration.

Moore's history in the theatre seemed inevitably to rest on collaboration. In 1879 he published *Martin Luther*, written in collaboration with his Paris friend Lopez; *The Strike at Arlington* was written with Arthur Kennedy; he had helped Martyn with *The Heather Field*, *Maeve*, and *The Tale of a Town*; he and his friend Alexis had made a French version of Gilbert's *Sweethearts*. Later he was to write *Elizabeth Cooper* with Mrs. Pearl Craigie, a revision called *The Peacock's Feathers* with Dujardin, and still a further revision, *The Coming of Gabrielle*; a "very intelligent young man" contributed to the first dramatization of *Esther Waters* (produced by the Stage Society on Bernard Shaw's recommendation) and Barrett Clark later helped revise it. He was constantly considering scenarios for operas (including one based on the story of Deirdre, and one borrowed from Synge's *Well of the Saints*). He bombarded Yeats with criticisms and suggestions for scenarios, and finally in 1901 their *Diarmuid and Grania* reached the stage.

Their collaboration on this play has been described amusingly and fairly accurately by Moore in *Hail and Farewell*, more discreetly by Yeats in *Dramatis Personæ*. The idea apparently first came from Moore and work had already begun when they turned their attention to *The Tale of a Town*. In a letter to his sister in 1899 Yeats describes the "compact" agreed upon:

We have made the first draft and have got, as I think, a very powerful plot and arrangement of scenes. It will be a wonderful part for a great actress if she can be found. Moore is in boundless enthusiasm. The play will be in prose. . . . Moore is now writing the play out fully.

He will then give it to me and I will go over it all putting it into my own language so as to keep the same key throughout and making any other changes I think fit and send it back to Moore.

In theory, Yeats was willing to recognize Moore's superior knowledge of the stage, "a power of construction, a power of inventing a dramatic climax far beyond me"; Moore in turn was content to allow Yeats's authority on question of style. Despite occasional outbursts of impractical enthusiasm (according to *Ave*, they once considered carrying the plot through three different languages before turning it into Anglo-Irish) and heated disagreements (at another time Arthur Symons was called in as mediator), the play was finally completed, and produced by F. R. Benson's company in October 1901, in the third year of the Irish Literary Theatre's experiment.

The collaboration was more successful than the performance or the audience's reaction: the English company could not pronounce the Irish names; nationalists objected to Edward Elgar's "English" music; critics denounced the "coarse English society play presented to us in fancy dress" as "a heartless piece of vandalism practised on a great Irish story." The nationalist campaign against the Irish Literary Theatre had begun. Both Yeats and Moore replied to their critics, asserting the right to interpret the legend as they saw it, "the tragedy of a hero who has married a frail woman." The emphasis upon the "moral idea" and "the essence . . . as an escapement from formal life" is reminiscent of Moore's earlier pronouncements on the drama, and much of the staging (the banquet-hall setting, Diarmuid's sheep-shearing, the unrealistic love-scenes) appears to be his work also. But although the storm scene in the last act, one of the most powerful scenes in the play, may owe something to Moore's experiences at Bayreuth, it smacks even more strongly of Yeats's recent visits to Stratford-on-Avon. The defects of *Diarmuid and Grania* are obvious: the plot, as Yeats himself remarks in his preface to *Gods and Fighting Men*, "is indeed but a succession of detached episodes"; incidents and language swing from the lyrical and abstract to the prosaic and sensuous; the characterization of Grania, although more vivid than Diarmuid's, betrays the authors in two minds. As Susan Mitchell remarked, the authors passed each other on the journey. The play is neither a failure nor a success, and Yeats's comments years later perhaps most clearly define the reason for both:

Lady Gregory thought such collaboration would injure my own art, and was perhaps right. Because his mind was argumentative, abstract, diagrammatic, mine sensuous, concrete, rhythmical, we argued about words. In later years, through much knowledge of the stage, through the exfoliation of my own style, I learnt that occasional prosaic words gave the impression of an active man speaking. . . . Our worst quarrels, however, were when he tried to be poetical, to write in what he considered my style . . . we made peace at last, Moore accepting my judgment upon words, I his upon construction. To that he would sacrifice what he had thought the day before not only his best scene but "the best scene in any modern play," and without regret: all must receive its being from the central idea; nothing be in itself anything. He would have been a master of construction, but that his practice as a novelist made him long for descriptions and reminiscences.[9]

The greater playwright, because he was capable of learning more, perhaps gained most.

After the production, several attempts were made to improve upon the collaboration, and letters to Lady Gregory indicate Yeats's willingness to accept criticism of *On Baile's Strand* from both Martyn and Moore. But meanwhile new faces had appeared: the Fays, encouraged by AE, had replaced the English actors; Synge joined the movement; Lady Gregory, having learned her trade with *Diarmuid and Grania* ("Mr. Yeats used to dictate parts . . . to me, and I would suggest a sentence here and there.") began to write her own plays. The forces of folk drama and verse plays for the moment had the upper hand, and the rival stage tradition represented by Martyn and Moore was effectively routed. The uneasy friendship between the two cousins continued in a new theatre venture, but Moore, who had "never pretended to have any great claims on the theatre," returned to a happier means of expression and a new enthusiasm in that "angelic anarchist," AE.

Referring to their unfortunate collaboration over *The Bending of the Bough*, Yeats comments in his *Autobiographies*,

The finished work was Moore's in its construction and characterization, but most of the political epigrams and certain bitter sentences put into the mouth of Deane, a dramatization of Standish O'Grady, were mine. A rhetorical, undramatic second act about the Celtic Movement, which I had begun to outlive, was all Moore's; as convert he was embarrassing, unsubduable, preposterous.

It is those qualities of unashamed exuberance and preposterous proselytizing, embarrassing as they may have been to Yeats and painful as they certainly were to Martyn, that ensure the fame of this impudent comedian and grant him his part in the chaotic collaboration of the Irish Literary Renaissance.

9 *Autobiographies* (London: Macmillan, 1955), 434-36.

Division and Unity: AE and W. B. Yeats

ROBIN SKELTON

Gᴇᴏʀɢᴇ Wɪʟʟɪᴀᴍ Rᴜssᴇʟʟ, who chose to write under the initials AE, was a second-rate writer, a third-rate painter, a politician of minor significance, but a phenomenon of major importance in the Ireland of his lifetime.

He was born in Armagh in 1867, and his early education was that of an art student. He attended, in the 1880's, evening art classes at the Metropolitan School of Art, Dublin, and at the Royal Hibernian Academy. He showed considerable ability as an artist, but never pursued his talent to a conclusion; the majority of his paintings are technically unsatisfactory, and many of his oil paintings have grown dark and cracked. He gave up his art studies sometime before 1890. W. B. Yeats, whom he first met at this period, said in *Reveries over Childhood and Youth*, "One day he announced he was leaving the Art School because his will was so weak and the arts, or any other emotional pursuit, could but weaken it further." AE himself, however, while appearing to support this view in some of his autobiographical writings, once told Thomas Bodkin that "though he had always desired to be a painter, he gave up painting because his lack of means forced him to enter into some more paying, if less congenial, business."

These two explanations indicate the extremes present in AE's character. On the one hand he was a deeply religious, even mystical, thinker, willing to subdue any of his personal desires or ambitions for the sake of the truth and the health of his soul. On the other hand, he was a highly efficient practical man, fully aware of economic realities, and determined to use his abilities as an organizer, writer, and economist to better the condition of rural Ireland.

It was the visionary AE who first attracted Yeats, and who was most admired as a young man. He early discovered a capacity for intense imaginative visualization bordering upon the hallucinatory. In *The Candle of Vision* (1918) he wrote:

I was aged about sixteen or seventeen years, when I ... became aware of a mysterious life quickening within my life. ... I began to be astonished with myself, for, walking along country roads, intense and passionate imaginations of another world began to overpower me. They were like strangers who suddenly enter a house, who brush aside the doorkeeper, and who will not be denied. Soon I knew they were the rightful owners and heirs of the house of the body, and the doorkeeper was only one who was for a time in charge, who had neglected his duty, and who had pretended to ownership.

He felt, at this time, that "there were comrades who were speaking to me."

They seemed to be saying to each other of us, 'Soon they will awaken; soon they will come to us again,' and for a moment I almost seemed to mix with their eternity. The tinted air glowed before me with intelligible significance like a face, a voice. The visible world became like a tapestry blown and stirred by winds behind it. If it would but raise for an instant I knew I would be in Paradise. Every form on that tapestry appeared to be the work of gods. Every flower was a word, a thought. The grass was speech; the trees were speech; the waters were speech; the winds were speech. They were the Army of the Voice marching on to conquest and dominion over the spirit; and I listened with my whole being. ...

Whether AE read at any time Richard Jefferies' *The Story of my Heart* (1883) we cannot now know, but there are similarities between Jefferies' nature-worship and idealism and AE's. To Jefferies, as to AE, the world of natural beauty is only an emanation of, and a veil across, Eternity. The "Sun Life" of Jefferies and the "Earth Breath" of AE are similar in more than their phraseology.

Whether or not AE knew Jefferies, he did admire Blake, and shared his enthusiasm with W. B. Yeats. With Yeats he also discussed the work of the Theosophical Society with which they both became involved in the late eighties. With Yeats, too, he discussed in letters and in conversation many aspects of oriental mysticism, which also appear in the early poems of both writers. With all this in common, it may seem surprising that the two men did not work in closer harness. True, both were founder members of The Irish National Theatre Society, Yeats being its president; and the beginning of the Irish dramatic renaissance was, perhaps, the production of AE's *Deirdre* and Yeats's *Kathleen Ni Houlihan* by W. G. Fay's Irish National Dramatic Company in April 1902. Moreover, Yeats issued a book of AE's poems from the Dun Emer Press, and, in 1932, invited him to draft the rules for the proposed Irish Academy of Letters. Nevertheless, the relationship was always a little uneasy, and the reason may lie partly in the two men's quite opposed approach to the visionary.

The key to the difference may be seen in another passage from *The Candle of Vision*, where AE condemns the vanity of his early feeling that his visions were personal, and shows an aversion to any kind of self-dramatization or egoism. He says

... for some years my heart was proud, for as the beauty sank into memory it seemed to become a personal possession, and I said 'I imagined this' when I should humbly have said, 'The curtain was a little lifted that I might see'.

This contrasts sharply with the attitude expressed by Yeats towards the spiritual teachers who, he maintained, dictated the material of *A Vision*. In his Dedication to the first edition of 1925 he says of the whole philosophical system,

... I am longing to put it out of reach that I may write the poetry it seems to have made possible.

In the revised edition of 1937 Yeats describes how the spirit or dæmon who was responsible for his wife's automatic writing responded to his offer to

spend what remained of life explaining and piecing together those scattered sentences. 'No', was the answer, 'we have come to give you metaphors for poetry.'

Later in the same preface Yeats jettisons the whole of the mystical element in his "system," which he says he now regards as

stylistic arrangements of experience comparable to the cubes in the drawing of Wyndham Lewis and to the ovoids in the sculpture of Brancusi.

Yeats's attitude towards the occult was at once more sceptical and more intellectually organized than AE's. Though loving, like Sir Thomas Browne, to pursue his reason to an "O Altitudo," he felt it always necessary to attempt rational investigation of psychic phenomena. Hence he tried "experiments," testing the power of arcane symbolism upon his friends and visitors; hence he questioned, indeed tried to cross-examine, his instructors. Finally, he qualified his Vision of Eternal Truth with suggestions that it amounted to a psychological and historical system, rather than a religious one. This is even present in his early, and important, analysis of Blake's Symbolic System, made at a period when he was more uncritically involved in the occult that he was in later years.

Thus the two men were, in this respect, opposed types. For Yeats, art and poetry had primacy over vision; to AE the vision might even make poetry and art an indulgence to be avoided. To Yeats the vision was one vouchsafed to the individual heroic seer; to AE it was common property, and opposed to the vanities of the ego. Nevertheless, it sometimes seems as if Yeats was envious of AE's visionary experiences; he longed to see, but never saw, a ghost, and his own occult phenomena were restricted to strange sounds and scents, and to his wife's automatic writing. AE produced *A Candle of Vision* in October 1918. In the second edition of *A Vision*, Yeats states that his wife's visions began exactly a year earlier in October 1917; in the first edition he dates his meeting with the fictional Michael Robartes as "Spring 1917." *A Vision* was published in 1925. I cannot help suspecting the presence here of a degree of psychic "one-upmanship."

There are certainly similarities between the thought of Yeats in *A Vision* and in the poems arising from it, and the thought of AE in another philosophical work, *The Interpreters* (1922). *The Interpreters* is a series of discussions between various characters who each represent one philosophic outlook. AE said in his preface,

The Interpreters may be taken as a symposium between scattered portions of one nature dramatically sundered as the soul is in dream.

In this book there is a passage which is strongly reminiscent both of the basic contention in *A Vision* and of Yeats's description of Byzantium.

"The Earth spirit throws itself into innumerable forms of life," answered Lavelle. "Did you expect it to make its children all of one pattern? For every race its own culture. Every great civilization, I think, had a deity behind it, or a divine shepherd who guided it on some plan in the cosmic imagination. 'Behold,' said an ancient oracle, 'how the Heavens glitter with intellectual sections.' These are archetypal images we follow dimly in our evolution."

This could easily serve as a preface to the whole of Yeats's account of the changing shapes of western civilization in Book III of *A Vision*. AE's book continues:

"How do you conceive of these powers as affecting civilization?"

"I believe they incarnate in the race: more in the group than in the individual; and they tend to bring about an orchestration of the genius of the race, to make manifest in time their portion of eternal beauty. So arises that unity of character which existed in the civilization of Egypt or Attica, where art, architecture, and literature were in such harmony that all that is best seems almost the creation of one miriad-minded artist."

Yeats, on page 191 of *A Vision* (1925) wrote:

I think that in early Byzantium, and maybe never before or since in recorded history, religious, aesthetic and practical life were one, and that architect and artificers — though not, it may be, poets, for language had been the instrument of controversy and must have grown abstract — spoke to the multitude and the few alike. The painter and the mosaic worker, the worker in gold and silver, the illuminator of Sacred Books were almost impersonal, almost perhaps without the consciousness of individual design, absorbed in their subject matter and that the vision of a whole people.

It would take more space than I have at my disposal to list the many other instances where *The Interpreters* and *A Vision* bear upon one another. In some cases it seems clear that both books have been influenced by common source material in theosophy and neo-platonic philosophy. The descriptions of the characters in *The Interpreters* remind one of similar descriptions by Yeats of symbolic personages in books published both before and after 1922. The analyses of types of humanity in *The Interpreters* are similar to those used by Yeats though shorn of his special jargon.

In 1922, however, Yeats was, in other respects, moving farther away from AE. Since 1897 AE had been deeply concerned with the co-operative movement in Ireland. In that year he was appointed banks organizer for the Irish Agricultural Organization Society. In this capacity, and later as editor of *The Irish Homestead*, he fought for the establishment of cheap credit facilities for farmers, in order to release them from the clutches of the commercial banks, and the petty loan sharks or "gombeen men." He also, continually, supported the trade union movement, and spoke at an Albert Hall meeting in support of the Irish and General Transport and General

Workers Union strike in 1913. In *The National Being* (1916) he spoke out on social and economic matters from a left-wing viewpoint, and with a trenchancy absent in his philosophical writings. His championship of freedom of speech and religious tolerance, and his insistence that a narrow nationalism must be replaced by an international outlook, met much opposition from many quarters. Yeats, writing to H. J. C. Grierson on November 6, 1922, gave his own view of the situation:

We are preparing here, behind our screen of bombs and smoke, a return to conservative politics as elsewhere in Europe, or at least to a substitution of the historical sense for logic. The return will be painful and perhaps violent, but many educated men talk of it and must soon work for it and perhaps riot for it.

A curious sign is that AE who was the most popular of men is now suffering some slight eclipse because of old democratic speeches — things of years ago. I on the other hand get hearers where I did not get them because I have been of the opposite party. AE has still however his great popularity in co-operative Ireland. The Ireland that reacts from the present disorder is turning its eyes towards individualist Italy.

This gives a false impression of AE whose democracy was less than complete. In *The National Being*, indeed, he makes many statements with which Yeats appears to agree. Far from substituting logic for historical sense, he says that a "powerful Irish character has begun to reassert itself in modern times." He sees the ancient Irish clan as "aristocratic in leadership and democratic in its economic basis," and sees this ancient character persisting in the work of "Swift, Berkeley, O'Grady, Shaw, Wilde, Parnell, Davitt" who were "intensely democratic in economic theory, adding that to an aristocratic freedom of thought." He thinks this character still persists "in the mass" and that

it is by adopting a policy which will enable it to manifest once more that we will create an Irish civilization, which will fit our character as the glove fits the hand.

He uses the word "individualism" pejoratively, however, saying,

... we allowed individualism — the devilish doctrine of every man for himself — to be the keynote of our economic life; where, above all things, the general good and not the enrichment of the individual should be considered.

He states the necessity for leadership by the aristocracy, "not the aristocracy of birth, but the aristocracy of character, intellect, and will." And, like Yeats, he expresses his own and Ireland's love for the aristocratic character of Parnell. Moreover, like Yeats again, he believes in the Irish "respect for the aristocratic intellect, for freedom of thought, ideals, poetry, and imagination as the qualities to be looked for in our leaders...."

The degree of agreement between Yeatsian "conservatism" and AE's vision of "democracy" is so considerable that it is hard to see why Yeats felt himself to be of "the opposite party." Partly, of course, Yeats feared the levelling process of even "economic democracy." In *On the Boiler* (1939) he wrote:

Instead of hierarchical society, where all men are different, came democracy; instead of a science which had re-discovered Anima Mundi, its experiments and observations confirming the speculations of Henry More, came materialism: all that whiggish world Swift stared on till he became a raging man.

In passing, we might note that AE's version of Swift is a good deal closer to the author of *The Drapier's Letters* and *A Modest Proposal* than is Yeats's. We must also note that the same difference of temperament which made agreement upon the significance of visions impossible, also made disagreement about politics inevitable, even though in both cases the two men based their thought upon mutually acceptable premises.

As in philosophy and politics, so in literature. AE was as much the guiding spirit of a group of writers and poets as Yeats. He edited *New Songs* in 1904, which included work by Padraic Colum, Eva Gore-Booth, Thomas Koehler, Alice Milligan, Susan Mitchell, Seumas O'Sullivan, George Roberts, and Ella Young. None of these were perhaps very remarkable as poets, though there are lovely things in O'Sullivan, and Susan Mitchell's verse deserves more notice than it has yet received. When *The Irish Homestead* was merged with the new *Irish Statesman* with AE as its editor he became, says John Eglinton in *A Memoir of AE*, "the most noted disseminator of culture in Ireland," and "at his Sunday evening gatherings he acquired the ascendancy of a minor Dr. Johnson." At these gatherings, says C. P. Curran,

He made no difference of persons: the latest and youngest new-comer had his attention as if he were the long-awaited Avatar.... A kindly wisdom throned over debate, comprehending and all-forgiving. The most divergent opinions found patient hearing, but the immoderate appeared a little ridiculous.

Yeats contributed to *The Irish Statesman* under AE's editorship very few times. He contributed twice during his lifetime to *The Dublin Magazine* under the editorship of Seumas O'Sullivan. It seems that membership of the AE circle was quite distinct from that of the Yeats circle, or felt to be so by Dublin literary society. In fact, Gogarty, Frank O'Connor, F. R. Higgins, were common to both groups; these were all published by the Cuala Press, and were also all published with prefatory material by AE.

It is hard to say whether Yeats felt AE's Sunday gatherings presented any rivalry to his own At Homes, though references in Yeats's letters to AE's Ely Place circle do suggest that he was aware of an element of faction in the situation, while being sure that AE was in no way creating faction deliberately. It is clear, too, that the lines of demarcation were partly drawn by talent. AE's acceptance of the most weakly fledgelings was in contrast to Yeats's preference for singing birds with a touch of the hawk about them. Yeats went out of his way to befriend, tutor, and derive excitement from the younger poets whose vigorous talent he admired; Dublin gossip even speaks of him, on occasion, as setting out to "capture" young men from the circle of their acquaintance. AE was, as a social convener, less militaristic; friends and disciples happened to him; he did not seek them.

While gossip of this kind may seem out of place in an essay such as this, it does indicate, once again, the temperamental differences between the two men, and emphasizes that Yeats's burning zeal for the advancement of his own and others' poetic abilities was in opposition to AE's essentially less professional approach.

It is in the poetry and painting of AE that this difference shows most clearly. He was vain about his poetry, says John Eglinton, though he was vain about nothing else, and he could recite all his poems from memory, often with deep emotion. Yeats, on the other hand, could recall no poem without the aid of a manuscript, and was much more open to suggested revisions. Indeed, he reworked his poems to an extent impossible to AE, showing in this an impersonal devotion to the art remarkable in a man otherwise so wedded to the notion of the importance of the individual voice. AE's poetry is imaginative, insubstantial, mellifluous; it does not alter very much from its beginnings to its end, and even though it sometimes relinquishes its gentle idealism for definite political statement, it never achieves the vigour and passion of Yeats. Clearly influenced by pre-Raphaelitism and the brightly coloured vocabularies of some of the poets of the nineties, it has a faintly defeated charm; the emotional depths may have been touched by the writer, but they are rarely plumbed by the poem. There are occasional Blakeian poems of tense symbolism, but these are often marred by outmoded or commonplace epithets. Behind them all there is clearly a vision of great power, but the execution blurs it; almost always a powerful opening is deprived of its effect by following weaknesses. Take "Fantasy," for example. It opens magnificently:

> Over all the dream-built margin, flushed with grey and
> > hoary light,
> Glint the bubble planets tossing in the dead black
> > sea of night.
> Immemorial face, how many faces look from out thy skies.
> Now with ghostly eyes of wonder rimmed around with
> > rainbow dies.

The Vaughan-like power of the opening two lines is destroyed by the two clumsy and near-comic lines that follow. The simpler poems are often more successful, but, here again, the poem rather demands the sympathy of the reader than creates it. Sympathy with and love of the man could transform the reader's resistance into assent, and for many people AE's poetry was as emotionally sensitive and as warmly human as its creator. The paintings are much the same. His swiftly executed drawings and water-colours are often radiant with light and filled with ideal presences. Frequently they portray divine beings, gods, spirits and powers of the air; almost all were painted in the open air, either on his sketching holidays in Donegal, or on his Sunday morning excursions. The composition is, however, frequently weak, and the forms are irresolutely disposed. In poetry and in painting AE remained, if we are to adopt acceptably high standards, a talented and sensitive amateur. In a letter to W. B. Yeats of 1900 he wrote about a suggested revision:

I don't agree with you about "planets". You can do as you like about excluding it from your selection — but change it I will not. . . . I am obstinate about words which are a part of my idea and which cannot be altered without altering my meaning. I do not care whether another word is more beautiful if it does not convey the idea.

This is the statement of a teacher rather than a poet.

I cannot, however, dismiss AE on such a note. He was, judged against the giant stature of Yeats, a minor figure. He was, however, enormously influential for good, both in politics and in literature. Not the least of his achievements was the way in which he continually, whether by accident or design, challenged, instructed and disturbed his lifelong friend and occasional amicable opponent, W. B. Yeats.

Aide to Immortality:
The Satirical Writings of Susan L. Mitchell

ROBIN SKELTON

USAN MITCHELL was not a major writer, but she contributed much to the Dublin literary scene, becoming a jester extraordinary in a city where mockery has never been rare. She was well-fitted for the position, for she was intimately acquainted with the Yeats family and with the AE circle, and her jokes at the expense of Irish men of letters were informed by a knowledge of character as well as of books.

She was born in 1866 in Carrick on Shannon. Her father dying in 1873, she was adopted by her three aunts, living first in Dublin and later at Birr. Later still she lived with the Yeats family in London, and just after the turn of the century she became a sub-editor and chief assistant to AE on *The Irish Homestead*. She worked with AE on *The Irish Homestead* and then upon *The Irish Statesman* until her death in 1926.

Her serious poetry is pleasing, sensitive, melancholy, and in its imagery and near-mystical tone often reminiscent of AE's verses. She achieves, however, on occasion a simplicity which is moving, and an economy of diction that qualifies sentiment with decisiveness. Her small poem "The Crib" is a good example of her simplest manner.

> Day closes in the cabin dim,
> They light the Christmas candle tall,
> For Him who is the Light of all.
> They deck the little Crib for Him
> Whose cradle is earth's swinging ball.

This is a late poem. Her earlier work tends to be more elaborate and rhetorical. Her verse, however, is always well made, and, perhaps because her vision was uncomplicated, it never suffers from those lapses of taste and sudden absurdities which mar AE's more ambitious writings. *The Living Chalice,* both in its first 1908 and in its expanded 1913 version, is a thoroughly pleasing collection of sensitive verses.

It was not, however, the sensitive and lyrical work which took Dublin by the ears; it was the tough-minded, deft, satirical work. *Aids to the Immortality of Certain Persons in Ireland: Charitably Administered by Susan L. Mitchell* was first published in 1908, and its cover bore a cartoon drawn by "Mac" in which the better known Dublin literary folk are depicted in typical poses. The books opens with the author's review of her own work in which she quotes, about herself, Yeats's statement about Lady Gregory's *Cuchulain of Muirthemne,* "This is the best book that has come out of Ireland in my time," thus hinting her delighted disapproval of those who puff their friend's books. The collection closes with a page of mock publishers' announcements. The books listed are:

No Ideas Good or Bad. By W. B. Yeats. A Sequel to *Ideas of Good and Evil.*

Supernatural Law in the Economic World. A Treatise by AE.

The White Flower of a Blameless Life. An Autobiography by George Moore.

Women of No Importance. A Series of Sermons by Edward Martyn.

In between these two splendid gestures are "George Moore — A Ballad History" of rollicking allusiveness, "The Voice of One," a conversation piece in which the voices of Moore and Yeats can be distinctly heard, "The Ballad of Shawe Taylor and Hugh Lane," "The Irish Council Bill 1907," a bitter poem to which the author added another verse in April 1910. This verse was never printed in a book, but is an excellent demonstration of her most vigorous and downright manner.

> Home Rule is far off still
>   Says the Shan Van Vocht
> And we've got an empty till
>   Says the Shan Van Vocht
> Budgets four we've had since then
> And we still are asking — When?
> God Almighty, give us men
>   Says the Shan Van Vocht

The book concludes with "Ode to the British Empire," which parodies Kipling's "Recessional." It is a small, but a gay volume. The second edition of 1913 is much larger, and ranges farther into politics as well as letters for its prey.

Susan Mitchell was a lampoonist rather than a satirist; her best jokes are both local and ephemeral, but on occasion she can wield the weapon of parody with some force. Her "Anti-Recruiting Song" concludes with two verses as direct and angry as one could hope for.

He didn't see much glory, and he didn't get much good,
In most unrighteous causes he bravely shed his blood;
The best years of his manhood he spent across the foam,
And when they'd no more use for him they took and sent him home.

He'd bullets in his right arm, he'd bullets in his leg,
He had no *grá* for working and he had no leave to beg;
The peelers had an eye on him, twice he's been in quod,
Now he's in Carrick Workhouse — Glory be to God!

This contrasts in both tone and intention with the gaiety of "George Moore Becomes High Sheriff of Mayo."

We've some bright boys in Ireland, we've got our W. B.;
Faith, Martyn, we have got yourself, we've also got AE.
When Plunkett isn't writing books, he is our pride and joy,
And though MacDonnell may be glum he's not a bad wee boy.
We love our own O'Grady, we love our Douglas Hyde,
And from this pleasant company there's one we won't divide;
'Tis yourself, Moore, you're the playboy, but you're faithful to the green
Though you're hangin' men and women down in Ballaghadereen.
    Down in Ballaghadereen, down in Ballaghadereen,
    Sending souls to instant glory down in Ballaghadereen.

The dexterity of Miss Mitchell's comic talent shows itself even more strikingly in *Leaguers and Peelers; or the Apple Cart*, a two-act musical farce, which was published in *The Irish Review* for October 1911, but has never been reprinted. This is Gilbertian in plot and in structure, owing a good deal to *Trial by Jury*. In it an apple-vendor is brought into court for having disobeyed the law and followed the counsel of the Gaelic League in painting the owner's name on his cart in Gaelic. He is about to be sentenced when it is discovered that the cart belongs in fact to the judge's daughter. The judge is about to proceed stoically to sentence when it is pointed out that as his daughter is legally an infant, he is the guilty party.

This situation is resolved by the nobility of the Hero who confesses to owning the cart, and who is willing to go to jail if he can marry the judge's daughter at the expiration of his sentence.

There are several splendid moments in this playlet, which makes ironic use of the tunes of both Irish and English patriotic songs. Thus the R.I.C. sergeant sings, to the tune of *Rule Britannia*:

> When Dublin first at our command
> Arose up in the emerald pale,
> Upon this law we took our stand
> That Dublin Castle should prevail.
> Rule R.I.C. men, rule, rule these Irish knaves,
> Do your duty and they ever will be slaves.

Later in the play the foreman of the jury sings, to the tune of *God Save the King*,

> No Connaught Rangers we
> To bow the traitorous knee
> Merely for gain;
> What are we packed for here
> If not to close the ear
> To every fact we hear?
> Down with Sinn Fein.
>
> My lord, we are agreed
> That Irish is his creed
> Well may he swing.
> Who speaks a foreign tongue
> Good Irishmen among,
> Oh, let his neck be wrung.
> God save the King.

While we, in the 1960's, may feel such satire to be merely amusing, to many people in the Dublin of 1911 it must have seemed an outrage. The parody of the National Anthem would have seemed close to blasphemy, and Susan Mitchell did not avoid a similar accusation from Irish Nationalists, for her parodies of revered Irish songs are just as cruel, and her portrayal of the Irish is as comic as that of the British. *Leaguers and Peelers* may not be of the stature of Swift, but it is written with a similar courage, and if it is, on the whole, cheeky and smart rather than subtly witty, it is the more efficient as a social weapon. Urbanity and subtlety are characteristic of only a few satirists. We have our Peter Pindars and John Skeltons as well as our Popes and Swifts. It is clear that Susan Mitchell intended her lampoons to act with maximum efficiency in a particular situation, and did not expect them to interest posterity. As a consequence her work is now largely forgotten, but, when rediscovered, brings back the feel of her times more strongly than the work of many of her more distinguished contemporaries.

Miss Mitchell was not only a wit herself, but also a source of wit in others. She marshalled many talents together in her anthology *Secret Springs of Dublin Song* (1918). Here, protected by anonymity, are parodies by Oliver Gogarty, AE, R. L. Tyrrell, Seumas O'Sullivan, Lord Dunsany, G. M. Redding, and "Michael Scott." Many of these squibs are hurled at no particular target, but simply thrown for the hell of it. Some are, however, dropped neatly at the heels of the unsuspecting Moore, and the meditating Yeats. George Moore aroused amusement in Dublin much more frequently than W. B. Yeats, however. Moreover, he also aroused anger. Susan Mitchell's one prose work was called *George Moore*. It was published in 1916 in Maunsel & Co's sober *Irishmen of Today* series. An idiosyncratic, witty, excoriating analysis of all Moore's works and foibles, it exposes, with relentless lucidity, his literary sophistication, his ruthless exploitation of friendship, his pretentiousness, his innocence, and his malice. It also presents us with an acutely sensitive portrait of the world of Irish Letters, and lays bare, quite as amusingly as Moore's own *Hail and Farewell*, the confusions and absurdities of the Irish Renaissance. The book is filled with comments of Shavian pungency and concision. We are told that "'Impressions and Opinions' are very much Moore weighted with all his sincere and unreasonable personality." Moore, the self-confessed hedonist and womanizer, with the amoral man-of-the-world outlook, is neatly revealed as a poseur.

Perhaps the Latin races can sin gracefully, the Irish cannot. And Mr. Moore's sinning? He cannot escape from his birthright, Lough Cara set her seal on him, "islands lying in misted water, faint as dreams." As Silenus he is a poor thing. His leer is so much "make-up", and it is the more revolting because he is naturally sincere. He has no genius for the gross. It is a creed with him not to be ashamed, but here I catch him tripping for he is ashamed of being ashamed.

Miss Mitchell makes very merry over Moore's conversion from a previously unstated Catholicism to an unconvincing Protestantism. She detects in him a zeal to appear zealous in a cause, and an ardour for the role of ardent believer in any available faith. Like many

Irishmen, he found himself drawn towards "Movements," but (also like many Irishmen) once involved in them he found his disputatious intelligence and thirst for drama only satisfied by comedy or rebellion.

Moore is regarded as being typically Irish also in his love of a public gesture, and in his natural talent for passionate buffoonery. His conversion to Protestantism, we are told, "was conceived in the mood of light comedy." The prologue occurred when he

wrote to the papers and announced his intended reception into the Protestant communion as a protest against the decoration of Maynooth with King Edward's racing colours. The chorus in Dublin, in a mood rightly related to the mind of the protagonist, commented gaily upon the spiritual state of one whose protest against a King took the surprising form of adopting the religion of that King against whom he protested . . . it was suggested by the chorus that Mr. Moore was trying to kill two birds with the one stone. He hoped to destroy one religion by explaining his reasons for leaving it and another by explaining his reasons for joining it.

This is hardly profound criticism, but it is distinctly illuminating of the religio-political confusions of Dublin in the Edwardian period. Moore, indeed, served Ireland well, for he parodied in his own sincerities those which also afflicted his contemporaries, and exposed, all unknowing, the bland absurdities of much of the intellectual ferment of the Ireland of his time. Miss Mitchell is fully aware of this and her book is as much a study of Dublin as of Moore, whose arrival in that city is presented with trenchant wit:

We in Ireland are gifted beyond most peoples with a talent for acting, and in Dublin especially, while scorning culture, which indeed we have not got, we are possessed of a most futile and diverting cleverness. Mr. Moore's entrance on the stage in Dublin was marred by an audience having as much dramatic talent as he himself, and each so full of admiration for his own exercise of it that he had only a fierce criticism and no appreciation to give a rival player. We Irish are very much aware of our art as actors, we seldom lose ourselves in it, but Mr. Moore's dramatic concern with himself is so much interwoven in his nature that he can only be really himself in the various poses he assumes. He is absolutely sincere in each, and his Gaelic pose had for him a momentous importance that provoked the merriment of Dublin, where no one really believes in anything and where nothing matters at all save as providing a subject for conversation, and where if by chance a noble aspiration arises in some heart, the effect of its utterance is exploded in the percussion of a drawing-room jest.

The candour of Moore's comments upon Ireland in *The Untilled Field, Parnell and his Island,* and *Hail and Farewell,* is no more extreme than that of Susan Mitchell, whose acerbity, however, is more frequently qualified by affection and dictated by principle. Nevertheless, her own version of the collaboration between Yeats and Moore in the writing of *Diarmuid and Grania* is just as funny as anything in Moore:

What an alliance! Literary Dublin sought in the play with intense interest for the footmarks of the writers and when it found God Angus described as "A ragged old man wandering along the mountains prodding a boar," it cried "Lo Yeats" and behold it was Moore, and coming on the description of Conan scratching his head and complaining of lice it said "Lo Moore" and behold it was Yeats. Yeats had come to the collaboration determined to be substantial and material like Moore. Moore had resolved to rise to the heaven of the picturesque and beautiful to meet Yeats. They had passed each other on the journey.

In spite of its rich comedy this book is more than "a collection of jokes against Moore, disguised as a biography" as Alan Denson has described it. It is a plea for freedom of discussion and for self-criticism by the Irish intellectuals. Moore's candours, though attacked for their malice, are praised for their courage. His naturalistic Zola-esque novels are admired for their insight into human necessities. Even his later religious stories, though regarded as perverse and wilful, are complimented on their attempt to re-examine Christian belief and story. Moreover, throughout this book there are many occasions on which the author dares herself to discuss religious problems in Ireland, and to examine critically all those articles of faith held so passionately by the leaders of the Irish Renaissance. In the last pages of the book, the whole situation of Irish culture is briefly examined and the conclusions stated there are as courageous —for this is 1916—as anything ever written by Moore. A few sentences from different parts of this last chapter make the point.

There has always been a certain sterility in Irish ideals; we reach for a star or we scramble lower down for a terrestial bauble. In all their aims high and low Irishmen have a tragic alienation from life. They became peasant proprietors more because their fields were symbolic of the four fields of Kathleen ni Houlihan than because they might be sown and harvested and produce the food of man. They value their municipal privileges more for the sense of power these confer than from any serious intention of using these powers for simple human needs and comforts. Their political power has been treated as a game as diverting as musical chairs at a children's party, sitting, acting and voting to meaningless party tunes played at hazard and stopped at hazard. If this were not so, would we have our land in grass, our towns and cities in slums, and our country without a human hope to break down the barriers that our several quests have imposed upon us?

A little later, in a passage written after the Easter Rebellion, we read:

I often wonder what effect upon our normal constitution here in Ireland had all the movement of that febrile time that we call the Irish literary revival. Has any intellectuality at all emerged out of it, any public opinion, any essentially nationalistic flavour in our life?... our public life in Ireland is as barren of thinking as it ever was and there is no true cohesion amongst us, though there are many enforced unities.

This view of the situation contrasts sharply with the blurred optimism and "Nationalist" enthusiasm of other writers of this time. Miss Mitchell was unable to find heroic majesty in muddle, or detect self-abnegatory mysticism in political ineptitude. In spite of her own firmly held and gracefully expressed religious faith, she was not one to suspect portent and miracle in every strange event; the gods that visited AE and sent symbols to Yeats were more inspired but less shrewd-eyed than hers. When she died in 1926, Ireland lost one of its most valuable citizens: a jester of strong moral principles and equally strong affections, who had the courage to speak her mind and the wisdom to make it worth the speaking.

"A Share in the Dignity of the World": J. M. Synge's Aesthetic Theory

"Every life is a symphony and the translation of this sequence into music and from music again, for those who are not musicians into literature or painting or sculpture, is the real effort of the artist."

(From an unpublished play)

THE ACHIEVEMENT of John Millington Synge the playwright is by now assured in the canons of literary criticism; recent revelations concerning his development as a poet have further entangled him in the web of Yeatsian dialectic; however, the extent to which Synge's critical attitudes also disturbed Yeats has not received much notice. Indeed apart from recollections by Yeats himself and Synge's own prefaces, little concerning his æsthetic theories has been available, but evidence from his unpublished notebooks and diaries indicates that like his older colleague Synge began very early to establish his artistic creed.

"Real art is always a suggestion," Synge commented in an early diary; "an intangible emotion lurks behind the things that we produce as life lurks within the body."[1] Unlike his fellow dramatists, Synge rarely explored or elaborated a philosophical concept in his plays and poetry; rather, as can be observed in his essays and especially in *The Aran Islands,* he allowed the world outside to play on his feelings and emotions as a violinist handles his violin, reflecting and intensifying the mood and atmosphere to which he is attuned. All his work was subjective, coming out of moods in his

---

[1] Unless otherwise stated, all notebook material is in the possession of the literary executors of the Synge Estate, with whose kind permission it is produced.

207

own life, he once confessed to Padraic Colum. He preferred to
look on life "as only a play, a dream, scened for my single delecta-
tion."² It was this interested passivity which puzzled Yeats. "I really
don't think him selfish or egotistical," he explained in a letter to
Lady Gregory about 1906, "but he is so absorbed in his own vision
of the world that he cares for nothing else."³ Whereas Yeats eagerly
and publicly sought "correspondences" for his own work and frequently found them in unlikely places, Synge published few references to other writers, and then mostly with disdain. In fact so
anxious was he to assert his independence, he might on occasion
have been guilty of snubbing a fellow traveller. "For him," Yeats
wrote in his autobiography, "nothing existed but his thought. . . . I
do not think he disliked other writers — they did not exist. . . . In
the arts he knew no language but his own." Not even Yeats realized
that Synge's rare critical comment, startling in its incisiveness and
bewildering in its implications, was the product not of sudden insight but of much thought and almost encyclopedic study.

The story of Yeats's first encounter with Synge reads like a fairy
tale and has often been turned into one. The year was 1896. Yeats
was on revolutionary activities in Paris with Maud Gonne; he had
just returned from a tour of western Ireland with Arthur Symons,
where he had stayed with Edward Martyn at Tulira, met Lady
Gregory at Coole, and visited the Aran Islands. Synge, having renounced music for literature, had moved to Paris from Germany;
he had just returned from a visit to Italy, and was studying Petrarch
and French literature at the Sorbonne, reading Thomas à Kempis
and works on socialism, and dabbling in the occult with his comrade
Stephen MacKenna. Lady Gregory had acted as a catalyst to Yeats;
now Yeats in turn affected Synge. As Yeats confesses, he no more
recognized Synge's genius than he had Lady Gregory's, and at first
encouraged him in his efforts to play "second fiddle" to Arthur
Symons as a critic of French literature. But Yeats's imagination was
full of "those grey islands where men must reap with knives because
of the stones," and soon he urged Synge to seek in Aran "a life that
had never been expressed in literature, instead of a life where all
had been expressed." Two years were to pass before Synge visited

2 See also John Masefield, *John M. Synge: A Few Personal Recollections*
(Cuala Press, 1915).
3 Letter to Lady Gregory, 1906, quoted by Greene and Stephens, *J. M. Synge*
(New York: Macmillan, 1959), 232.

Aran for the first time; the rest is Abbey history. Here was the man the founders of the Irish Literary Theatre sought; through them, Synge found the expression he had been seeking. But although his arrival was to alter the course of the movement and profoundly influence Yeats's own ideas and style, ideals and much of the practice had already been established. Synge's own basic tenets too had already been formed. "Many of the older poets, such as Villon and Herrick and Burns, used the whole of their personal life as their material," he was to write in his last preface, and in this remark we find the key to his own work. The foundation to his art was laid long before the encounter of 1896.

"All emotions have neither end nor beginning, they are part of a long sequence of impulse and effect. The only relative unity in art is that of a whole man's life time." Synge's childhood was in many ways similar to Yeats's. Neither had regular schooling, Yeats because of the family's frequent removals, Synge because of ill-health. Both early had a scientific curiosity in nature and wandered at large collecting and observing. But Synge was more systematic in his naturalist studies: he was a founder-member of the Dublin Naturalists' Field Club; with his cousin Florence Ross he made an extensive collection of butterflies, moths and beetles; and he read Darwin. Besides creating an even greater gulf between him and his evangelical family, this keen interest in nature remained with Synge the rest of his life. His notebooks are full of careful observations made on his walks and cycling trips through the Wicklow mountains, and he transferred this delight in the details of the natural world to his writings:

I believe that the art we feel and recall among the greater moods of nature is the only art which is begotten of a mood in harmony with nature, of a mood then that is healthy and worthy of a place in the temple of the things that we admire. The thin and sickly artist fears nature. A life spent in the making of paste jewels seems wasted among the flowers of the country; and the poor player of dances is distressed by the music of the spheres. . . . The art we call decadent, or at least the more unholy portion of the art we call decadent, is not the fruit of disordered minds but rather the life of a people far from the real fount of all artistic inspiration.

At the age of eighteen Yeats had entered the Metropolitan School of Art; at the same age Synge enrolled in the Royal Irish Academy of Music and entered Trinity College, Dublin. His college studies were desultory, and apart from a natural gift for languages which earned him prizes in Hebrew and Irish, he made little impression on that bastion of Anglo-Irish ascendancy. For the rest of his life, however, music remained an important influence; he became proficient in the violin, flute, and piano, studied musical theory and counterpoint, and joined a student orchestra which, he states in an autobiographical sketch, gave him "extraordinary pleasure":

The collective excitement produced in each player by a band working together with one will and ideal is unlike any other emotion. To be lost in a living tempest that wails round one with an always beautiful passion, to lose one's identity yet be greater than before, to build cathedrals with the purple waves of a hurricane, to play with mountains in the mist, yet be alive, human, are some of the sentiments I have experienced. And the Adagios! The suave balm that draws out intricate charities from places not open to the world.

To realise that all emotions depend upon and answer the abstract of ideal form, and that humanity is God, is but the first step towards a full comprehension of this art.

This inter-relationship between music and natural beauty is also reflected in Synge's work. During his first visit to Aran in 1898 he commented in his diary,

When the sun is covered six distinct and beautiful shades still blend in one another — the limestone, the sea leaden at my feet and with a steel tinge far away, the mountains on the coast of Clare and then the clouds transparent and opaque...no pictorial wording can express these movements peculiar to our humid insularity unknown in the more radiant South — today three delicious movements differ only from a symphony in that the finale is always the opening of a new design.

There are these — the dim adagio in six tones, the presto of the quick colourless rain followed by a glorious allegro con brio where sun and clouds unite in brilliant joy.

His first play, *Riders to the Sea,* became a lyric in tragic mood, its rhythm the steady relentless beating of waves against a rock gradually increasing in strength to the accompaniment of the low moan of the *caoine.* Against this eternal rhythm of nature the characters move in dream-like measures towards their inevitable destiny. In his last play, *Deirdre of the Sorrows,* the mingling of two worlds —of ancient prophecy and of mortal longings—is set against a verdant tapestry of "the life that is richest," until the ridge of the

world again narrows to the space of a new-made grave and dream
and myth are one.

A human being finds a resting place only where he is in harmony with
his surroundings, and is reminded that his soul and the soul of nature
are of the same organization.[4]

In a letter to his German translator, Dr. Max Meyerfeld, Synge
explained his defection from music as a career: "I saw that the
Germans were so much more innately gifted with the musical faculties than I was that I decided to give up music and take to literature
instead."[5] A further and more likely reason was his extreme nervous-
ness in public. The playwright is twice removed from the process of
self-revelation, by means of his dramatization and through the
actors; the performer has no place to hide. But like his passion for
nature, Synge's love for music remained constant throughout his
life. A keen ear contributed to his skill in languages and appreciation
of the sounds of nature (Mary and Martin Doul tell the season and
hour by the noises about them); a highly-developed sensitivity aided
the evocation of scenes and situations (the Tramp sings sweetly of
the joys of the world beyond shadowy glens); perhaps most important of all, assiduous training in harmony and counterpoint encouraged the rhythmical balance and formal intricate structure of his
plays (scenarios for his three-act plays indicate his conscious effort
to build up "currents" of tension through crescendos and contrasts,
juxtaposing tragedy and comedy through exposition and poetry).
His notebook for 1901 includes the following comment:

Contrast gives wonder of life. It is found in
(a) Misery of earth consciously set against Heaven, see pious writing.
    Happy other World, Hearn, etc.
(b) Wonder of world set against the misery of age and death (see
    Villon).

Like Yeats then, Synge retained a lively interest in the various
literary movements of his time; his notebooks abound in comments
on every aspect of literature. As could be expected, he was especially
concerned with the problem of style, that "portrait of one's own
personality, of the colour of one's own thought." A scrap of paper
preserved among his manuscripts is typical of his method of evalua-
tion:

4 Early notebook, about 1896-98.
5 September 1, 1905. The original is in the National Library of Ireland.

Scott — best in pieces with dialogue where there is style formed of
    living language
O. W. (Wilde) — style formed of brilliant language spoken in good
    London circles
Pater — style formed of written language
Wordsworth — peasant language without style
Borrow —   "   "
Mallarmé — Pater
Huysmans —   "
Anatole France — O.W.
Shakespeare — makes a style from language of each of his characters
Molière — ditto
Ibsen — Wordsworth
Scott — makes his characters speak with a written language

His public denunciation of Zola, Ibsen (whom he first read in
German), and "the Germans" for "dealing with the reality of life
in joyless and pallid words" is elaborated in his notebooks to include
Villiers, Mallarmé and Huysmans, although Huysmans' "curiously
brutal slang" is given a passing nod. The trio Burns, Villon and
Herrick, who gained approval for using "the whole of their personal
life as their material" is extended to include Wordsworth who is
"more at one with nature" than Coleridge or Shelley. ("In Shelley's
poetry there is the *trifling* of a soul.") Maeterlinck's work receives
praise for signs of "a virile — an almost transcendental common
sense of the greatest interest and importance"; Anatole France is
also given tentative praise for his "exquisite prose style" in the treatment of "a plain local mood"; Pierre Loti might have certain
commendable qualities, but is ignorant of the peasants he chooses
as copy. George Borrow, Rabelais, Le Sage, Balzac and Standish
O'Grady, however, are read and enjoyed. And again he uses nature
as a touchstone:

In the old poets — as Ronsard — who give the delicate lyric one feels
their delight in their own art first of all and then beyond that a direct
delight — not a thinking or a moralizing about it — in the objects of
nature with [which] they unwittingly identify themselves.

He too was prone to cyclical theories:

It may seem for a moment that the essential movement of thought from
Voltaire to Anatole France is unimportant, that two centuries have
achieved little and negation has no fertility or change of outlook. Such
is not the case. The change between these two writers is a clearly

marked if small one and humanity cannot complain if two centuries have led one step upon this way. Voltaire destroyed. Anatole France has cleared the debris of destruction and the soil is again virgin and smooth watered though barren as yet and warmed only by an occasional wintry sun.

Nor does he ignore the interests of his countrymen in this roll call of the arts. The draft of an article on Irish folklore compares the current interest in the peasantry to a revival of popular folk music, the "Volklied"; an essay on Mallarmé compares the attitudes of Maeterlinck, Yeats and Lionel Johnson. It was as a cosmopolitan that Synge returned to Ireland, then, and throughout his life he considered himself a European writer. Frequently in his essays he refers to Ireland as "the most westerly point of Europe." It is singularly appropriate that his were the first plays of the Irish literary movement to be produced in other languages.

It is apparent, therefore, that long before Synge met Yeats and avowed allegiance to the Irish cause he was actively concerned with the development of his own æsthetic theory and that here also he called no man master. In fact, although his studious and questioning temperament led him to greater probings and analysis, his independence of mind forced him to approach any attempt at synthesis with caution:

All theorizing is bad for the artist, because it makes him live in the intelligence instead of in the half-subconscious faculties by which all creation is performed.

Moreover,

Young and therefore living truths, views, what you will, have a certain diffidence or tenderness that makes it impossible to state them without the accompanying emotional or imaginative life in which they naturally arise.

However, "in applying, for ourselves, to our own life, what is thought in different ways by many, we are likely to hit on matters of some value."[6] It is with this warning in mind, then, that we must approach any examination of the general theory underlying Synge's critical annotations and creative works. "Art is so essentially synthetic that if it can be classed as idealistic or realistic it is nearly always inferior."

[6] These three extracts are taken from his notebooks as quoted in the 1932 edition of the plays.

Three distinctions must be sought in a work of art, Synge felt: "it must have been possible to only one man at one period and in one place."

Although only two suffice to give us art of the first importance such as much of the Gothic architecture, folk songs and airs, Dutch painting, etc., the great artist [such] as Rembrandt or Shakespeare adds his personal distinction to a great distinction of time and place.

It is the combination of personal originality with "the characteristic of a particular time and locality and the life that is in it," that gives work its uniqueness or artistic value. Hence national art, which interprets the whole intellectual mood of the time, is "broad, serious, provisionally permanent" in contrast to the individual mood which is "often trivial, perverse, fleeting." This universality can be achieved by allowing our true emotions free flow rather than emphasizing instead the historical or naturalist details which either depend on artificial form with no sense of the immediate, or slice the immediate life so thin that the breadth and permanence disappear.

The emotions which pass through us have neither end nor beginning, are a part of eternal sensations, and it is this almost cosmic element in the person which gives all personal art a share in the dignity of the world.

Biography, even autobiography, cannot give this revelation, for the deeds of a man's lifetime are impersonal and concrete, might have been done by anyone, while art is the expression of the abstract beauty of the person.[7]

Beauty equals perfection; "a thing perfect of its kind gives the sentiment of Beauty." But although Beauty is an attribute of art, it is not the end or essence of it any more than goodness is of life. Beauty, like goodness, is only a quality, and if sought instead of the essence of art itself, will lead only to the sickliness of the extreme æsthetes, in the same way that the search for health as the object of life leads to morbidity. "A dramatist has to express his subject and to find as much beauty as is compatible with that, if he does more he is an æsthete," he once remarked to Yeats. The artist should therefore seek intensity and richness in his art, which will result in natural perfection or universality and lead to health or sanity, since all insanities in art, as in life, "are due to a one-sided excitement." "Sanity in sane conditions leads to beauty (art), good-

7 From his unpublished play.

ness (morals), health (bodily condition)." It is this wholesomeness which gives art its *human* value as opposed to the uniqueness which gives a work its *artistic* value. Only by combining the two can art remain permanent and universal. The criterion for the arts is therefore to be found in "testing art by its compatibility with the outside world and the peasants or people who live near it." And it is this healthy balance between the personal contribution of the individual and the richness drawn from the universal qualities which creates the synthesis of "stoicism, asceticism, and ecstasy" Synge felt so essential to great art.[8]

Nietzsche fails by seeking the sub-human and thus yoking life and joy to an hypothesis in time.

A truer morality would find everything in the instant. — Compare perhaps Pater noting that his views were city views rather than cosmic.—

In his theory as in his drama Synge was striking out on his own, aiming at a union of the realist qualities of naturalism with the symbolism of æstheticism:

The rhythm of verse is to the rhythm of prose as the harmony of Bach is to the harmony of Brahms. In the rhythm of prose you have a strict art — once you have a style — which is perfectly subconscious, that is the hope of it.

Verse is not only conscious but *self-conscious.*

And elsewhere from his notebooks:

What is highest in poetry is always reached where the dreamer is leaning out to reality, or where the man of real life is lifted out of it, and in all the poets the greatest have both these elements, that is they are supremely engrossed with life, and yet with the wildness of their fancy they are always passing out of what is simple and plain.

(Hence Yeats's poetry is acceptable, but AE's is not.)

The first step in attaining this union is, as he points out in his preface to *The Tinker's Wedding*, to discard all ideas of didacticism. "We should not go to the theatre as we go to a chemist's or a dramshop. . . . The drama, like the symphony, does not teach or prove anything." In a letter to Stephen MacKenna he objected, "The stage . . . would not regenerate — or for that matter unregenerate —

<hr/>

[8] Recalled by Yeats in *Autobiographies* (London: Macmillan, 1955), 346 & 509. Yeats then applied the same "trinity of spiritual values" to Lionel Johnson in *A Treasury of Irish Verse* (1900).

Ireland any more than the symphonies of Beethoven can regenerate Germany." The theatre should, however, reveal the artist's vision, that expression of "ordinary life" as the playwright sees it, "the reality, which is the root of all poetry." The artist's duty is to record, not to judge or expound. (In following the Tramp, Nora is obeying a higher moral law, the call of her own nature; in worshipping the Playboy, Pegeen too is answering the gypsy's call.)

If the artist is to read life truly and strike the balance necessary to wholesome art, he must be occupied with "the whole of life," "for although exalted verse is the highest," he wrote to Yeats, "it cannot keep its power unless there is more essentially vital verse at the side of it." Only then can he provide "the nourishment, not very easy to define, on which our imaginations live." And that nourishment, the power of exalted verse, is found in the reality and zest of life, the "strong things of life," rather than in the "seedy problems" of modern plays.[9] "On the stage one must have reality, and one must have joy," he was to write in his preface to *The Playboy of the Western World*; it is when we combine the ecstasy of a life superb and wild with the stoicism and simplicity of the realities of life that we achieve art that is lasting. Art in this sense escapes both the extremes of æstheticism and naturalism; rather, it brings the enlargement of life detached from the ordinary problems of every day and yet with "strong roots among the clay and worms." "He loves all that has edge, all that is salt in the mouth," Yeats wrote in "J. M. Synge and the Ireland of his Time."

Furthermore, by seeking to express the whole of life, the artist will achieve not only the universality he requires, but the uniqueness as well:

The profound is always inimitable. . . . Profound insight finds the inner and essential mood of the things it treats of and hence gives us art that is absolutely distinct and inimitable, — a thing never done before and never to be done again.

But in choosing a life that is "superb and wild" one cannot expect to find only sweetness and light. When men preserve "their poetic feeling for ordinary life" and use "the whole of their personal life as their material," they preserve the bitter and the harsh as well as the sweet and the gentle; very often it is the bitter that makes the sweet. "It may almost be said that before verse can be human again

9 Prefaces to *The Tinker's Wedding* and *Poems and Translations*.

it must learn to be brutal," Synge wrote in his preface to *Poems and Translations*. And this may require the presentation of wildness as well as strength, evil as well as good, tragedy as well as humour.

We all of us delight in strength, whether we see it in other things, or feel it in ourselves. There is joy in the mad rush of a mountain torrent, in the flying foam of waves, and in the storm itself when it comes rushing to us through the terrified pine trees,

he wrote in his diary in 1888. Almost twenty years later he commented concerning *The Playboy,* "the wildness, and if you will, vices of the Irish peasantry are due, like their extraordinary good points of all kinds, to the *richness* of their nature—a thing that is priceless beyond words." ("I notice that when anybody here writes a play it always works out, whatever the ideas of the writer, into a cry for a more abundant and a more intense life," Yeats wrote to Charles Ricketts in 1904.)

Similarly, the artist must accept life in the mixture in which it comes:

The man who feels most exquisitely the joy of contact with what is perfect in nature and art is the man who from the width and power of his thought hides the greatest number of satanic or barbarous sympathies.

Squeamishness was not only dishonest, but a disease: "Ireland will gain if Irish writers deal manfully, directly and decently with the entire reality of life. I think the law-maker and the law-breaker are both needful in society." "No drama can grow out of anything other than the fundamental realities of life," whether these realities are innocent or otherwise:

There are beautiful and interesting plants which are deadly, and others that are kindly. It is absurd to say a flower is not beautiful nor admire its beauty because it is deadly, but it is absurd also to deny its deadliness.

Consequently the artist may find himself outside the sympathies of both orthodox religion and morality. In 1904 after reading Anatole France he commented in his diary,

In reading French literature one is tempted to wonder what nature literature is likely to take in the perhaps distant years when the science of men like Huxley and Haeckel . . . will have taken a place definitely in the intelligence of writers and readers. . . . It makes one ask . . . what in the new literature I have dreamed of will be the conception of love for on it will depend a good deal of the fortunes of humanity. . . . What form in this case would the new representatives . . . of St. Theresa and St. Thomas à Kempis take with an outlook on the world like Haeckel's? In what way will they create for us a romance of reality. . . . Most important of all — How will they rescue love — the word is not too strong — from the French?

It was this "romance of reality" Synge sought in his own work, and to achieve it he was willing to reach not only towards the zest and joy of life, but also among the clay and worms. Like Yeats and Lady Gregory, he was willing to forego popularity and friendship for the sake of his belief, and before he died he had foresaken both family and friends. Like Lady Gregory and Yeats also, he would defend the *Samhain* principles even against his fellow-directors. "I am prepared to stake everything on a creative movement even if we all go to the work-house at the end of four years," he wrote in a memorandum to Yeats over a disagreement in policy.

Art which deals with the whole of life will by its very nature encompass both tragedy and comedy, for "it is only the catastrophes of life that give substance and power to the tragedy and humour which are the true poles of art." Humour, he felt, was "the essentially poetic quality" in vital verse. Moreover, humour is the true test of morals, both in art and in life, "as no vice is humorous."

Bestial is, in its very essence, opposed to the idea of humour. All decadence is opposed to true humour. The heartiness of real and frank laughter is a sign that cannot be mistaken that what we laugh at is not out of harmony with that instinct of sanity that we call by so many names.

But the sorrows and bitterness of life will in turn leave their mark on humour, and again he points to "the frank philosophy of large classes among the French, who are kept healthy by an ironical attitude towards their own distress." Comedy, like tragedy, will inevitably contain brutality as well as beauty, and as in life itself, the mingling of the two will provide the richness which nourishes.

But where can one find in this modern world the "strong things of life" that will make the drama the powerful nourishment it once was? Synge's wanderings among the hills of Wicklow, the wild wastes of Connemara, and the bare grey islands of Aran provided the answer — the peasant folk of Ireland, a people in whom there still remained "a popular imagination that is fiery, and magnificent, and tender." "For the present the only possible beauty in drama is peasant drama," Synge wrote in his notebook. "For the future we must await the making of life beautiful again before we can have beautiful drama. You cannot gather grapes of chimney pots." But in the lives of these people, in whom "the spring-time of the local life has [not] been forgotten," there was ample material for his pen.

With these tenets in mind, then, Synge wrote his plays, seeking not the didactic interests of a particular moment in history, but the rich joy of a life "superb and wild," keyed much higher than the "overcrowded wretchedness" of the towns. Nor was his joy confined to comedy, his seriousness to tragedy, his reality to plays of modern life. Drama, whether tragedy or comedy, had to answer first as the expression of his sympathy and enthusiasm for life. His comment concerning *The Playboy* applies to all of his work:

I wrote [it] directly, as a piece of life, without thinking, or caring to think, whether it was a comedy, tragedy, or extravaganza, or whether it would be held to have, or not to have, a purpose.

Drama must first provide that "nourishment, not very easy to define, on which our imaginations live." What else it does depends upon the personal vision of the dramatist.

"Unarrangeable Reality":
The Paintings and Writings of Jack B. Yeats

ROBIN SKELTON

But all wild sights appealed to Synge, he did not care whether they were typical of anything else or had any symbolical meaning at all. If he had lived in the days of piracy he would have been the fiddler in a pirate-schooner, him they called 'the music —' 'The music' looked on at everything with dancing eyes but drew no sword, and when the schooner was taken and the pirates hung at Cape Corso Castle or the Island of Saint Christopher's, 'the music' was spared because he *was* 'the music'.

THIS COMMENT UPON SYNGE by Jack B. Yeats reveals as much about its author as its subject and hints at attitudes which persisted throughout his paintings, writings, and life.

Jack B. Yeats was born on August 29, 1871, and was the youngest of John Butler Yeats's children, W. B. Yeats being the eldest. He spent the greater part of his childhood in Sligo, where he early showed his fascination with both drawing and the theatre, writing and illustrating childish plays and acting them out in a toy theatre. He studied art at Westminster School, and before the turn of the century, first in London then in Manchester and later at Dartmouth, he had established himself as a cartoonist and illustrator. His work of this early period is bold in line and dramatic in concept; the drama often approaching in mood the melodramatic directness of folk tale, or of those pirate stories he delighted in reading.

His childhood experiences and enthusiasms clearly coloured his imagination. He showed a love of the fantastic and of the savage innocence of Irish peasantry. His delight in dreams of far lands and strange countries was one he shared with the poet John Masefield, who contributed verses to his early plays for children, and who clearly intensified his interest in things piratical. Indeed, in old age, when told that there was a rumour that, as a youth, he had fallen out with his brother and gone to sea for seven years, after commenting, "I was never at sea in my life," he explained the influence of the sea upon his work with the single name "John Masefield."

The rumour, however false, indicates the apparent lack of sympathy between the two brothers, but it must be remembered that the younger continually contributed to the Cuala Press broadsides of which W. B. was an editor. Both were admirers and friends of J. M. Synge (though the younger was more his intimate). Each has recorded his admiration of the work of the other. And both were interested in folk anecdotes, ballads and the supernatural, though they expressed their interest in different ways.

It was in the first decade of the century that Jack Yeats began to show his paces most clearly. In 1902, with Pamela Colman Smith, he produced a series of broadsheets, each of which contained verse and two illustrations, one at least of which was hand-coloured. This clearly emanated from a feeling which he shared with his brother that art could be "taken to the people" in this way, and reflected the strong influence of the thought of William Morris upon the Yeats family generally. These broadsides led W. B. Yeats and his sisters to issue a similar monthly series from the Cuala Press from 1908 to 1915, and later series in 1935 and 1937. W. B. Yeats contributed poems to the broadsheets, just as Jack Yeats's drawings appeared in the broadsides. Moreover, it was these broadsides which led W. B. Yeats, especially in his later years, to develop his earlier ballad style, and to write songs for which music was often specially composed, with the wish expressed in *On the Boiler* to become himself part of a folk tradition.

In 1905, Jack Yeats first began to paint consistently in oils. His work in this medium between 1905 and 1924 still made use of the heavy outlines he had used as a book illustrator, and he took his subject matter frequently from his memories of the peasants, beggars, and tinkers of Western Ireland whom he knew so well, and whom he also portrayed in his illustrations to Synge's *Aran Islands* and to the articles on "The Congested Districts" which Synge wrote for the *Manchester Guardian*. He also, however, made great use of the circus, which he used to visit with Masefield. These circus and peasant paintings have a solidity reminiscent of Millet; the paint is applied with heavy insistence, and the colour is much more drab

than in his later work. His work of this period has been associated
with that of the London group, and, in its strange combination of
anecdotal realism and symbolic distortion has been compared with
that of Sickert. Even though realism seems a part of his work at
this time, he never painted from actuality, but always from memory;
the distortions are less the product of a fallible memory than of an
intention to transform, dignify, dramatize, and elucidate the actual,
and cast over it "a colouring of the imagination." Moreover, in
even the most serious or pathetic of these works there is a quirkish-
ness, a flicker of humour, a fascination with a delight in oddity.
This is particularly evident in his picture book, *Life in the West of
Ireland*, which was published in 1912.

This delight shows itself even more openly in his writings of this
period. Jack Yeats was the author of a number of plays for children
with hand-coloured illustrations. Their titles are indicative of their
contents: *James Flaunty: or, The Terror of the Western Seas*; *The
Scourge of the Gulph*; *The Treasure of the Garden: A Play in the
old manner*. This last is advertised by Elkin Matthews, who published a whole series of *Jack Yeats's Chap Books* with the note:
"Stages with Prosceniums designed by the Author, Footlights, Slides,
and scenes, can be had, price 5s net each." Apart from these plays
he wrote a story, *The Bosun and the Bob-Tailed Comet*, and an
account of the toy boats made by himself and his friends as children,
with the title *A Little Fleet*.

Setting aside the exuberant drawings with their superbly rhythmical use of line, and their masterly compositions, the plays themselves
include, for all their manipulation of the clichés of childhood adventure, a disturbing juxtaposition of the ebullient and macabre. The
plot of *The Scourge of the Gulph* is as follows:

Captain Carricknagat, a black-bearded pirate, aboard his ship off
The Isle of Plumes, learns that his wife has been captured and eaten
by cannibals. The message is brought by Bosun Broad, who has lost
an arm in the fight but has escaped with a letter from the unfortunate woman. This letter asks the Captain to find her body, remove
her skull, place it in a black box with silver hinges and bury it on
the round hill on The Island of Plumes. The Bosun and the Captain
find the skull, but the Bosun dies of "the black thirst" before the
Captain is able to dig a grave with his sword to bury what he calls
"This sad piece of ivory." At that point Joe Miles, a sailor who has
earlier been marooned, comes upon the Captain, and, believing the

box contains treasure, kills the Captain. On opening the box he discovers the skull, and brings the play to an end with the words "An empty skull, a black box, a dead skipper! Have I done anything or nothing?"

This curtain recalls similar moods at the close of some of W. B. Yeats's plays for the most adult audiences, in which, after all the agony, the question is again put.

The Herne's Egg (1938) ends with Corney commenting:

> All that trouble and nothing to show for it,
> Nothing but just another donkey.

This is, indeed, that dying fall, that weary or appalled asking of the cosmic riddle, with which much poetic tragedy ends. The note of soliloquy is necessarily frequent in these plays, for the nature of the cardboard theatre, with its figures held perpetually in the pose in which they have been painted, requires a somewhat static drama. Thus Jack Yeats's plays for children have the same restricted or formal pattern of movements as that provided by W. B. Yeats for his plays, though with a different reason.

Ernest Marriott in his small monograph on the work of Jack Yeats makes the point:

It seems to me that these diminutive dramas shew something of the fanciful simplicity and directness of phrase which we find in the work of the better-known dramatists of the Irish movement. . . . Bosun Hard-bite addressing McGowan who is seated on a mooring post on the quay says, "Sit there on yer old iron mushyroom till the seaweed grows you." An Emigrant replies, "The poor captain is feeling sad in his heart. The poor man, like the rest of us, doesn't like leaving the dear silk of the kine." At the beginning of [*The Treasure of the Garden*] the captain ruminates, "What a roaring life it is too, chasing the rich ships — the big fat pigeons with crops full of gold. But it's the other thing that sickens — fighting two great ugly frigates in a little ditch of a creek . . . they fall across you and lie on you like a dead horse." The impressive scene where he makes this speech is a battered deck with bullet-riddled pirates hanging from the shrouds in the last horror of bodily death.

If Jack Yeats took the role of "The Music" in his Pirate Drama, he also took it in many of his drawings and prints of this period. The series of hand-coloured prints by him which were issued by the Cuala Press almost all belong to his earlier manner. In them one can see certain themes emerging over and over again. The solitary watcher, caught up in reflective nostalgia; the sailor, with his eyes full of strange places, walking alone through the city street; the ballad singer, a vehicle for songs even odder and older than himself; the peasant inextricably a part of the rude barren landscape. These are often accompanied by images of physical exuberance and energy, even of a kind of brutality, as they are also accompanied in the work of his friend Synge and in much of the work of Masefield. In these prints, he makes use of the bright colours and bold forms of an art both emanating from and directed at popular tastes and notions.

Sometimes this leads him into an over-crude simplicity as in the print of St. Patrick where interpretation and reinvigoration have been replaced by hagiography; on the whole, however, his prints are superior to those of the majority of his contemporaries. Their "Gælic" quality attracted AE who wrote in 1909,

We have had abundance of Irish folklore, but we knew nothing of folk art until the figures of Jack Yeats first romped into our imagination a few years ago. It was the folk feeling, lit up by genius and interpreted by love. It was not the patronage bestowed by the intellectual artist on the evidently picturesque forms of a life below his own. I suspect Jack Yeats thinks the life of a Sligo fisherman as good as any, and that he could share it for a long time without being in the least desirous of a return to the more comfortable life of convention.

The folk art quality which AE detects not only emerges from the use of themes which excite the common "folk"— races, hurling matches, circuses, outlaws of land or sea—but also from a curious wonderment and rhythmic stridency. His coloured prints and drawings frequently use large areas of bold colour and contrast them simply. His greens and blues are more intense than natural, just as his figures are also exaggerated in shape and gesture. In the black and white drawings he uses a multitude of lines, covering earth, sky and clothing with closely packed ripples, so that the whole picture is often throbbing with rhythm. The heavy outlines are not, thus, imposed upon the figures, but are developed from the pressure of life within them. This is, for all the apparent calm of many of the resting or idly talking figures, a tumultuous art.

It was not until 1924 that a similar tumultuous quality emerged in his oil painting and in his writing. Perhaps his best prose work is *Sligo*, first published in 1930. This is a helter-skelter of freely associated memories, reflections, fantasies and jokes. There is no shape to it; its form is that of the rhythms of the mind alone, and in this it occasionally reminds one of Joyce's *Ulysses* and *Finnegan's Wake*. Yeats, however, is an original, not a disciple. His high jinks are like nobody else's, though his methods in this, and in his later *The Amaranthers*, do seem to anticipate many of those used by Flann O'Brien in *At Swim Two Birds* (so praised by Joyce) and by T. H. White (especially in *The Elephant and the Kangaroo*). His particular vein in *Sligo* emerges clearly from his account of the reason for the title. It is given after forty pages.

About a name for this book. I was making some notes one day while travelling in a train through a boggy country in Ireland when a melodeon player opposite me asked me if I wouldn't stop and "give out a tune" and he handed the melodeon towards me. "I have no ear," I said. "Ah, to hell with ears," he said "I play it with my body. Are you writing a book?" he said. "Well I am making notes for one," I said. "What are you going to call it?" he said. "I don't know yet," I said. "Call it Sligo. It's the name of a town," he said, "the only town in Ireland I never was in. I was near it once but I stopped on the brink and took the long car with a unicorn yoked to it for a town called Ballina. Call it Sligo, it ought to be a lucky name." So Sligo it is. When he asked me to play a tune he pronounced it Chune, a very good way too. If they give me music to my grave I will sooner they will call it a Chune than a Toon: there is a want of dignity about the word 'Toon' and I would not look forward to it.

This, in its inconsequence and dry humour, is reminiscent of Sterne. In other passages, however, we find a satirical absurdity that is Swift without Swift's anger.

But why tow, why not let others tow as they like it. There are more up-lifters in the world than subjects of uplift. Let them uplift us, shoulder high. Then we will be able to see over their heads to the several promised lands, from which we have come, and to which we trust to go. When the uplifters are wedged and milling together, and we are tired of sitting, we can stroll about on their solid heads, and view these lands. There will be very few of us and so, like weeks of Sundays, the time will pass pleasantly, each in turn doing the honours of each's own promised land. I suppose walking on heads will be a little like walking on cobble stones. Of course all Uplifting heads are exactly the same size and Uplifted come to the same level, the skulls are thick and we will be wearing pampooties, so they will not mind our strolling over the tops.

An even more Swiftian quality emerges in the passages about the Ropes family and its ancestors in which the evolution of a society is parodied. Jack Yeats, however, unlike Swift, wrote from affection, and believed in the basic goodness of humanity; compare Swift's accounts of sectarian conflicts, political and religious, with Jack Yeats's account of how the Ropes family explained the nature of the tides.

... they all sat in a ring on the warm sand and settled about it. Not all at once. But after a good many days they reduced the idea to two parties. Those who held that the sun drew the water up and down and those who held that the water was working the sun. The usual thing. And there was very little hope of anything being settled, until a small wedge party got up an idea that the whole place was pulsing any way it liked if you were satisfied. So they all agreed on that.

The light-hearted, but in no way trivial satire of *Sligo* is attached to a pseudo-autobiographical thread of narrative and reflection, as it is also in later works, the most notable of which is *And To You Also* (1944). This book is even more exuberant than *Sligo*, and its prose is even more carefully slapdash. Here also, he expresses yet again his strong feeling of the limitations of language as a medium of expression, and attempts to expand its boundaries in a number of ways. One of these is the use of the incantatory and absurd list — as practiced by Rabelais. His introduction to one magnificent list is as follows:

Now — thinking of you also I would like to give you from my store a really full-waved chapter heading, and we are in luck for I have under my hand a list of suggestions for the contents of a chapter which I will not write. But I will not waste the list so here it comes, and as you have been standing up to breast the gravelly storm as far as this without a breather, I'll call it

Chapter Two,

and here goes:

J. Toole, and Cook, and James Sullivan, and his great poster. Swede turnips, Weight-lifting, man in his walking clothes grunting. Swan song, heard record and refused to die. Vale of Aylesbury and all the falls. Waterfalls everywhere — Jem Mac. Jem Smith. The Lord Mayor's Coachman. Paintings outside booths at the Fairs. The private performance of the little play called Hand Knocks. Bob Habbijams. The M. C. Harris. Pictures on walls of Inns, and of the Lambeth School of Arms. Shapes the bus conductor. Rain. Glissade. House Boats. Walking by Seashores. Song Book Shops.

And so it continues for four pages, showing a dexterity in free association, a verbal music, a capacity for pattern making, that are truly astonishing.

Jack Yeats is, in fact, a prose artist of real importance, and an innovator. His prose contrasts sharply with his brother's hieratic and stately periods, and has far more flexibility and range. It is, perhaps, less sonorous; it is certainly less solemn. It is as capable of epigram, but incapable of pretension. It is not, however, less profound, only less earnest.

Jack Yeats's novels and stories are as original as his memoirs. His first full length novel, *The Amaranthers*, divides itself into two parts. In the first one the members of the Club are introduced to us, and are shown to be (among other things) devoted to the making of toy boats behind the sober façade of the island's only (small) skyscraper. The remainder of the book chronicles the adventures of James Gilfoyle, who finally reaches the island and befriends the Amaranthers, who have suffered the effects of an earthquake.

In *The Amaranthers*, as in *Sligo*, digression is frequent and amusing. We have a full description of the performance of a play which sounds, in some respects, like a drama concocted by a combination of Anouilh, Ionesco, and Jean Genet, with Robert Louis Stevenson supervising. We have the life stories of several bizarre characters. There is sudden death, banditry, high finance—it is a gallimaufry of a book. Some parts of Gilfoyle's adventures are distinctly reminiscent of the adventures told by Masefield, especially in *Odtaa*, but they are odder, and parody the adventure story more than exploit it seriously. The book is also, however, filled with radiance, gaiety, and intense enjoyment of physical beauty, so that even while the reader is laughing, he is also being charmed.

In *On the Boiler*, W. B. Yeats wrote of his brother's *A Charmed Life*:

He does not care that few will read it, still fewer recognize its genius; it is his book, his "Faust", his pursuit of all that through its unpredictable, unarrangeable reality least resembles knowledge. His style fits his purpose for every sentence has its own taste, tint and smell.

This is true also of *The Amaranthers*. It is one of the most original of books, though it clearly relates to the Irish tradition, having Swiftian passages, as well as passages that remind us of the broad and magical comedy and adventure of Irish epic. Moreover, as in Irish epic, the magical adventure often approaches farce, but is countered and qualified by an underlying romantic seriousness, so that the grave and the gay remain in tension and give the book a fundamental ambiguity of outlook as they do so often in Joyce. It is perhaps this balance of the grave and gay, this combination of the tragic and comic, that is characteristic of much of the best Irish writing. It is notable in Synge, O'Casey, Joyce; it is present, though to a muted degree, in Goldsmith; it is characteristic of the best of Wilde and Congreve, and it appears in heroic proportions in Swift.

It is also present in Jack Yeats's paintings of his last period. In these the colour has become hectic, challenging, expressionist. The rhythmic vitality of line in his earlier drawings has now been translated into thick oil colour, so that the landscapes and figures are all trembling with gay vitality, even though the total symbolism of the picture may be tragic or pathetic. Moreover, just as in the earlier drawings the rhythm of the figures takes up the rhythm of the landscape, so in the later paintings man and environment are possessed by the same vitality and animated by the same force. These later paintings do not reproduce well, and Jack Yeats himself set his face against their being used for prints; as a consequence his stature as one of the greatest of twentieth-century European painters is recognized only by those who have a first-hand knowledge of his work. This later work has been compared to that of Kokotchka (who admired it) as well as to Eduard Munch, but it is really quite distinct from the main tide of expressionism. In painting, as in writing, Jack Yeats is an innovator and a master.

The later plays are no less original than the paintings. *La La Noo* (1942) is set in a lonely pub in Ireland. The Publican and a Stranger are chatting when seven women arrive to shelter from the rain. They have been to a nearby fair and must catch a bus on the road which is a little distance away. After some talk of life and death, they set out again, are drenched by a sudden shower, and return. The Stranger puts them into another room, and they hand all their clothes out to him round the door; he then dries them by the blacksmith's fire. When they are dressed again they realize there is no time to catch the bus. One of them runs for it. The others wait for the Stranger to drive them off in the Smith's lorry, which he has decided to borrow. He has never driven an automobile before, and, on his way to pick up the ladies, he crashes into a tree and is killed.

This curious little fable is not attached to any moral. The talk throughout seems inconsequential, and the characters are unheroic. Nevertheless, with a hint here and there, the author indicates his theme, which is of the frailty of life, the inevitability of death. The theme of the nude (la la nu) is really an understated version of Lear's "unaccommodated man"; the number of women adds both a farcical element of crowded confusion and, because of the number seven, a touch of magic. The Stranger's sacrifice is not a parody, but an echo of all sacrifices for humanity. The conversation, full of small talk and the bywords and commonplaces of country people, is a microcosmic reflection of the grander talk of theologians and philosophers. Hell, death, mortality are the themes, as they are so often in country talk.

FIRST WOMAN: I would hate to see any man die. I didn't see my father die. He was away from me when he died. I have no brother or sister and my mother died when I don't remember her. And I thought I was going to see that Jockey boy die there on the Strand to-day. I was sick at it. I didn't want to see it. I am glad now, not only for him, but for myself. But surely I cannot expect to live all my life and see no man die. 'Tis too much to expect.

FOURTH WOMAN: I never seen them die. I seen them wither and when my back was turned they died on me. Wouldn't they put the life across you. They'd like to with their tricky ways. They're in hands with death the whole time, the dirty twisters.

FIFTH WOMAN: I don't care what you say, I'll see a man die and then I'll die myself and it won't be long either.

Behind this, as behind much of the play, is the conflict between the urge towards life, which is represented by the women's yearning towards men, and the resignation to death, which is represented by the fearful bachelordom of the Publican, the Stranger, and the Smith. The more one reads *La La Noo,* the more one gets from it. It differs, not only in style, but also in general approach from W. B. Yeats's drama. It is unaggressive. It avoids ritual. It uses realism in the interests of symbolism, and does not attempt esotericism or prophecy.

Jack Yeats was out of sympathy with his brother's interest in the use of masks. In *Sligo* he wrote:

Oh Masks, such a lot of talk about Masks — everyone knows about Masks being just about the last thing but three.

He was, however, very much in favour of "Theatre in the Round," and derisive about the Picture Frame Stage. In *Sligo* again he commented:

That fender and fire-irons and fender seat which producers slap down
bang in front of the footlights never to my mind comes off completely.
It is hard for the audience to keep remembering that they are in the
place of a fire or just came down a chimney like Santa Claus.

It was with *In Sand*, first produced in 1949, but not published until 1964, that Jack Yeats fused all the themes of his writings into one
whole. This play concerns, once again, an isolated community on
an island, and presents us, as in the Ropes sections of *Sligo*, and
The Amaranthers, and the later romance *Ah Well*, with many parodies of the growth and nature of the society in which we live. The
play is in several acts, each one taking place some years later than
the one preceding; they are linked together by the recurrence of the
words written in the sand of the seashore below high water mark
at the dying wish of Anthony Larcson. The words, "Tony, we have
the good thought for you still," being, after the passage of some
years, almost meaningless, take on the force of a magic charm, or
of a long-known but little understood passage of scripture. "Who
was this Tony?" asks the Governor, in the last act, and receives the
reply "I don't know, sir — he just brings us luck." This joins scepticism and faith with powerful simplicity. We may, ourselves, see the
whimsical and trivial origin of the message, and doubt its value,
and yet to all the characters in the play it brings comfort and understanding of the human condition. The fundamental ambiguity
present here may remind us of a similar ambiguity, more harshly
expressed, in the equally fantastic *Waiting for Godot* by Samuel
Beckett, another Irishman, whose scepticism is less qualified by
affection for the human race. The drama with which *In Sand* is
most allied is, however, expressionist. *In Sand* is of the same family
as Wilder's *The Skin of Our Teeth*, and Tennessee Williams' *Camino
Real*, and in its free-wheeling wit may recall Ionesco and Alfred
Jarry, though it never approaches the surrealistic. It is, however,
very much a part of twentieth-century drama. The way in which
each character creates his own version of reality, and uses fantasy
to satisfy his own and others' irrational human necessities, making
all things into a game he may manipulate according to his own
rules, is something which has much in common with the very
different worlds of Pirandello, Eugene O'Neill, and Jean Genet.

Jack Yeats's drama is not merely of its time, but central to it. His
work fits into the European scene much more easily than the drama
of his brother, and yet retains its distinctive national characteristic

just as completely. It is, moreover, absolutely original. No other dramatist has the same strange combination of realism and fantasy, affection and satire, regional authenticity and universal significance, gaiety and pathos.

Jack Yeats's paintings have now come to be recognized as among the most powerful and important of the work of the century. His writings have received less attention, partly because his own reputation as a painter and his brother's as a writer have overshadowed them, and partly because he allied himself to no "school," of either professional Irishmen, or socially-conscious didacts. His human sympathies were too intense to permit him the follies of sectarianism, and his distrust of pretension prevented him from stating any single message for the world. If Jack Yeats had any overriding message it is the one hinted at in a passage of *Ah Well* (1942) in which he describes a concert at which a young woman sang, receiving no tribute of applause.

But yes, she got something, for everyone hung the head to one side, or lifted its weight in his hand, resting a round cheek on a hollow palm or vice versa. I think now, with those people, it was as it was with me, for all the time the woman sang I heard nothing of the strange coloured lands she sang of. I saw only before me, as if she stood by its grey walls, an old, old house standing by a wide lake, gloomy to the centre, but fringed with dry old reeds, bone rattlers in a small breeze, blowing always for the Americas, across rock and heather and buchalawns, and sandy shore, and wide deep ocean. I hung my head as they hung theirs. We weep together, we laugh together, we die in one deep grave.